D0743562

A HISTORY OF SMITH COUNTY, KANSAS TO 1960

by

VERA EDITH CROSBY FLETCHER

B. S., Kansas State University, 1956

————————

A THESIS

submitted in partial fulfillment of the

requirements for the degree of

MASTER OF ARTS

Department of History, Political Science, and Philosophy

KANSAS STATE UNIVERSITY
OF AGRICULTURE AND APPLIED SCIENCE

1960

MAPS

TABLES

MUELLER SCHOLARSHIP

This study was made possible through the generous assistance of the Mueller Scholarship for Graduate Research in Kansas history. This annual scholarship was established at Kansas State College in 1956 by Colonel and Mrs. Harrie S. Mueller of Wichita, Kansas, for the purpose (1) of preserving the history of Kansas which includes attention to South Central Kansas; (2) of giving incentive to students to become teachers of history, especially of Kansas history, in the public schools of the state; and (3) to increase the knowledge, understanding, and appreciation of the Kansas heritage.

PREFACE

Smith County is located in the north central part of Kansas, bordered on
the north by Nebraska, and on the other three sides by counties quite similar
in physical features, and economic and industrial development. The economy,
except for a few minor industries, is based wholly on agriculture. The towns,
none large enough to be classed other than rural, range from hamlets to a population of approximately 2,400 at Smith Center, the county seat. Since there
have been no industries to bring in "outsiders," most of the people are descendants or related in some way to the early settlers of the area and are
intensely proud of their county.

The writing of this thesis on the history of Smith County has had a particular interest for me because I belong in this category. My grandfather,
Daniel H. Crosby, was one of the early homesteaders in the county. He was one
of the incorporators of Cedarville, the first town in the county, and later
was a business man in Kensington for many years. He and his wife who came to
the county with her parents in a covered wagon, were married by the first probate judge of the county, John Harlan. The grandparents of my husband, John
Pletcher and William Barcus, both homesteaded in the area then known as Crystal
Plains. I lived in Smith Center all of my girlhood and graduated from high
school there in 1935 so my ties to the county extend over three generations.
For this reason the writing of the history of Smith County, while seemingly
an insurmountable job, has been a pleasant and a fascinating task.

The purpose of this thesis has been to give a brief survey of the history
of Smith County from the pre-settlement days to comparatively recent times, including the history of the settlement of the various towns, and some representative families and people who have contributed to its development. As no

my indebtedness. Special appreciation is given to my husband and mother for their patience and inspiration throughout the months I have been occupied in this work.

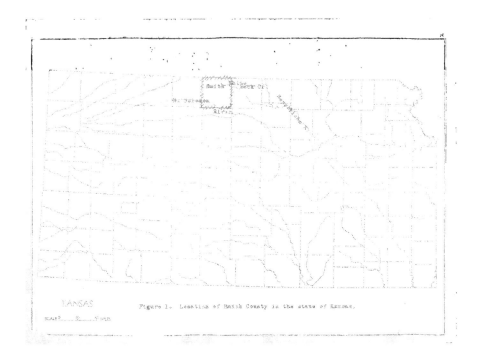

KANSAS

Figure 1. Location of Smith County in the state of Kansas.

CHAPTER I

AS GOD WROUGHT

Smith County lies in the extreme northern tier of counties in what is generally termed the north central area of the state of Kansas. It is bounded on the north by Webster and Franklin counties of Nebraska; on the west, east and south respectively by Phillips, Jewell, and Osborne counties of Kansas. It is 900 square miles of gently undulating grasslands except where the north fork of the Solomon River cuts across the southwest corner. Here chalk-rock hills border a valley which varies in width from one to five miles. Another rough area is the edge of the foothills of the Republican River in the extreme northwestern part of the county, which were good grasslands before settlement.

In the twentieth century, Smith County is cut by ravines and ditches, many too deep to cross, due to erosion, but in 1876 it was optimistically described as "scarcely a ravine in the county where the plow or reaper can not be run in or across the same without any inconvenience. Along the streams the bottoms are wide and sloping.... There is not more than 3 per cent of our land, exclusive of the timbered portions, that cannot be tilled, and this 3 per cent affords the most excellent pastures and stock grazing lands in the world."[1]

The ground was covered with a short, native grass commonly called buffalo grass which browned under the sun but turned green with light showers of rain.

---

[1] Rev. W. M. Wellman, "History of Smith County", address delivered at Smith Center July 4, 1876, "in the presence of 2,000 honest pioneers."

This grass deceived the first travelers who thought its height and dead appearance showed the country infertile and unproductive, but they soon discovered that it cured on the ground, and not only the buffalo but cattle and horses could graze all winter and keep in good condition. Grass roots closely entwined in the sod held the soil firmly so that no silt was carried into the streams and river to muddy its waters. It was said "the water in the Solomon River was clear as crystal and the fish could be seen plainly."[2]

The entire area is drained by tributaries of the Solomon River, which are Beaver Creek, East Beaver Creek, Cedar Creek, Middle Oak, West Oak, and Oak Creeks, Spring Creek, and Twelve Mile Creek, all of which flow in a southeasterly direction. There are also two arms of White Rock Creek which drain east into the Republican River. These creeks and the river were bordered by timber consisting of black walnut, oak, elm, hackberry, boxelder, willow, cottonwood, and cedar.[3]

A state survey in 1875 showed two per cent of the land in timber and 98 per cent in prairie.[4] Wild plums, currants, and chokecherries were found. There were native flowers, although several early settlers note there were no weeds until settlers came and plowed the ground. It is said that as soon as the sod was broken, sunflowers were seen.[5] "They lined the trails; for miles one could see them."[6]

The early animal life was that of the contiguous counties in Kansas and Nebraska; rabbits, antelope, wild turkeys, prairie chickens, quails, squirrels,

[2] Rev. W. M. Wellman, op. cit.; Margaret Nelson, Home on the Range, p. 44.
[3] A. T. Andreas, History of Kansas, p. 908.
[4] Annual Report of Kansas State Board of Agriculture, V. 4, Topeka, 1875.
[5] Minnie D. Millbrook, Ness Western County Kansas, p. 26.
[6] Margaret Nelson, op. cit., p. 44.

blacksnakes, rattlesnakes, ducks, geese, fox, deer, beavers, wolves, coyotes, and buffalo. Areas several acres in extent in the Solomon River Valley were covered with prairie dog mounds.[7]

Smith County was in the area that was the grazing ground for the huge buffalo herds on which the Indians depended for existence, and these large herds were seen by the earliest settlers in the county. Mrs. Margaret Nelson, a daughter of homesteaders and author of the book, Home on the Range, writes, "The buffalo was the department store of the Plains Indian. When the millions that roamed the prairies were exterminated, the Plains tribes were starved into submission. It is the shame of the white man that within three years of his arrival the plains were almost stripped bare of meat for both the Indian and the homesteader...."[8] The same idea was expressed by Minnie Millbrook when she wrote, "The buffalo was not only the trade goods of the Indian, it was also his commissary...."[9]

Various accounts tell of buffalo in Smith County the first years of settlement. Charles Biermann was building a log house in 1871, but did not have the roof on yet when he saw what looked like a black cloud rolling up on the horizon. "There was buffalo as far as I could see...a moving mass." He climbed on the corner of the logs and watched for several hours as they passed by.[10] Harry Ross told of men who were hunting buffalo in Smith County being caught in the Easter storm of 1873. One, Ed Howell, lost his team and most of his fingers and toes. His companion, named Gates, died.[11]

---

7 The plants, grass covering, and the extent of the prairie dog villages are also described in Fremont's account of his trip through this area: John C. Fremont, Report of the Exploring Expedition to the Rocky Mountains, 1843-1844, pp. 108-109.

8 Ibid., p. 11-12.

9 Millbrook, op. cit., p. 27.

10 Smith County Clippings, Vol. I, Kansas State Historical Library.

11 Harry Ross, What Price White Rock, p. 34.

Edna Chase Cowan came with her family to Smith County in 1871 and settled west of Gaylord near the Solomon River. One day they heard a distant rumble. Her father yelled that there were buffalo coming. They sat by the window and watched them circle the house several times. As they left, her father shot a calf.[12] William Allen, who settled on Oak Creek in 1871, stated that the big hunters estimated 10,000 buffalo were in the radius of fifty miles of their place. In 1872 a buffalo, apparently wounded by hunters, wandered into a homesteader's yard and chased the children into the house. In the southeast part of the county in 1872, buffalo, chased by hunters and consequently "on the prod", attacked two settlers who barely escaped being killed by running from tree to tree until the hunters arrived. "In '72 and '73 many settlers came and the buffalo disappeared rapidly."[13]

The last wild buffalo recorded as seen in Smith County was a lone animal about two years old captured by Lee and Lon Cook, Harve Hayworth and Shube Carruthers on Loss Creek in the northwestern corner of the county in 1877. He was little and thin so they fattened him up. People came from miles around to see the buffalo. They finally took him back to Indiana thinking to make some money showing him, but their project was disappointing, so they butchered him and sold the hide for five dollars.[14]

---

12 Bess Cowan, Reminiscences of Edna Chase Cowan as written by her daughter, 1951. Manuscript in the Kansas State Historical Library.

13 Errol Allen, "Incidents of Homestead Days," unpublished manuscript by son of William Allen, found in Kansas State Historical Library; Robert C. Venable, "The Kansas Frontier, 1861-1875," unpublished M.S. thesis, Univ. of Oklahoma, 1936. Venable stressed in his thesis that it may be the killing of the buffalo and wild game that was a determining factor in the passing of the frontier, for these herds provided the principal sustenance of life for the Indians and after their disappearance the Red man was more easily induced to accept ways of civilization. Since Smith County was settled after the great buffalo hunts had moved west and south, this may account for less Indian trouble there.

14 Margaret Nelson, op. cit. p. 235. Verified by the author in an interview with Mrs. M. Nelson.

The sport most enjoyed by the men after the buffalo were gone was jack-rabbit hunts. Between Christmas and New Year's, 1876, a grand hunt was organized in Smith County. The county was divided equally between east and west and the hunt ran for an entire week. Ten thousand rabbits were slaughtered and taken to Hastings, Nebraska, which was the nearest railroad point, where they were sold. The losing side gave a big supper to the winners on New Year's night.[15]

The fertility of the soil was not apparent to the first travelers through Kansas. The scarcity of trees, the short, dead-looking grass and the infrequent rain did not look like signs of an productive area to the men from the green, timbered valleys east of the Mississippi river. Smith County was part of the area Pike designated as the Great American Desert.

The key climatic factor then and now is the amount and variability of rainfall. The average annual rainfall in Smith County is approximately 22 inches but a low of ten inches and a high of thirty-eight inches in a single year have been recorded. The climate is the variable climate of the plains area: hot, dry summers with sudden showers, considerable wind, and occasional tornadoes. The winters may be characterized by many days of cold but with sunshine, or there may be heavy snowfall, usually with much wind and deep snowdrifts. The drier air tends to register lower temperatures, often zero or near zero for days in succession.

The weather is always an element of risk in an agricultural area, and in this "temperamental" region it is a constant topic for conversation. It spelled joy or sorrow, success or failure for the settlers in the 1870's

6

Table 1. Annual precipitation, Smith County, Kansas. 1898-1952.*

Year	Inches of Precip.	Year	Inches of Precip.	Year	Inches of Precip.
1898	16.34	1916	18.27	1934	10.02
1899	18.25	1917	16.69	1935	29.07
1900	22.96	1918	22.95	1936	10.11
1901	16.54	1919	29.49	1937	14.39
1902	33.80	1920	21.41	1938	20.07
1903	32.94	1921	13.87	1939	14.85
1904	21.50	1922	16.49	1940	16.43
1905	27.95	1923	29.86	1941	30.26
1906	20.00	1924	18.09	1942	25.56
1907	16.29	1925	20.66	1943	15.78
1908	28.33	1926	16.49	1944	32.93
1909	26.95	1927	23.95	1945	22.53
1910	17.53	1928	30.99	1946	35.47
1911	20.25	1929	18.49	1947	24.06
1912	20.41	1930	18.58	1948	—
1913	20.96	1931	21.73	1949	28.99
1914	17.81	1932	—	1950	23.67
1915	34.13	1933	15.01	1951	38.18

Average precipitation, 1898-1914   22.29

Average precipitation, 1915-1930   21.71

Average precipitation, 1931-1952   22.20

* Climatic Survey of the United States, Report of United States Department of Agriculture, Weather Bureau, 1952.

TABLE OF CONTENTS

and continued to do so in the twentieth century.

Archaeological and geological surveys of Smith County have been made but natural resources have been undeveloped to a great extent. Fossils found along the Solomon River and in Oak Creek tributaries show evidence of three different periods of the earth's past. First, the sea silt shows it was part of the ancient inland Chalk Seas; fossil vegetation found marks the tropical climate of the dinosauric age; later deposits of the glacial age are found.[16] These different periods made a soil of a fertility hard to duplicate, but left little known mineral deposits.

The finding of what was apparently mammoth skeletons in a sand pit on the Merrill Lyon farm four miles southwest of Smith Center in July, 1953, seems to further confirm this. The story, as told by the Smith County Pioneer, was that Gale Reilly of the local state highway crew found a broken part of a tusk. The engineer, Charles Vinckier, and foreman, Charles Springer, stopped work in that part of the pit and notified Kansas State College. Three men from the geology department removed a head and one vertebra. Unfortunately, as soon as the air strikes the bones they start to deteriorate unless shellacked. The head was broken by a careless souvenir hunter before it could be removed. The skull was three feet across and the tusks were estimated to be at least eight and one-half feet long. A mammoth thigh bone dug from the same pit in 1907 is in the University of Nebraska Museum.

A later find was made across the pit some 75 to 100 feet east of the earlier discovery. The skull was larger than the first with one tusk about nine feet long. The tip, estimated at another foot, was missing. The other

16 Smith County Pioneer, April 16, 1936.

tusk, broken off within a foot of the head by the bulldozer, measured nine
inches in diameter at the break. There were two teeth in the head, one meas-
uring ten inches in length and five inches in width, both in the upper jaw.[17]
Another tusk and some bones were found by Robert Maxwell northwest of Smith
Center. They had apparently been uncovered by a heavy rain and were in a
strata about five to six feet below the normal surface of the land in that
vicinity.[18]

Limestone abounds and is of good quality for construction purposes.
Sandstone is plentiful, but is of an inferior quality, while there are small
quantities of gypsum of fine industrial quality.[19]

Chalk deposits have been found from Jewell County southwest to Finney
County. They have been scenic wonders for years while the United States im-
ported chalk from England. In 1952 the Kansas State Geological Survey made
investigations that revealed some exceptionally pure chalk in Smith County.[20]
It is now mined on the Giese farm in Harvey township and the Walter Hofer
farm in Valley township. Chalk shipments have been made from Gaylord and
Harlan. It is the only place in the United States that chalk is mined on a
commercial basis. An estimated 50,000,000 tons make up the largest and
purest commercial reserves on the continent.[21]

Oil and gas seeps have been reported in Smith County for years and were
reported in a Kansas Geological Survey in 1917. In 1916-1918 much of the land

17 Smith County Pioneer, July 30, August 6, 1953.
18 Smith County Pioneer, October, 1959.
19 Charles R. Tuttle, New Centennial History of Kansas, p. 650-651.
20 Alvin Leonard and Walton Durum. Geology and Ground - Water Resources
of North Fork of the Solomon River, State Geological Survey of Kansas,
Bulletin 98, p. 23; John D. Bright, Kansas, The First Century, p. 202.
21 Smith County Pioneer, November 7, 1940.

around Athol in the western part of the county and Bellaire in the central part was leased for oil development. A few tests were drilled but with no favorable results. Kenneth Landes and John Jewett made trips to Smith County in 1938 and in visits with M. R. Dimond and other citizens they got the following story. About sixty years ago oil that was similar to kerosene and used in lamps was obtained from dug water wells little more than twenty feet deep in Old Germantown. Later neighboring wells here and around Bellaire became unfit for water use. At Bellaire the town became infuriated because they thought some person was putting oil in the town well. "Coal oil" was rediscovered there about 1917 in a shallow well and used for automobile fuel. In 1917 it was reported that crude oil — one hundred or more barrels — was taken from a well about twenty-five feet deep in Athol. It ran into a cistern that was being dug and was pumped out with an ordinary pitcher pump at the rate of five gallons a day to heat a commercial garage. A well near the hotel had to be abandoned because of oil pollution.

In 1938 oil similar to kerosene accumulated on a cistern in Athol to the depth of several inches. Test holes were made by state geologists near the cistern in Athol and kerosene-like oil along with water was bailed out. Sand with a strong odor of crude oil was found at twenty-four feet. Analyses of incomplete samples showed that this does not resemble any of the crude petroleum of Kansas. The unusual character can possibly be explained as the result of filtration.

Surface geology of Smith County is very simple. It has an Ogallala formation of Tertiary Age in the northwest corner of the county and in a narrow outlier extending southeastward from the southern part of T1S, R13W, to a mile or two west of Bellaire. No seeps have been reported from either of these two areas of Tertiary rock. The rest of the county, except for a relatively small area in the south and southeast parts is floored with the chalky shale of the Niobrara formation. This formation is the thinnest in the southeast part of the county where the underlying Carlile shale is exposed and is the thickest beneath the cap of Tertiary rocks in the southwest corner. All but one of the seeps shown in the map occur in the area floored by the Niobrara formation -- mostly where the chalky shale has broken down through weathering into a veneer of soil several feet thick. The gas seep in Section 3, T5S, R11W in the southeast part of the county is the only seep known in the area of the outcrop of Carlile shale.

It seems unlikely to us that the source seeping is to be found in the shallow formations. These formations are notably devoid of oil in other parts of the state where they have been adequately tested, except of sandstone layers in the Dakota.

Under the circumstances the best guess that can be made is that the source of oil is in the formations of Pennsylvanian age which occur in Smith County at depths in excess of 2,000 feet.... Recent chemical studies of soils, especially in the Gulf Coast area, have shown that the lighter, more volatile components of crude oil can travel upward through a considerable thickness of rock strata.... In the course of upward migration the crude oil has been fractionated so that only the light constituents have appeared at the surface. The presence in commercial quantities is a possibility without the presence of seeps. The presence of seeps strengthens this possibility.[22]

22 Kenneth K. Landes and John M. Jewett, Oil and Gas Seeps in Smith County, Kansas. State Geological Survey of Kansas, Mineral Resources Circular 12, 1939. (Summarized by the author.)

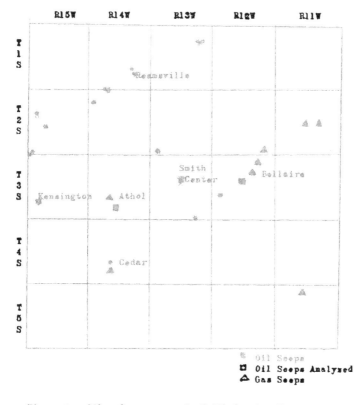

Figure 2. Oil and gas seeps in Smith County, Kansas. **

**Map from State Geological Survey of Kansas, Mineral Resources
Circular 12, 1939.

CHAPTER II

TEPEES, TREATIES, AND TRAILS

Smith County, historically speaking, goes back to the sixteenth century when the Spanish Conquerors of Mexico extended their explorations into what is now Kansas and claimed it by right of discovery and conquest as part of the Spanish Empire. Coronado's march in 1541 placed the first white men in Kansas, but Smith County lays no claim to his presence.

In 1682 La Salle claimed all the land drained by the Mississippi River and its tributaries for France and named it Louisiana in honor of his king. There were French explorers in Kansas during the eighteenth century such as Dutisne, Bourgmont, Mallet Brothers, but again as far as is known none of them followed the north branch of the Solomon River through Smith County.

At the end of the French and Indian War in 1763, France was forced to cede all of Louisiana lying west of the Mississippi to Spain. Then in 1800 Napoleon traded with Spain and received Louisiana back again. This area was part of the Louisiana Purchase from France in 1803 and thus became part of the United States. In 1805 the Louisiana Territory was divided, but this area remained in the north part carrying the same name until Louisiana became a state in 1812 and the name was changed to Missouri Territory. In 1821 when Missouri was carved out and became a state, Kansas became part of unorganized territory, but in 1830 it was merged into the Indian Territory.

From time immemorial Smith County had been the home and hunting grounds of nomadic tribes and the pasture land of millions of buffalo. In early historic times the Pawnee Indians controlled all the area between the Arkansas

12

and Platte rivers although no evidence of permanent settlements have been found in the county.[1] Since they knew little of boundaries except rivers, undoubtedly Comanches from farther west and Wichitas from the south probably followed buffalo herds through this area, too. Other tribes seemed to acknowledge Pawnee superiority until about 1832 when the tribe was ravaged by smallpox and lost an estimated one half of their population. In 1833 by treaty they relinquished to the United States their claims south of the Platte and west of the Missouri and agreed to stay north of the Platte. This was the country of the Sioux who were old enemies of the Pawnees. The Sioux constantly slaughtered them until they became practically obliterated.[2]

Inconclusive stories of a large encampment of Pawnees having fought the warlike Sioux southwest of what is now Lebanon with the Pawnees nearly wiped out have been reported. This may be the same story reported in the Smith County Pioneer.[3] Due to the lack of definite landmarks and conflicting names of creeks, early events are often placed many miles apart by different narrators. Here is the Headley story.

> It is interesting to note from the early files of the Smith County Pioneer that about twenty years earlier in 1852 a desperate Indian battle was fought at the spot at the forks of the Beaver, southwest of Smith Center, as recorded by a French trapper, Moncravia, who was an eye witness to the conflict. The battle was between the Pawnee, Delaware and Omaha Indians on the one hand and the Cheyenne, Comanches, Arapahoes and Apaches on the other. The French trapper reported that the Pawnee party numbered some seven thousand warriors and that the Cheyenne confederation numbered about nine thousand. This battle resulted in the slaying of over two thousand Pawnees and over three thousand of their

---

[1] Waldo Wedel, An Introduction to Kansas Archeology, Bureau of American Ethnology, Bulletin 174, pp. 6-7.

[2] Annie H. Abel, "Indian Reservations in Kansas and the Extinguishment of Their Titles," Kansas Historical Collections, V. 8, p. 107.

[3] Smith County Pioneer, January 27, 1876. Republished April 16, 1903.

opponents were killed outright, some seven hundred taken prisoners and a number of them afterward burned at the stake. According to the trapper this battle was brought on by the Pawnees who at that time were the most powerful and warlike tribe west of the Mississippi and resisted the incursions of the Cheyenne, Comanche, etc. The fight lasted three days and is regarded as one of the most bloody conflicts between opposing bands of Indians ever fought in the Middle West. The Cheyennes were led by O-co-no-mo-woe of whom Sitting Bull of the Sioux is said to be a lineal descendent. In this desperate conflict the Pawnees were successfully led by the celebrated chief Tar-po-no-ha who at that time was renowned as the most daring chief of the federation. This story is said to be further substantiated by the testimony of an old Indian trapper and hunter who for many years lived on the extreme headwaters of Frenchmen's Fork of the Republican river, and was told the story by Pawnee friends.[4]

If these stories are true and the setting can be placed in the area of Lebanon, it may account for some of the archaeological findings on Oak Creek.[5]

The Osage, Kansas and Sioux moved in behind the Pawnee for hunting but the real occupants of this area seemed to be the Arapahoes and Cheyennes. These hunting expeditions often led to disputed rights and battles like the one described above. Brigadier-General Henry Atkinson of the U. S. Army and Major Benjamin O'Fallon, Indian agent, negotiated treaties with the various Plains tribes of Indians from June 22, 1825 to October 6, 1825. This included treaties with the Cheyenne, Ogallala Sioux and Comanche tribes in the north central Kansas area in which these tribes pledged not to molest American citizens passing through their territory.[6]

---

[4] A. L. Headley, "Smith County, Kansas," unpublished manuscript, 1959.

[5] Waldo Wedel, op. cit., p. 535. Smith County finds were reported in 1938-1939 by Smith and Kiseley, but not developed. Blaine Pletcher, the author's husband, has helped to dig out some places revealed by high water erosion on Oak Creek, but they have never been developed.

[6] Smithsonian Institution, Bureau of American Ethnology, Bulletin 30; U. S. Congress, Senate, Indian Affairs, Laws, and Treaties, Vol. 35, Senate Doc. 452, 57th Cong., 1st sess., (1901-1902), pp. 161-164.

In 1834 it was the purpose of the United States to set aside the land west of the Missouri River as a perpetual Indian Territory. The government made treaties with the Indian tribes whereby they were assigned land in what came to be Kansas. The area of Smith County was not affected as far as records show; however, a map in the Archives of the Kansas State Historical Society shows the Delaware Outlet extending west through the southern part of the present county.[7]

The Indians claimed to have designated a "dead line" in 1860 beyond which, to the west, no white man should settle. This line was used as an excuse for raids and atrocities against the settlers west of it, and as it supposedly extended north and south about the location of Cloud and Republic Counties, this made Smith and Jewell Counties in the Indian territory.[8]

Sub-committees of Congress were sent to the southwest to conclude a treaty of peace with the Kiowa, Comanche, and Kiowa-Apache tribes at Medicine Lodge, October 21, 1867. The treaty provided for the withdrawal of these tribes from the region between the Platte and Arkansas rivers, and agreement not to molest railroad construction through the area. This area of course included Smith County.[9] About 1868, the state and federal government actively set to work to open up the country to settlement, by giving security to the settlers. This was done by maintaining troops for short periods at camps on the Republican and the Solomon, and at forts along the railroads, and by keeping up a patrol on the border. This action was reported efficient by the year

7 Issued from Indian Office, Washington, D. C., Aug. 5, 1845.

8 Z. T. Walrond, "Annals of Osborne County, Kansas," Osborne County Farmer, July 22, 1880.

9 Indian Affairs, Laws, and Treaties, op. cit., pp. 754-764.

1870.[10]

However, there were many accounts that mention hardships to be faced from the Indian danger. Reports of Indian atrocities east of Smith County in more settled areas would infer that the more sparsely settled frontier was in danger, regardless of army reports.

On White Rock Creek, northeast of Lebanon and over the line in Jewell County, attempts were made at settlement from 1866 to 1870, but the groups were continuously driven out by Indian attacks. Harry Ross in his book on White Rock Creek, calls the year 1869 "the last bloody year" and has one chapter listing loss of life and property from Indian atrocities in that area. This was the year the first permanent settler also arrived in Smith County and settled on White Rock Creek.

Settlers built Ft. Jewell (now Jewell City) after an Indian scare May, 1870. Nearby settlers stayed there about six weeks. On June 28, after the Indian scare was past, a company of mounted artillery of the regular army came and occupied the fort, remaining until fall to protect the homesteaders of that section.[11]

Another Indian incident found in numerous accounts of this area is the basis for the naming of Higgins' Bluff on Oak Creek two miles north and one mile west of the southeast corner of the county. In the early 70's, Jim Higgins, Sam Owens, and Matt Freeman went on a buffalo hunt from Concordia. They had made their kill and were drying meat on top of the bluff so as to

---

[10] Annie H. Abel, "Indian Reservations in Kansas," p. 14. From original M. A. thesis, Kansas University, 1900. Only forts found on record were Ft. Riley, established 1852; Ft. Harker, 1864; and Ft. Hays, 1865, with Hays the closest to Smith County.

[11] Harry Ross, op. cit., p. 18-26.

watch for Indians. Higgins went after brush for the fire, saw the Indians, and lay down in the tall grass to hide. Owens shot the leader, ran to the east edge of the bluff and jumped off. He ran to Oak Creek, hid under some driftwood, and thus escaped. Freeman ran another direction and escaped, but Higgins was shot while trying to escape. His scalped body and the remains of the burned wagon was found a few days later. Thus the name, Higgins' Bluff.[12]

May 9, 1870, the Indians attacked four white settlers hunting on Twelve Mile Creek, but they were able to escape to Cawker City which is just outside of Smith County in northwest Mitchell County. May 9, 1870, twenty-five Indians attacked settlers below Cawker City. Three of the settlers were killed and two escaped. Dr. Lyon was killed in the same community in 1869. May 29, 1870, the Indians stole a number of horses in this area. In July they appeared again but did no harm. Mrs. Nelson and other early settlers report more or less friendly encounters with Indians in the early seventies.

Kansas lay across the trails to the West. Her central geographic position, slightly inclined land and wide river valleys opening mostly to the West were ideal for the trader and the settler. Kansas became a highway to all the farflung West from time immemorial. But it would appear that Smith County and the northern tier of counties adjoining lay between all the early trails, expeditions, railroads, and settlement which usually followed the major rivers of the Arkansas, Blue, Republican, Smoky Hill, and Platte.

Early explorers apparently followed one or another of these rivers. Bourgmont's route apparently followed the Saline River for a distance. Pike cut southwest through Jewell County in 1806 to hit the Arkansas River, Major

---

[12] One such report was written by A. E. Gledhill, Smith County Pioneer, March 1, 1900.

Long had groups on the Platte, Arkansas, and Kansas rivers in 1819-1820 but none came close to Smith County. It is thought that Fremont may have crossed Smith County on one of his five trips through Kansas. In 1843 he cut from the Kaw River northwest to the Platte River in Nebraska (see accompanying map, Fig. 3).[13]

The early trails also missed following the Solomon River which would have taken them through Smith County. The Santa Fe Trail was far to the south of the Arkansas River and a Mormon Trail cut the northeast corner of Kansas. One of the most used trails to California and Oregon went from Kansas into Nebraska in Washington County. The Pony Express followed the same route, as did the Overland Stage route. The Butterfield Overland Dispatch went up the Smoky Hill River and across Kansas to Denver.[14]

With the discovery of gold in the Pike's Peak region and "the prospect of a huge migration to the West, the 'jumping off' places on the border began to vie with one another for a share of the business...Ft. Leavenworth had long been the chief military depot for supplies bound for the West" and had grown rapidly during the 1850's with a freighting business increasing by leaps and bounds. By 1858, Russell, Majors, and Waddell had become known as the largest freight contractors for the government in the West. In 1859-1860 plans were made to establish one of the most noted transportation companies ever to serve the Rocky Mountains. The Leavenworth and Pike's Peak

---

13 According to the map included with John C. Fremont's report (J. C. Fremont, op. cit.) drawn under the orders of Col. J. J. Abert, Chief of the Topographical Bureau, and using the longitude lines for location, the author concluded that John C. Fremont traversed Smith County on this trip. In his written report (pp. 108-109), descriptions placed him in the area June 18 and 19.

14 Kansas Historical Collections, 1905-1906, V. 9, map on p. 576.

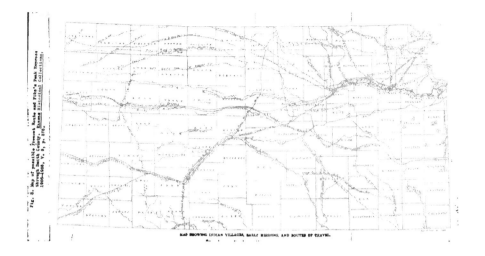

Fig. 3. Map of possible Fremont Route and Pike's Peak Express through Smith County. Kansas Historical Collections, V. 9, p. 576.

MAP SHOWING INDIAN VILLAGES, EARLY MISSIONS, AND ROUTES OF TRAVEL.

Express Company was the one famous freight line or trail that Smith County can definitely claim. Although it did not last long, it received much publicity. The New York Daily Tribune carried announcements of the new firm and classified advertisements for it.[15]

The promoters, W. H. Russell and John S. Jones (of the famous freighting firm of Russell, Majors, and Waddell) bought 1,000 fine Kentucky mules and a sufficient number of Concord coaches to supply a daily coach each way between the Missouri River and Denver. They sent out a surveying party in March which planned the route from Leavenworth to Junction City, then along the divide northwest, across the southwest corner of Jewell County, then nearly straight west through Smith County. They planned twenty-seven stations on the route, twenty-five miles apart, with six men at each station — four drivers and two to remain permanently at the station. Tents were furnished at each station for the summer, and they planned to build adobe or log houses by winter. Station 12 was located in Smith County (see Fig. 4).

There is some disagreement as to where this station might be located in Smith County. According to the map, the station was northeast of the farthest north point of the Solomon River, "probably a little south of the forks of Beaver Creek, about seven miles southwest of present Smith Center."[16] This would place it on the bend of the Solomon between Gaylord and Cedar. The Smith County Pioneer had an article written in 1881 by James Scarbrough

---

[15] George A. Root and Russell K. Hickman, "Pike's Peak Express Companies"; Kansas Historical Quarterly, V. 13, No. 3, August 1944, p. 167. George A. Root was on the Kansas State Historical Library staff for over fifty years and was considered an authority on trails, ferries, roads and bridges in Kansas as he made this a lifetime project.

[16] Ibid., p. 227. The original map signed by Geo. A. Root is in the Kansas Historical Library Archives.

telling of his visit to the East Cedar Creek farm of Ed Stevens, then County Clerk of Smith County, where the old Jones and Russell Overland Stage and Express Line Stage and Express Line Station was located. He said that near the old trail crossing on Cedar Creek was a miniature "Pawnee Rock" standing alone on the bank of the creek. The rock was about ten feet high and twelve feet in circumference and not another one of its kind is found in the surrounding country, so Scarbrough said. It is inscribed with a large number of names and dates back to 1840. Some names that were decipherable were R. S. Rook, 1859; Simon Mullen, 1859; Omahas, 1852; J. T. Vanduzen, 1870. In one place the date 1840 was readable but the names were almost entirely gone.[17] Unless the survey maps could be found, this station can not be more definitely located.

The first stage that traveled through Smith County left Planter's House in Leavenworth, April 18, 1859, and arrived in Denver May 7. The return trip from Denver began May 10, 1859, and reached Leavenworth May 20, 1859, to the accompaniment of a great celebration that lasted two days. May 19, 1859, two coaches arrived in Denver and on them was a noted passenger, Henry Villard, correspondent of the Cincinnati Daily Commercial, who wrote an account of his trip for his paper. The most famous passengers ever carried by this stage line through Smith County were Horace Greeley and his journalist companion, Albert D. Richardson, correspondent for the Boston Journal. They wrote interesting accounts of this trip which each later published in books.[18] To settlers "it is doubtful if at that time the arrival in Kansas of any other

---

17 Smith County Pioneer, August 29, 1881.

18 Horace Greeley, Overland Journey, 1860; Albert D. Richardson, Beyond the Mississippi, 1875.

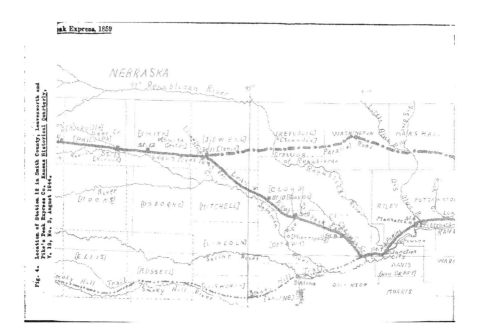

Fig. 4. Location of Station 12 in Smith County, Leavenworth and Pike's Peak Express Co., Kansas Historical Quarterly, V. 13, No. 3, August 1944.

man would have created such a sensation. Greeley's paper, the New York
Tribune, was widely read in Kansas. He had been a constant and devoted
friend of 'Free Kansas,' and his pen and voice had been effective in secur-
ing her freedom."[19]

The express that arrived on June 19 brought to Leavenworth conclusive
proof of gold in the Western Mountains. It carried $2,500 in gold dust. It
also brought the "Greeley Report" which substantiated the claims of rich dis-
coveries and convinced the people. The coach would have made the trip in
seven days from Denver but it was delayed a day by an accident which took
place near Station 12 (Smith County area). The coach was moving at a fast
pace while thousands of buffalo were swarming on the plains and in the trail.
A herd passed directly in front of the mules which were frightened and ran.
The driver dropped the reins and jumped for the mules, but he was dragged.
In a few moments mules, coach, and all rolled over a bank. Luckily, neither
animals, driver nor coach were injured, but a day was lost in getting lined
out again.[20] Another incident that happened in the same area is recounted
by Albert D. Richardson in his diary.

> At Station 12 where we dined, the carcasses of seven buffaloes
> were half submerged in the creek. Yesterday a herd of 3,000 crossed
> the stream, leaping down the steep banks. A few broke their necks
> by the fall; others were trampled to death by those pressing from
> behind.[21]

---

[19]Martha B. Caldwell, "When Horace Greeley Visited Kansas in 1859,"
Kansas Historical Quarterly, V. IX, pp. 115-150.

[20]George Root and Russell Hickman, op. cit., pp. 219-221.

[21]Albert D. Richardson, op. cit., p. 169.

On May 11, 1859, Jones, Russell and Company purchased the mail contract of John M. Hockaday and Company. It ran from St. Joseph to Salt Lake by way of Forts Kearney and Laramie. July 2, 1859, the first express ran to Denver via the Platte, and north central Kansas, including Smith County, lost its Express.

CHAPTER III

SURVEY TO SETTLEMENT

Smith County was created on March 3, 1867, in one of the laws passed
by the Kansas State Legislature. Thirty-two other counties in the territory
east of range line 26 west of the sixth principal meridian had their boundaries defined. Neighboring counties of Jewell, Osborne, and Phillips were
covered by this legislation. Each county, covered by this act could be organized when it had 600 inhabitants.[1]

Since the area of Smith County was in unorganized territory in the
eighteen-sixties, Governor Samuel J. Crawford wanted the area organized for
law enforcement. He later stated that:

> It was the rendezvous for thieves, robbers, and roving bands
> of Indians. Ranchmen were there with herds of taxable property,
> and traders, whose principal business was to supply hostile In-
> dians and outlaws generally with arms, ammunition, and bad whiskey...
> to reach these knights of the plains and bring them within reach of
> the law, I proposed and had introduced in the House of Representa-
> tives, a Bill establishing 36 new counties, and attaching them to
> organized counties along the western border for judicial purposes.[2]

Prior to 1867, the organization of new counties was determined by
settlement. With the Bill of 1867, however, a comparatively uninhabited
territory was divided into counties, not because of the needs of settlement,
but in the interest of law and order. Thus these counties, including Smith
County, had a rather unique beginning. Another unusual thing was that Smith

---

[1] Helen G. Gill, "The Establishment of Counties in Kansas," Kansas
State Historical Transactions, V. 8, p. 456; Laws of Kansas, passed at the
Seventh Session of the Legislature, 1867, pp. 51-57; General Statutes of the
State of Kansas, 1867, Ch. 24, Sec. 1, p. 228; Sec. 72, p. 246.

[2] Samuel J. Crawford, Kansas in the Sixties, p. 248.

County was one of twenty-two counties that were bounded in thirty mile squares with no attention to geographical conditions when organized later. It was one of eleven to remain as originally planned (see maps, Figs. 1 and 5).

In 1864 an order was issued by the federal government for a survey and dedication of Smith County. During 1865, a party of surveyors, guarded by federal troops, ran the lines and established the section corners.[3] William Brake, later a Gaylord shoe cobbler, was a member of the cavalry company that accompanied the surveying party.[4]

There is a great deal of discrepancy in reports of the first settlement in Smith County. This possibly is due to two reasons. First, settlers came into Smith County from three directions, following the different waterways. This is learned from the stories of their trips in which they identified various points that were definitely named by 1869. One general route was to follow the Solomon Valley, then up some of the rather large tributary creeks which flowed into the Solomon River. There were four such systems in Smith County, namely: Oak, Twelve Mile, Cedar, and Beaver Creeks. Another was to follow the Republican up from Concordia (a kind of "jumping off place" as the Federal Land Office was located there July 7, 1870), then turn west up White Rock Creek, which was practically a river at this time, and on into Smith County. The third route used by settlers was to come through Nebraska and

---

3 39th Congress, 2nd Session, 1866-67, Report of Secy. of Interior, 1866, Exec. Doc. No. 1, Vol. 2, pp. 448-453. No. 11D was report from Surveyor General's Office, Leavenworth, Kansas, Aug. 25, 1866 reporting that surveys contracted for out of appropriations approved July 2, 1864, had furnished to Western Land District, Junction City, Kansas, during year ending June 30, 1866 triplicate plans to fulfill contract. Plans for particular sections and ranges of Smith County were furnished Feb. 10, 1866. Reference No. in libraries, Serial Doc. 1284.

4 Smith County Pioneer, September 3, 1936.

27

Figure 5: Map of counties created by legislature in 1867, including Smith.

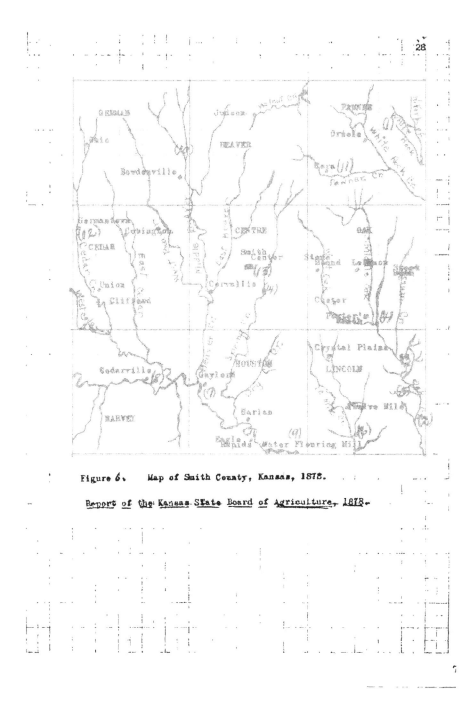

Figure 6.   Map of Smith County, Kansas, 1878.

Report of the Kansas State Board of Agriculture, 1878.

follow branches of the Republican into northern Smith County. These available routes caused the settlers to be widely scattered and often unknown to each other until much later.

The second reason is conflicting reports. As Mr. Headley said in a speech before the Smith County Historical Society,

In compiling the history of a state or county there will always be many minor and seemingly conflicting accounts. Aside from the meagre facts to be found in official records, many of the most interesting incidents of the early settlement days have been handed down by word of mouth from one generation to another. This is especially true of Smith County. In the rugged environments of the early days there was little incentive or opportunity to make a permanent record of the daily incidents which at the time seemed commonplace but which, from a historical standpoint, provided the foundation upon which the intimate history of those days could be assembled.

The first reference to any settlement in Smith County is found in the story written by Harry Salmons when he was about 75 years old. He said that he and his parents left England when he was ten years old. They came to Ft. Riley where his father hired out as coachman to Chaplain Reynolds. In 1867, they took a claim on the north fork of the Solomon near present day Gaylord. The father returned to Ft. Riley to work. Harry and his mother stayed on the claim, where they hunted wild game for food. His father claimed this must be the grazing land of the main buffalo herd, but added that few people realized the immense number on the plains in the 60's. He said he stood on a bluff above the Solomon and looked down the valley ten miles and all that met his gaze were buffaloes.[5]

5 Harry Salmons, "Some Incidents of Pioneer Days," Spokane, Washington Chronicle, date unknown; cited in the Smith County Pioneer, Sept. 8, 1932.

Horace Greeley in his Overland Journey described a similar sight between
Station 10 which was located in Cloud County and Station 13 located at Kirwin.
His observation covered an area across Jewell and Smith Counties.

> Thence nearly all day, the buffalo in greater or less numbers
> were visible among the bottoms of the Solomon on our right — usually
> two or three miles distant. At length, about five in the evening we
> reached the crest of a "divide", whence we looked down on the valley
> of a creek running to the Solomon some three miles distant, and saw
> the whole region from half a mile to three miles south of our road
> and for an extent of at least four east and west fairly alive with
> buffalo. There certainly were not less than 10,000 of them; I be-
> lieve there were many more.[6]

The first record of continuous settlement was of Joseph Cox, his wife
and five children, who homesteaded on section 35, White Rock Creek, in what
is now Logan Township, April 1869. His occupancy held the land and he never
filed until a year later. He built a windowless dugout in which the family
lived for two years. In 1871 Cox built a log cabin which Mrs. Cox in later
years described as "leaking like a sieve." Six more children were born to
the Cox family in Smith County. Mr. Cox, an English coal miner from Pennsylvania, was thirty when he came to Kansas and lived to the age of seventy-
eight on his original homestead, giving him a "longer continuous residence
in Smith County than any other man in 1912."[7]

His son, Joseph Cox, Jr., was born in Wilkes Barre, Pennsylvania, and
was six when he came to Smith County. He died July 1948, at the age of
eighty-five years. He was able to tell many interesting stories of early
life in Smith County such as a buffalo stampede by their dugout in 1869.
Another time an Indian came to the door, entered, and after looking around,

---

[6] Horace Greeley, op. cit., pp. 81-83.

[7] Souvenir Booklet of Old Settlers' Association, 1912. Mrs. Joseph
Cox died in 1902 and was buried in Oriole Cemetery, the oldest female settler
in Smith County at the time of her death.

signified by motions that he wanted the coffee pot. Mrs. Cox gave it to him
in spite of the men's protests that she would never see it again. The next
day the Indians broke camp on White Rock Creek near the Cox home and started
to leave in single file procession. As they went by the Cox dugout, one
Indian left the line, galloped into the yard, and returned the coffee pot.
Five years later the same Indian came into the Duckerville store (located
four miles west of the Cox homestead) where Mr. Cox and eleven year old
Joseph were standing. Recognizing them, he gave them a friendly greeting
and putting his hand on Joseph's head, he said, "Papoose growed heap."[8]
Some other members of the family were Mrs. Jess Green, one year old in
1869, Mrs. Nancy Upp, Mrs. Letitia Baylor, and Tom Cox.

The next settler in Smith County was probably Lotrip Darling, who arrived the latter part of September, 1869, and established a home on a claim
about three miles southeast of the present townsite of Gaylord. Darling had
made a journey across the plains from California where he had gone to hunt
gold. He had gone to California by ocean voyage around Cape Horn, then came
to Smith County across the plains. He filed on his claim (now NW¼, S19,
Harlan Township) at Concordia, December 20, 1870, and being a blacksmith by
trade, he quarried stone and built a blacksmith shop. He kept in repair the
tools used in the first breaking of the sod along the Solomon Valley. He
sold out in 1883 and went to Osborne, but returned to Gaylord in 1899 and

---

[8] Told by Joseph Cox, Jr. and reprinted in the Smith County Pioneer,
February 6, 1950.

ran a hotel for awhile.[9]

After these earliest settlers, there was a steady increase of arrivals in Smith County.[10] An examination of the records in the National Archives, Washington, D. C., showed that the first twelve homestead entries for land located in Smith County were made by Josiah Crick, Henry M. Blue, Daniel Hopkins, Chancy Williams, James Thompson, G. W. Jeffrey, Clarence Blinn, Rufus Brown, Herman Potter, Bella Merrill, and James Richard. However, an examination of the records at the office of the Register of Deeds, Smith Center, Smith County Kansas, showed that apparently only four ever received patents to the original homestead claims, namely: C. W. Jeffrey, Clarence Blinn, Victor Blinn, and Rufus Brown. Patents to the remaining claims were received by A. P. Hester, Nancy Custer, John Watson, Johan McCullough, Hans

---

[9] Smith County Review, September 3, 1936. In A. T. Andreas, op. cit., pp. 908-910, Lotrip Darling was listed among earliest settlers at Gaylord, reference was made to first white child born in county as Maggie Fowler, born June 16, 1871, on homestead of Lotrip Darling. Henry Abercrombie, one of the first Houston township officers elected, settled at Gaylord in early 1871. James Clydesdale homesteaded later in the spring of 1871. Clydesdale's daughter, Mrs. Dick Godney, wrote a manuscript, based on material told her by Abercrombie and her father that told Darling's story. This was later published in the Smith County Review, Sept. 3, 1936. References are made in local news items in Gaylord newspapers (Gaylord Herald) 1879-1883 and to his blacksmith shop which he ran until 1883. A letter from the County Clerk, Smith Center, Kansas, dated April 28, 1960, showed he received a patent to $NW\frac{1}{4}$, Sec. 19, T5, R. 13. The story of his arrival in Smith County and filing on the claims as described above was given in the Souvenir Book, 1912, published for the Old Settlers' Association.

[10] An attempt has been made to list these earliest settlers in groups according to the earliest possible records found with the supposition that people were living at the time who gave the information or personally knew the party mentioned. Birth records also supplied valuable information. Another problem encountered in accurately locating places of settlement was that until 1885 Smith County was divided into nine townships. Reports after 1885 generally located people in one of the twenty-five townships of the present county (see Figs. 6 and 7).

Clemann, Wm. Sheppard, Alvin Culley, Charles McCullough, George Kyger, James Clark, Julius Harris, Wm. Coop, and James McColm.[11]

These first entries, considered alone, gave little idea of actual conditions, however, because many early arrivals had not yet made the long trip to Concordia to file on a claim. They were "squatters" for the time. Even written accounts disagree when a record of early settlers is examined and the above records do not correspond with homesteaders' records.

Rev. William M. Wellman, who wrote his speech while living in Smith County in 1876 and at a time that most of these people were still there, says L. B. Graves took out the first homestead papers January 8, 1870, but the claim was later abandoned. Apparently this was one of the early homesteads, not the first. Since White Rock Creek, or Old Salem as it was called, had one of the first permanent settlers, others there may be mentioned first.

(1) This community[12] was really on the Smith-Jewell County line and, without surveyed descriptions, it is practically impossible to separate the early settlers as to county. The west edge of the town plat itself was only three-fourths of a mile inside Jewell County. Old Salem was the early trade center, post office, and community center for northeast Smith County and as such is interwoven into its history. Settlers listed for 1870 are Bill and Henry Stone. B. F. Myers settled up the creek northwest in 1870. Some that

_____

11 National Archives and Records Service, Washington 25, D.C. Section numbers and dates shown in a letter in the Appendix. These first twelve entries were made between October 29, 1870 and November 18, 1870. Final disposition of land shown in letter in Appendix from Office of Register of Deeds, Smith County, Kansas. These entries, located after township organization, would be as follows: No. 1 to 5, Webster Township on Oak Creek; No. 6, Houston west of Gaylord; No. 7 to 9, Harvey Township north of Gaylord on Beaver Creek; No. 10, Valley Township on Solomon River; No. 11, Harvey Township adjoining Cedar; No. 12, Garfield on Twelve Mile Creek.

12 These settlements are approximately located on Figure 7 by the designated numbers.

arrived in 1871 were the Hartman family, the Beardslee family, Charlie Prevost, Miles George, "Pickle" Smith, John Argyle, Fred Nussbaumer, Pete Heinline, Joe Jolly, George Morrison, James Bailey, Henry Basford, Jasper Bailey. Isaac N. Kimsey and Joel Bartlett homesteaded in the fall of 1870, then returned east for their families. Kimsey came back to settle two miles southwest of Salem with four sons, Michael, Jarrett, William, and Charles in September, 1871.[13]

(2) Another county line settlement was in the extreme southeast corner on Oak Creek, the first large tributary of the Solomon in Smith County, and was near the Jewell County settlement of Dispatch. Early settlers from Holland settled on the east side of the road in Jewell County, but later ones settled on the west side in Smith County. Records indicate that John Deters, George Walbert, and John Renken arrived in 1869. George DeBey and family came from Holland in 1869 and started West. They bought a covered wagon at Solomon City and "headed for Dispatch where other Hollanders had settled."[14] They arrived in 1871 and homesteaded in Smith County. Some arrivals for October 14, 1870 were A. Stegink, C. Klinkenberg, J. Wolberd, and J. Walters. In 1871, a funeral of a Mrs. DeYoung was held in her dugout and burial was made on the farm. A subscription school was started and held in a log house and the Dutch Reformed Church was organized that year, with Minister Deingerman (or Dangermond), Elder Peter Klinkenberg, charter members John Deters, George Wolbert, and Renken. Also arriving in 1871 were the families of Koop, Vander Giesen, Rychel, Kuiken, Snellers, D. Van Donge, Folger, B. Rosendale,

---

[13] W. E. Kimsey, manuscript published Smith County Pioneer, March 8, 1956. He was a son of Isaac N. Kimsey.

[14] Peter DeBey, son of George Debey, in interview. Printed Downs News, August 3, 1939. A. Stegink lived to be 103 years old.

Huiting, Van de Riet, Verhage, and Builstra. Sena Deters was born July 4, 1871.[15] Higgins' Bluff, where the buffalo hunters were attacked by Indians and Higgins was killed is located about one and one-half miles from this early settlement.

(3) In Webster Township, which is farther north on Oak Creek, Frank Barnes homesteaded February, 1870, but he did not prove up and it was taken by Martin Rychel. G. J. Van De Reit, Henry Bode and J. V. Lenwen homesteaded March, 1870, as did two brothers-in-law, Samuel Mathei and Martin Sonnenberg.[16]

(4) In the northwest part of Webster on Oak Creek there was another group of settlers around what was to become known as Porter's Ranch. Among them were Thomas and James Decker, May 13, 1871, and William R. Allen from Warren County, Iowa, who had a son, Elmer O. Allen, born September 15, 1871. William H. Porter was appointed postmaster at Porter's Ranch, December 28, 1871.[17]

(5) Another group of settlers in this area were J. K. Belk and Ambrose Oldaker, who settled on Oak Creek north of the Dispatch group and south of Webster in Lincoln Township, May 1, 1870, and G. J. Peebles, October 20, 1870. Mrs. Martha (or Mary) Peebles is often named as the first white woman settler in the county but dates apparently do not confirm this. The first birth in Lincoln Township was Joseph Stone, September 4, 1871.[18]

(6) LaGrand Stone was president of the New Haven Colony and led two hundred families from Connecticut to settle in the Solomon Valley and creeks draining into it. Stone first came to Kansas in 1869 with buffalo hunters and

15 Ibid.

16 Smith County Old Settlers' Homecoming Souvenir Booklet, 1912.

17 First Biennial Report of State Board of Agriculture, Vol. VI, 1877-78, pp. 424-426.

18 D. W. Wilder, Annals of Kansas, p. 523; A. T. Andreas, op. cit., p. 908.

camped at the mouth of what was later named Twelve Mile Creek. In 1870 he
returned to Kansas and located his claim on Twelve Mile (section 30, Lincoln
Township), then returned to Connecticut. In the spring of 1871 he started
for Kansas with his family. Leaving them at Solomon City, he and other men
started for their claims. He built a log cabin and made other improvements,
then brought his family to the claim in the fall. Stone saw a possibility
for the stock business and bought Texas range cattle. In a few years his
herds were ranging the Oak Creek hills. After living in the log cabin for
five years, he built a frame house of lumber hauled from Hastings, Nebraska.
"As it was one of the first frame houses in Smith County, people came for
miles to see it." He paid nine cents a pound for the wire to build what was
believed to be the first barbed-wire fence in Smith County. He also planted
a large orchard. The first religious service conducted in this area was held
by Rev. Balcom of the Baptist Church in an old granary that still stands on
the home place. In later years he was justice of peace of Lincoln Township
and married many couples in his home. He was responsible for getting a school
district started, later known as Stone School. Mr. Stone died March 1922 at
the age of nearly eighty-eight. His granddaughter and family, Mr. and Mrs.
Martin Wiersma, are living in the 83 year old house on the original homestead.[19]

(7) An area of settlement farther west along the Solomon River itself
developed into the towns of Harlan, Gaylord, and Cedarville. Some 1870 arrivals in the fall at Gaylord were Peter J. Ott, John Rhodes, J. A. Scarbrough,
William D. Street, C. E. Gaylord, S. D. Houston, William Burns, Amos Cutter,

[19] Mrs. Martin Wiersma, manuscript written for Smith County Historical
Society, published in part in The Downs News, March 31, 1960.

Alex and George Parker, and William H. Kelley. The first grocery store was
started in the spring of 1871 by C. P. Newell. George G. Hartwell, Sr. from
Livingston County, Missouri, homesteaded on Drycreek. Baker and Keeler
started the first grist mill. H. D. Pratt arrived and he and W. H. Kelley
eventually built the Pratt and Kelley Gaylord Roller Water Flouring Mills at
a cost of $13,000 in 1882-1883. William D. Street began the first store on
the west side of Beaver Creek in a loghouse and had the first post office
there June 2, 1871. William M. Skinner, Harry Abercombie, and James Clydesdale arrived. Peter Ott, L. Darling, C. P. Newell, B. Ballard, N. H. Worth-
ington, Webb McNall, and C. E. Gaylord organized a Gaylord Town Company,
January, 1871. The town was laid out and named "Gaylord" after C. E. Gaylord
who had come from Irving.[20]

Jeremiah Gilman came to the area in 1870, built the first frame house
in Gaylord in 1871 and kept it as a hotel for five years. He hauled the
lumber for his building from Waterville in Marshall County. The first child
born at Gaylord and, as far as dates can be ascertained, the first one in
Smith County, was Maggie Fowler, born on the J. Darling homestead either
May 21, 1871 or June 16, 1871.[21]

(8) Cedarville, the westernmost settlement on the Solomon in the 1870's,
was first associated with a man named Billings, but little is known of him
except he came in the fall of 1870. Another group of enterprising young men,
James and John Johnston, Major John T. Morrison, A. H. Black, Andrew and
Joseph Marshall, V. J. and B. S. Bottomly, are recorded as arriving October 12,

---

[20] A. T. Andreas, op. cit., p. 908; Smith County Review, Sept. 3, 1936;
W. M. Wellman, op. cit. C. E. Gaylord was the brother-in-law of Senator
Samuel C. Pomeroy, Atchison.

[21] Smith County Review, Sept. 3, 1936.

1870, and locating the townsite of Cedarville at the mouth of Cedar Creek
where it flowed into the Solomon River, October 25, 1870. On January 28,
1871 the papers were filed in the United States Land Office at Concordia
in behalf of the Town Company of Cedarville.[22]

John Johnston opened the post office in his store July 3, or a month
after Gaylord's post office was established. It is related that when the
mail arrived from the east it was dumped into a big packing box and the
settlers sorted through the box whenever they came in for any mail that belonged to them or the neighbors. A government inspector happened along and
notified the postmaster that the practice was illegal and must be discontinued. Johnston asked if it were legal for him to appoint deputies. He
was informed that it was. When the inspector left, he called in the settlers who were accustomed to getting their mail there and deputized them
as deputy postmasters; each continued to sort out his own mail.[23] Johnston's salary was $12.00 a year, an amount based on the business of his
post office.

(9) Apparently there was another settlement called Dresden near or
on the Solomon where it left the county in Houston Township (now Garfield).
It is known that a post office was established in the house of Sylvanus
Hammond December 1, 1871, with him as postmaster.

(10) Settlers who came in the spring and fall of 1871 who did not come
with any group include Elder M. E. (Elisha) Grover, A. R. Henderson, and Asma
Walters, A. R. Barnes, Chesley Barnes, Levert and John Hibbard, George Roe,

---

[22] Wm. Wellman, op. cit.; Mrs. Margaret Nelson, op. cit.; A. L.
Hoadley, op. cit.; Old Settlers' Souvenir Booklet, 1912.

[23] A. L. Hoadley, op. cit.; John Johnston was later county treasurer.

Sam Yarrick, Luny Walters, Dave Nelson, Sam Sweeney, Eleanor Robertson and
her two daughters. These pioneers took claims in the Reamsville area or in
the original Beaver Township. Elder Grover was a Missionary Baptist pastor
and held church services in the Baptist Church in Cora, Shiloh Church, and
at Porter's Ranch on Oak Creek.[24]

(11) Cora, on a branch of White Rock Creek, had no record of settlers
but the first school was taught in the winter of 1871-1872. School organizers were S. M. Cupp, Julius Nelson, George Buckley, and Matt Duckworth, so
they must have settled near there. Julius Nelson became postmaster there,
December 11, 1871.

(12) There was an early German settlement, with Germantown as the center, on the branches of Cedar Creek in the extreme west part of the county in
what was then north Cedar and south German Townships. Recorded as arriving
January, 1871, were H. Menshoff, L. Binman (or Bierman), Jake Rider, Abe
Eldridge, and H. H. Graurholtz and wife.[25] Frederick Wagner, his wife, and
her parents, Mr. and Mrs. Michael Emme came June, 1871. Their daughter,
Anne Wagner, was born December 15, 1871. William and George Wagner also
came in 1871. Frederick Wagner opened a general merchandise store in April
and was made postmaster December 18, 1871.[26]

(13) The organization began for Smith Centre in 1871, but there was no
settlement until 1872. The legal spelling of the name was "Smith Centre" on

[24] Mrs. Margaret Nelson, op. cit.; A. R. Barnes, unpublished manuscript
dictated by A. R. Barnes for the Smith County Historical Society. The author
has a copy.

[25] H. H. Graurholtz was also listed as H. H. Grauerholz and H. H.
Granholz. It is assumed they are one and the same since no two are listed
together.

[26] A. T. Andreas, op. cit., p. 908; Mrs. Margaret Nelson, op. cit.

the town charter, but the spelling "Smith Center" was used interchangeably from 1873 and more frequently as time passed. In September, 1871, the Smith Centre Townsite Company was incorporated with a capital stock of $12,000; 120 shares at $100 each. The charter members were R. W. Reynolds of Belleville, Dr. Roe, H. A. Wilson, W. E. Stone, John W. George, and his son Nate George, all of Jewell County. Tom Comstock of New York was the principal promoter. The first building was not begun until May, 1872, so its growth will be treated in a later section.[27]

(14) Southeast of Smith Center, probably close to Spring Creek, the Thomas Lane family and Anthony Robertson family filed on claims about July 22, 1871. A son was born to Mr. and Mrs. Christopher Noggels on August 25, 1871. They had arrived in this area June, 1871.

Other early residents in Smith County by 1871, but no definite location given, were J. T. Burrow, J. F. Albright, Charles Stewart, T. J. Tompkins, Charles S. Myers, H. A. Barb, C. B. Harlan and parents, L. Kirkendall, N. J. White, Sr., George Windscheffel. Undoubtedly there are many more who had settled on the creeks and river in isolated areas of which there are no written records.

By January 1872 it was believed that enough settlers were in residence to meet the legal requirements of six hundred inhabitants necessary to formally organize the county. An informal census was taken which showed more than six hundred, although oldtimers contend the animals had names so were counted. A committee was appointed to appear before Judge Carnahan at Concordia, armed with a petition, asking for the organization of the county. By

---

[27] Mrs. Hattie Baker Collection, op. cit.; A. T. Andreas, op. cit., p. 909.

the following proclamation from the governor, James M. Harvey, February 1,

1872, Smith County was duly organized:

> Whereas: It appears from the records in the office of the
> secretary of the state, that a census of Smith County has been
> taken, according to law, properly sworn to by three resident free-
> holders of said county, showing a population of over six hundred
> (600) inhabitants, citizens of the United States, and
>
> Whereas: More than twenty inhabitants, freeholders in Smith
> County, have petitioned for the appointment of three special county
> commissioners and one special county clerk, and having selected
> Cedarville as the place for the temporary county seat, of Smith
> County, now,
>
> Therefore, by virtue of the authority vested in me, as
> Governor of the State of Kansas, I, James M. Harvey, have appointed
> and commissioned the special county commissioners and clerk asked
> for, in that petition, and do hereby declare Cedarville, the tem-
> porary county seat of Smith County.... Done at Topeka, this First
> day of February, A.D. 1872.[28]

German	Higley	Pawnee
Cedar (Harvey)	Houston	Holland

Figure 7. The original township division.

---

[28] Hangs in the County Clerk's office, Smith Center, Kansas.

Temporary county officers appointed were James H. Johnston, clerk;
James Anderson, Frederick Wagner and George Marshall as the Commissioners.
John Johnston had opened a small store in Cedarville April 17, 1871, and
as such it was the town meeting place. Here the first commissioners' meet-
ing was held March 9. James Anderson never qualified. They met again April
first and formed townships for voting precincts by dividing these into half.
These townships were named Pawnee, German, Holland, Houston, Higley, and
Cedar (changed to Harvey May 22, 1872).[29]

January 4, 1875, Higley was changed to Beaver, Holland to Lincoln, and
the new townships of Cedar, Center, and Oak were added (see Fig. 8). Smith
County was divided into nine townships for at least six years during most of
the early settlement.[30] In the early 1880's changes took place rapidly until
many people were uncertain what township they did live in. Perhaps at this
time the custom grew to identify oneself with a particular community, usually
centered around a little country store, school, church or post office regardless of the township. It is not surprising, in talking to the older inhabitants to have them refer to happenings in Twelve Mile, Oak Creek, Crystal Plains,
Germantown, Cora, Spring Creek, or similar communities.

May 3, 1881, Harlan Township was created from part of Houston. On
April 7, 1884, Cora Township was organized. Later townships created were
Blaine, White Rock, and Logan, October 7, 1884; Martin, Crystal Plains and
Valley on January 8, 1885; Webster, Washington, Banner, Garfield, Pleasant,
Lane and Dor, July and August 1885. No subsequent change in the external

---

29 Old Settlers' Souvenir Booklet; Mrs. Hattie Baker Collection; interviews with Trube Reese, one of Smith Center's first settlers; A. T. Andreas,
op. cit., p. 909.
30 Mrs. Margaret Nelson, op. cit., p. 108; Trube Reese, article published
in Smith County Pioneer, Nov. 28, 1935.

43

SMITH COUNTY, KANSAS

NEBRASKA

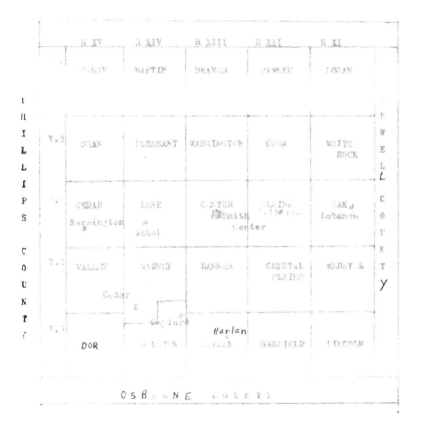

Figure 8. Townships as organized by 1885.

boundaries of the twenty-five townships, each containing 36 square miles or 36 sections of land has been made (see Fig. 8).[31]

At the special election, June 25, 1872, the poll books of all but Higley and Cedar were declared illegal. By the votes counted W. R. Allen, was elected county clerk, W. M. George, county treasurer, E. C. Benton, probate judge, Browster Higley, register of deeds, Mont Phillips, sheriff, and Levert Hibbard, W. Angel, W. D. Covington, commissioners. The bond of Charles Newman previously had been approved as Justice of Peace. Cedarville remained the temporary county seat with a vote of 77 to Smith Center 55, and Gaylord 22.[32]

In the meantime the Smith Center Town Company had been busy. It was a profitable enterprise to lay out the plat of a successful town. Land could be bought from the government for $1.25 an acre. A townsite one mile square — 640 acres — cost the promoters $800; laid out in town lots, eight to an acre and sold at $100 per lot, a profit of $798.75 per acre over the original $1.25 investment. A county seat town would have added assurance of success.

William George and A. J. Watson began the first building on the townsite May 10, 1872. Their helpers were L. T. Reese, John Goodale, and Hank Batchelder. It was a small building, 16 by 24 with a lean-to in the back, and was used by Wate George and his wife for a boarding house. It was built of green, heavy cottonwood lumber sawed by Hi Browning at his sawmill on White Rock Creek, and hauled overland by ox teams.[33]

31 Records in County Clerk's office, Smith County Courthouse, Smith Center, Kansas.

32 Ibid.; Smith County Pioneer, Apr. 4, 1878.

33 This building was later sided with pine and continued in use for the "Hotel Kansas Central" until 1885 when it was converted into the Smith County National Bank. While a hotel it was used as a political headquarters for the county. March 13, 1898 it was moved to the Frank Blaylock farm one mile north of town to be used for a dwelling, and a block of new brick buildings was built across the place where it stood. Smith County Pioneer, March 17, 1898.

Smith Centre was a good name for the new town. It was located exactly in the center of Centre Township and exactly in the center of Smith County and in the center of continental United States. It was the only town in the township and the only post office town in the United States by that name. As far as it known, Smith Centre is the legal spelling but is never used now (1959-60).[34]

During that fall of 1872 people began to move in. Albert J. Allen began a store with a stock of goods valued at $150; R. K. Smith had the second one with $300 capital stock. Both of these stores were located on the west side of the square, the Smith store on the corner, later occupied by the First National Bank, and the Allen store farther north. The third store was owned and operated by G. L. Gaylord, but later managed by Capt. J. S. McDowell. Several other business houses were soon built on the west and north sides of the square. Among the early homesteaders who proved up on their claims around Smith Centre were S. S. Reese, William Stevenson, Newton and David Hadden, R. A. Chandler, Frank Morgan, T. M. Hardacre, John Goodale, L. C. Uhl; Eli Stewart, C. S. Uhl, Martha Clark, G. D. Cordry, H. H. Springer, J. C. Harlan, Watis George, Albert Watson, L. T. Reese, E. M. Burr, Henry Batcholder, E. H. Ratliff, Thomas and W. D. Hardacre.[35]

At the first general election in November, 1872, the most interest was in the vote for county seat. There were 425 votes cast and Cedarville claimed the victory. However, J. W. George, president of the Smith Centre Town Company, persuaded the sheriff to go to Cedarville to get the county books and

_____

[34] Mrs. Hattie Baker, "History of Smith Center and Center Township." Unpublished 100 page notebook of typed material and pictures gathered by Mrs. Baker in her newspaper work and loaned to the author for this work.

[35] From a map made in the Smith County Register of Deeds Office, Smith Center, Kansas, for Mrs. Hattie Baker.

take them to Smith Centre. Sheriff Mont Phillips, and A. J. Watson went but
were met by about forty determined Cedarville men. At the show of force it
was decided to hold a legal meeting. Phillips contended the election was illegal and Cedarville was not the county seat. The answer was, "If the election was illegal, then you are not the sheriff and have no right to the county
records." It was agreed that if the promised election in the fall of 1873
showed a majority for Smith Centre, the books would be sent up the day after
the election.

Now the competition began in earnest. The Smith Centre Town Company
used part of their money in the contest. George, who was president of the
company, was running a hotel in Jewell. He kept a lookout for immigrants
and told them the claims in the valley were all taken; he then directed them
north to Tom Comstock who was superintendent of schools in Jewell County. He
in turn would direct them to Smith Centre where they would be located on claims
free of charge. Will Jenkins, with a claim adjoining Smith Centre, worked in
the printing office in Cawker City. He was to meet all incoming immigrants
there and direct them northeast to Crystal Plains, southeast of Smith Centre.

The Cedarville side had "a regular chain of land boomers" at various
points along the Solomon River from Waterville, 130 miles east, engaged in
steering immigrants to the valley to locate in the southern portion of the
county and advising them not to go to the northern or central portion because
the country was so rough they could not get through with wagons and the water
supply was inadequate. The result of the election was a decisive 275 votes
for Smith Centre, Gaylord 92, and Cedarville 81. The records were sent to
Smith Centre the next day as agreed and arrived in a shoe box.[36]

36 Mrs. Margaret Nelson, op. cit., p. 109; Mrs. Hattie Baker Collection.

Officers elected in the 1873 election were: John T. Morrison, first
Representative to the legislature; William M. Skinner, county clerk and
register of deeds; J. C. Harlan, probate judge; Nick Clemens, sheriff; W. M.
George, county treasurer; E. Hall, superintendent of schools, N. H. Withing-
ton, surveyor; J. T. Burrow, clerk of the district court; J. M. Stephen,
coroner; Vess Payne, Matt Wells, and Jesse Stranathan, commissioners. Levi
Morrell was placed on the ticket for county attorney although a printer instead of a lawyer.[37]

In 1873, it was discovered that the town company as such, could not
perfect titles to land and the company dissolved. The 640 acres of government land that had been set aside as a town site was given up except one
quarter section, including the east part of section 21 and the west part of
section 22. Block 22 of the town plat was reserved as a public square. This
was kept vacant for several years in hopes that a courthouse might be constructed there. But when it seemed no funds would be available for a long
time, the block was divided into lots and sold. All income from the sales
was placed in a Court House Fund.[38]

The courthouse story in Smith County is long and complicated due to
delay and lack of construction funds. There was no courthouse from 1873
until early in 1875. If a trial was necessary, it was held in the Uhl
building and otherwise the officers took care of their own books and records

37 Records in County Clerk's office, Smith Center, Kansas; Mrs. Hattie
Baker Collection; He afterwards went to the Ozarks in Missouri and served as
postmaster at Notch and is the "Unkle Ike" in Harold Bell Wright's The
Shepherd of the Hills; Smith County is in the Sixth Congressional District,
Fifteenth Judicial District, Fortieth Senatorial, and Eighty-sixth Repre-
sentative District of Kansas.

38 A. T. Andreas, op. cit., p. 909; Mrs. Hattie Baker Collection, op. cit.

in their homes or places of business. At an early election there was a
proposal submitted to bond the county for $2,000 to pay current expenses,
but it was defeated. Homesteaders, many of them recently discharged from
the Civil War, had very little with which to pay taxes. The first courthouse
was the rented building of Col. C. F. Campbell. It had two stories and a
cellar beneath, and was located at the northeast corner of the intersection
of Main Street and East Kansas Avenue. Campbell had built it for a store
early in 1873; shortly thereafter he was appointed register at the Kirwin
Land Office which opened January 4, 1875. The store changed hands several
times and the stock finally was moved out. It was then that it was rented
to the county. County offices were on the first floor, a courtroom above,
and the jail in the cellar. It was one of the best built buildings in the
town. At the time the only lumber available locally was green cottonwood
sawed at the mill in Salem, so Campbell sent to Manhattan to get the kind of
lumber he wanted. He employed six men, J. H. (Dick) Hill, A. J. Watson, Jim
Logan, Glen Campbell, Jim Oatis, and L. T. Reese, to haul the lumber with
teams and wagons. Jim Kindred, the blacksmith, made a novel device to hold
prisoners in the jail which was really only a pit dug under the floor. Trube
Reese described it as a "horse-powered tumbling rod...dropped through the
floor into the cellar and imbedded into the earth, together with an iron
clamp with hinge to go around the ankle and also there were leather puttees
or leggings and a heavy chain and padlock." There was only one prisoner before a complaint was filed that the device was a barbarity. He was a member
of the notorious Jack Allen and Loss Miller horse stealing gang and was being
held for state officers. In 1874-75 after the grasshopper invasion the jail
was used by the army as a distributing room for the relief provisions of beans,

bacon, flour, rice, potatoes, and coffee.[39]

The first district court convened in Smith Centre on May 5, 1874, with Judge A. J. Banta presiding. Nick Clemens was sheriff and O. F. Sheldon, Clerk of the Court. The court admitted as eligible to practice as attorneys, L. C. Uhl, E. M. Burr, and Levi Morrill.[40] A divorce was the first case on the docket — Phebe Cisco asking divorce from John Cisco.

Agitation began in the early eighties to build a new courthouse. Block number 25 was purchased and plans begun for the new building. The contract for a brick structure was let in 1887 to James Boddy and John Crandall in the sum of $5,000 and construction began. Disaster hit when, after the side walls were up and part of the roof on, the walls fell in. The material was damaged, the money gone, and the contractors ready to quit. The citizens of the town rallied to raise $1,000; in return they entered into a contract with the commissioners to use the courtroom for entertainments. The building was finished and the county officers moved in the first of March, 1888. It was later decided to take the money to repay the amount subscribed from the general fund so the county would be sole owners of the building. It was felt if the doors were opened to the public no other arrangements would be made for local amusements. If the courthouse was used just for county affairs, Smith Centre would soon have an opera house. The county commissioners who faced this problem were A. D. Barnes, Ora Jones, and John Brown. The money pledged was returned and four men, E. S. Barger, Dr. D. W. Relihan, Walter Darlington, and H. H. Springer, who had planned to build adjoining business houses that year added

39 Mrs. Hattie Baker Collection, op. cit.
40 Mrs. Hattie Baker Collection, op. cit.; another source listed S. M. Corn, G. W. White, and E. D. Morse but they may have come after this court term.

an upper story over all; this was called the "Opera House Block" for many
years. The wide stairway that led to the auditorium is under the figure
"1888" which may be seen as one drives through Main Street.

A new two-story jail, built of native stone at a cost of $3,995, was
erected during the summer of 1893. It was located just east of the courthouse, and remains in use (1959).

The old brick courthouse served its purpose for thirty years. In
1917 the county residents and commissioners, Joe Wolfe, Ed Shields, and
Emer Diggins felt the need of a larger structure and gave a contract for a
new building to M. C. Brady of Beloit. The corner stone was laid June 23rd,
with a parade, bands, and the Masonic Fraternities of the county in charge
of the program.[41] During construction, Smith County leased the Odd Fellows
Building on the west side of Main Street as temporary offices for the county
officials while the new courthouse was being built.[42]

The new building, one of the finest in the state, was finished January
1, 1920. It was 97 feet long, 81 feet wide, and 47 feet high, and was constructed of gray ozark granite up to the water table, from there up was
cream-colored Bedford stone. The flooring was of tile, all the stairways
were of marble, and the wainscoatings of tile. The total cost furnished
completely was approximately $98,000 and was all paid for when ready to be
occupied.[43]

---

[41] In the cornerstone were placed the Masonic Grand Lodge proceedings for
1918, list of the officers of all the Masonic Orders of the county, roster of
Smith County companies of Kansas State Guards, copies of the Smith County
Pioneer and Smith County Journal, names of the county officers, copy of the
contracts, one penny and a five-cent piece dated 1867.

[42] The Topeka Journal, January 25, 1917.

[43] The above material on courthouses was collected by Mrs. Hattie Baker,
and summarized by the author.

EXPLANATION OF PLATE I

Fig. 1. Joseph Cox, White Rock Township, first permanent Smith
        County settler. This picture represents four genera-
        tions: his daughter, Mrs. Nancy Upp; granddaughter, Mrs.
        Della Rice; and her daughter, Bernice Rice.

Fig. 2. First Smith County Courthouse, built in 1888.
        (Courtesy of Mrs. Hattie Baker.)

Fig. 3. Present Smith County Courthouse, dedicated in 1920.
        (Courtesy of Mrs. Hattie Baker.)

PLATE I

Fig. 1

Fig. 2

Fig. 3

CHAPTER IV

HOMESTEADERS AND HOMES

They crossed the prairies as of old
The pilgrims crossed the sea
To make the West, as they had the East
The homestead of the free.

John Greenleaf Whittier

During the summer and fall of 1872 and the beginning of 1873, more people
came into Smith County for settlement. They came singly, in families, and in
groups. This mass immigration was not a crusade of fanatics, or a raid of
filibusters, or a promoted exodus, but the measured march of earnest men and
women seeking homes and a future on the new frontier. The years of 1871-
1875 are a record of *firsts* in each part of the county, the first birth, the
first marriage, the establishment of the first schools, first churches, first
industries, the first post offices, the first doctors, all the things that
go to change the monotony of the prairies into flourishing farms and busy
towns. That these people came with the earnest desire to build a home is
shown by the fact that, in nearly every community, there is a record of a
school being organized a few months after settlement. Hand in hand with the
school, one finds records of church services held in dugouts, stores, and
even under trees on the creek bank until a church could be established, il-
lustrating that these people were endowed with a genuine Christian belief
and faith in God and the community and were not just transient speculators.

To record "first" events that happened in any particular community would
not reflect the life of the county as a whole; however, there were some general characteristics that did apply to the development of Smith County.

53

Where did Smith County settlers come from, what were their reasons for coming, and what were the population trends in the county, townships and towns? The heaviest increase in population in a short span was from 1870-1876 (see Table 4). The sources of the county's first settlers are disclosed in the state census returns of 1875. Smith County settlers came from twenty-eight states and territories, but apparently more came from Iowa and Illinois than from any other states. This total would have been larger for these states had the census considered birthplace instead of previous residence. The census in 1875 showed that of the 3,514 American-born in the population of 3,876, settlers came from the following states:[1]

Arkansas	1	Massachusetts	6	Pennsylvania	10
California	15	Michigan	6	Rhode Island	8
Colorado	1	Minnesota	140	Tennessee	5
Connecticut	16	Missouri	365	Vermont	6
Illinois	495	Nebraska	279	Virginia	24
Indiana	123	Nevada	2	West Virginia	4
Iowa	1,407	New Hampshire	7	Wisconsin	125
Kentucky	32	New Jersey	14	D.C. and Terr.	13
Maine	6	New York	60	Kansas	211
Maryland	1	Ohio	132		

Nell Waldron, in a study of colonization in Kansas from 1861-1890, found that "of all the states in the Union, Kansas is perhaps the most misunderstood. It is generally believed that Kansas is the offspring of New England."[2] The census figures in 1875 for Smith County followed the trend in the state and further supported the Waldron thesis that Kansas was not settled from New England. In a similar vein Henry Staack[3] found that more people went to Kansas from the state of Ohio than from all the New England states combined.

---

[1] Fourth Annual Report of the Kansas State Board of Agriculture, 1875.
[2] Nell B. Waldron, "Colonization in Kansas from 1861-1890," p. 151. Unpublished Ph.D. Thesis, Northwestern University, 1932.
[3] Henry Staack, "Frontier of Settlement in Kansas, 1860-1870," p. 26. Unpublished M. S. Thesis, University of Iowa, 1925.

In 1870 census showed that almost as many Kansans were born in Illinois.
(Second in settlement in Smith County. See information on 1870 census in
Appendix.)

In the proportion of immigrants from foreign countries, Smith County
and the surrounding north central counties differ from other areas in the
state in having a smaller percentage. The Tenth United States Census (1880)
showed the density of foreign population in Kansas that Smith County was in
the area of 4%-10%. This area was in the northwestern tier and the south-
central part of the then settled counties. There were approximately 28
counties in the 10%-20% area and approximately 7 in a 20%-34% area of immigrant settlement. In studying the census reports, one finds that Smith
County has had a decreasing percentage of foreign-born population since the
original sixty-six settlers in 1870 (see Table 3).

Most of the foreign-born settlers in Smith County came from Germany,
England, and Canada (see Table 2). Although the percentage of immigrants
was small, the contributions of these nationalities helped to form the
characteristics for which the county is known today. The German element
has always been the most numerous and has contributed much to the development of the western and northwestern areas of the county. The first Germans
settled on West Beaver Creek in 1871, namely, H. H. Granholz, H. Menshoff,
L. Bierman, J. Rider, and A. Eldredge.[4] By December, 1871, enough settlers
had arrived to justify the establishment of the Germantown Post Office with
F. W. Wagner as first postmaster. Most Germans came to Smith County as individuals but upon arrival settled near other Germans. Where one German

---

[4] A. T. Andreas, op. cit., p. 909; Biennial Report of the Kansas State
Board of Agriculture, 1877-78, pp. 424-426.

Table 2. Showing origin of foreign-born population in Smith County,
1875-1950.*

Country	1875	1890	1900	1910	1950
Australia	--	4	--	--	--
Austria	--	—	2	31	1
Bohemia	—	9	26	--	--
Canada	64	125	86	58	16
Czechoslovakia	--	—	—	--	9
Denmark	—	30 ·	34	25	4
England & Wales	70	172	146	91	7
France	—	1	--	--	—
Germany	120	406	467	389	94
Holland	—	53	58	38	2
Ireland	20	91	71	29	3
Norway	—	10	7	7	1
Poland	--	2	--	--	1
Scotland	10	33	28	15	—
Sweden	--	70	26	25	5
Switzerland	--	42	--	26	--
Mexico	—	--	--	64	—
North of Europe	36	--	--	--	--
South of Europe	19	—	--	--	—
Sweden, Denmark, & Norway	21	--	—	--	—
Other European	--	—	--	--	9
Others	2	—	--	8	11

* Federal and State Reports 1875-1950.

settled, others seemed to soon follow.

Table 3. Showing population of Smith County by origin of birth.*

Year	Native White	Foreign Born	Negro	% of Foreign Born
1870	57	9	0	15
1875	3,514	362	—	10
1880	13,002	881	15	6
1890	15,611	1,049	2	6
1900	15,384	999	1	
1910	14,554	806	5	$5\frac{1}{2}$
1920	14,430	545	10	3.6
1930	13,161	374	7	2.8
1940	10,339	243	0	2.8
1950	8,682	162	2	1.9

* Federal and State Reports 1875-1950.

Thousands of potential emigrants were prevented from leaving their homes by the Civil War. After the Civil War "exaggerated stories of drouth, famine, and Indian outrages deterred many from seeking a home in the state which was best known in Europe as the 'home of the free' until the early seventies."[5] As Smith County was one of the counties just ahead of the frontier line, as shown by the progression of the United States Land Offices (Concordia 1871, Cawker City 1872, Kirwin 1875), it was one of the counties to receive a substantial share of this immigration, as well as the many Civil War veterans

5 Nell B. Waldron, op. cit., p. 14.

who had by this time returned home and found that the opportunities for land
and advancement were gone in the more settled areas. The Kansas Pacific
reached Junction City in 1868, and the Chicago Company secured free transportation for purchasers of Kansas Pacific land. This brought a stream of
colonists from Illinois and the Scandinavian peninsula into the valleys of
the Republican, Smoky Hill, and White Rock Creek.

There was only one other foreign settlement in the county. That was the
Hollanders who settled in colonies in parts of Osborne, Mitchell, Smith and
Jewell counties and farther west in Gove and Sheridan counties. Waldron says
that "Kansas traditions and institutions no doubt appealed to the Hollanders,
but the Kansas climate did not. The Dutch farmer who controlled the water
supply for his crops was not eager to become a pioneer in the 'Great American
Desert'.... However, a colony of emigrants settled in the northeast corner
of Osborne County in 1871 and founded the little town of Rotterdam, later
called Dispatch. ...Additional colonists made their homes on the other side
of the boundary line in Jewell and Smith Counties. Oak Creek which makes
fruitful this corner of the four counties became a Dutch stream. Some of them
took land as far north as Reamsville.[6]

Charles Schwarz was the Hollander who built the now famous Dutch Windmill
in the Reamsville area. B. F. Koops homesteaded on Oak Creek. He was almost
penniless; however, he won a bride. As they were too poor to own a horse to
ride, they walked the twenty miles to Mankato, the county seat of Jewell
County, to be married and their honeymoon trip was the twenty mile walk back
to the homestead. "But they did not remain poor. Their wealth and family

---

6 Ibid., p. 97.

increased proportionally and finally, as their seven children came of age, the parents presented each of them with a Kansas farm!"[7]

Next may be considered the question, "Why did settlers come to Smith County?" Due to no direct evidence, this can be considered only in the light of what was true for the state as a whole in the early seventies. How interesting it would be to have interviewed a representative number of the first five thousand settlers with the question, "Why did you choose Smith County, Kansas?" As has been mentioned, Smith County was settled during the period of abundance of land. If a farm failed to produce profitably, or there was not opportunity to expand, the occupants would often move to the frontier and take up new land. This is what so many returning soldiers did after the Civil War. The location of Smith County, as a part of the frontier at this time, was inviting to immigrants hunting new homes.

Advertising, both private and commercial, had a lot to do with many settlers coming to Kansas and after they were here they spread out along the frontier. The first sod had been turned over and sown and some of the tremendous yields that were obtained with little work made good writing material to the friends and relatives "back East". Such an account is one found in the Report of the State Board of Agriculture for 1878, given by F. D. Morse, Smith Center:

> Corn — James Frazier planted 120 acres in T3R15 with yellow Dent corn. It was put in the first of May and was harvested in August and September, and was grown on bottom and upland, there being about equal parts of each in the field. The crop was ploughed three times with a cultivator, and averaged 98 bushels to the acre, at a cost of about $7.50.

---

7 Nell B. Waldron, op. cit., p. 96.

This was effective advertising and strong persuasion for those "caught close
to the bare margin of existence. Those who were economically independent or
had good positions were comparatively immune to the westward fever. It was
a restlessness that could be better explained in the terms of bread and butter
than a desire for elbow room."[8]

Commercial advertising was carried on by companies, the state, and individuals. Historians such as Fred Shannon, Ray Allen Billington, Thomas D.
Clark and A. Bower Sagesar agree that railroads with their advertising were
undoubtedly a great factor in the settlement of the state.[9] The exhibits at
the Centennial Exposition at Philadelphia in 1876 let the rest of the world
"discover Kansas." Henry Worrall, the only Kansas artist to achieve recognition on a national scale for a period corresponding to the early history
of the state, was employed by the State Board of Agriculture in 1875-1876
to collect, prepare and arrange exhibits for the exhibition.

> To appreciate fully the importance which the State Board of
> Agriculture attached to the Kansas exhibit it must be recalled that
> the drought and grasshopper year of 1874, with its widespread pub-
> licity, was, in 1875, a very tender spot in the conscience of Kansas
> enthusiasts and every possible aid in presenting the best aspects of
> the state to the nation were considered. One prominent Kansan, look-
> ing back many years after the exhibit, wrote, "The best effort for
> encouraging immigration ever made by Kansas was her agricultural
> display at the Centennial Exposition."[10] Twenty-five thousand copies
> of the Fourth Annual Report of the State Board of Agriculture were
> printed and distributed at the exposition....[11]

8 James Willard, The Trans-Mississippi West, p. 261.
9 Fred A. Shannon, The Farmer's Last Frontier, pp. 41-44; Ray A. Billington, Westward Expansion, pp. 706-708; Thomas D. Clark, Frontier America, p. 690;
A. Bower Sagesar, "Mails Go Westward," in John D. Bright's Kansas, The First
Century, pp. 234-253.
10 George Veale, "Coming In and Going Out," Kansas Historical Collections,
Vol. 11, (1909-1910) p. 5 as quoted in Robert Taft, "Pictorial Record of the
Old West," Kansas Historical Quarterly, Vol. 14, (1946) p. 252.
11 Robert Taft, op. cit., p. 252.

Several enterprising men of Topeka, realizing the advantage to be had in the state, had earlier organized an Emigration Society to aid the poor and needy in coming to Kansas. Through this Society's influence pamphlets had been printed and distributed throughout the United States and Europe in the spring and summer of 1875.[12]

Writings by individuals, some intentionally to influence immigration, publicized the state. Some of these were Horace Greeley, who had articles in the New York Tribune, Henry Villard in the Cincinnati Daily Commercial, and Albert Richardson in the Boston Journal. A group of Junction City men organized a company to survey the Solomon Valley for a railroad. Included in the group were Robert McBratney, lawyer in Junction City and leading organizer for railroads in Kansas; B. F. Mudge, professor at the Kansas State Agricultural College and former state geologist; and Richard Mobley, agent for sale of railroad lands. Governor Harvey ordered one hundred state troops to accompany them from the forks of the Solomon for Indian protection. McBratney and Mudge kept up a constant chain of letters to eastern Kansas newspapers giving most favorable accounts of the resources of the region. They were widely read and copied, and although they failed to attract railroad builders, they did cause many homeseekers to go up the Solomon Valley, which eventually induced the Union Pacific in 1879 to extend a branch line through the valley.[13] A Homestead Guide was published by F. G. Adams of Waterville in 1873. He included just about anything the prospective settler would want to know such as copies of all the Homestead Laws and extra provisions,

[12] Robert C. Venable, op. cit., p. 92; S. T. Crawford, Kansas in the Sixties, p. 226.
[13] Martha B. Caldwell, "Exploring the Solomon Valley," Kansas Historical Quarterly, Vol. 6, (1937), pp. 60-76.

elaborate descriptions of each county and town on the frontier open to settlement, with advertisements by merchants and of places for sale.

C. E. Hutchinson of Topeka wrote a book publicizing Kansas. He said it was based on "15 years of experience" and was designed to answer questions which were asked by persons contemplating a removal from some other region to Kansas. Another volume to "meet the popular demand for reliable information about "Kansas as it is" was the book by L. D. Burch of Chicago, published in 1878, entitled Kansas As It Is -- Resources, Advantages, and Drawbacks. He forgot most of the drawbacks in his enthusiasm.[14]

The J. W. Weyand and Co. formed at Smith Center, and J. I. Warner, Real Estate and Immigration Agent, published advertising pamphlets that were widely distributed through the state. Some sample advertisements were:[15]

> 90 acres in this farm, 25 of which is bottom land, 15 acres in cultivation, 10 acres under fence, sod house and barn, running water and a spring, 80 rods from schoolhouse and church. Price $824.

> 20 acres off of southeast corner of the southeast corner, Sec. 6, T4 R18 for $200 cash.

> SW¼ Sec2, T8 R13, 160 acres all upland, 85 acres in cultivation, 70 acres under fence, sod house and frame barn, 2 wells and one spring, 200 peach trees; 1½ miles to church and school. Price $2,500; $1,700 cash, balance two years.

As the spring of 1875 advanced the tide of immigration poured into Kansas. Smith County's greatest increase in population was in 1875, an increase of nearly four and one-half thousand for a single year.

---

[14] C. E. Hutchinson, Hutchinson's Resources of Kansas, Title page and introduction; L. D. Burch, Kansas As It Is - Resources, Advantages, and Drawbacks.

[15] J. W. Weyand and J. I. Warner, pamphlet at State Historical Society Library in Topeka.

EXPLANATION OF PLATE II

Advertisements from A. G. Adams' Homestead Guide,
published in 1873 at Waterville, Kansas.

SMITH CENTER,

—THE—

COUNTY SEAT OF SMITH COUNTY.

A COUNTY CONTAINING MORE GOOD LAND, BETTER DIVERSIFIED WITH

TIMBERED STREAMS OF UNFAILING WATER,

THAN ANY OTHER COUNTY IN THE HOMESTEAD REGION.

WITH GOOD BUILDING ROCK, NUMEROUS PURE SPRINGS, A DEEP RICH SOIL, AND SETTLING UP WITH MAR-VELOUS RAPIDITY.

THE COUNTY SEAT IS THE GEOGRAPHICAL CENTER OF THE COUNTY, AND IS THE

Center of Immigration.

IT IS A GOOD POINT FOR MECHANICS, TRADESMEN AND MANUFACTURERS, AND TO SUCH LIBERAL INDUCEMENTS ARE GIVEN BY THE

SMITH CENTER TOWN COMPANY.

JOHN W. GEORGE, President.

WM. A. GARRETSON, Secretary.

W. M. GEORGE. M. W. GEORGE.

GEORGE & BRO.,

REAL ESTATE AGENTS AND CONVEYANCERS,

Smith Center, Smith Co., Kansas.

Will locate settlers in that and adjoining counties. Proprietors SMITH CENTER HOTEL. Dealers in PROVISIONS and GROCERIES of all kinds.

A. J. SMITH,

Carpenter, Builder and Contractor,

SMITH CENTER,

Smith County, - - KANSAS.

PLATE II

F. D. MORSE,

Attorney at Law,

CEDARVILLE, KAN.

THE FRONTIER NEWSPAPER.

—THE—

Smith County Pioneer,

PUBLISHED AT

CEDARVILLE, Smith Co., KANSAS.

W. D. JENKINS, *Editor and Proprietor.*

Devoted to the development of the Solomon Valley. TERMS: $2.00 a Year.

E. P. HOBBS,

DEALER IN

GENERAL MERCHANDISE,

—SUCH AS—

Dry Goods, Boots and Shoes, Hats and Caps, Ready-Made Clothing,

GROCERIES, PROVISIONS, GRAIN AND FLOUR,

CEDARVILLE, - Smith County, - KANSAS.

64

Smith County was mainly settled by three big tides, with one major drop in 1882 which lacks explanation.[16] There was an increase of 3,810 the first five years of settlement; then the gain of 4,439 from 1875 to 1876; a growth of 5,570 the next four years; the unexplained drop of 3,015 in two years; than a gain of 5,514 in the next eight years to the highest peak of population ever recorded in 1900, when 16,384 inhabitants resided in Smith County.

Table 4. Population of Smith County, 1870-1959.*

Year	Pop.	Year	Pop.	Year	Pop.	Year	Pop.
1870	66	1884	12,663	1920	14,985	1946	9,098
1875	3,876	1886	15,361	1930	13,545	1950	8,846
1876	8,315	1890	15,613	1936	11,993	1954	8,500
1880	13,885	1900	16,384	1938	10,359	1956	8,288
1882	10,870	1910	15,365	1940	10,582	1959	8,016

* Totals taken from Reports of the State Board of Agriculture and U. S. Census Reports, 1870-1959.

After 1900 a gradual decrease set in for Smith County with a bigger drop in the decade of the "dust storm" years, 1930-1940. In contrast the state had an increase from an average population per county of 14,004 to 17,152 in 1940. Smith County had more residents than the average county in 1900, but 6,570 fewer than average in 1940, and has been decreasing ever

[16] The author considered and investigated climatic hazards, a possibility of new settlements in other counties or of unusual incidents peculiar to the area, economic trends, and compared population trends with neighboring counties without finding a satisfactory explanation for a change in trend and a decrease in population of 3,015 in two years, then a gradual increasing trend after the low in 1882. This offers a field for further research in the county.

since while the average county population for the state in 1960 is approximately 20,000.

Towns and cities in general over Kansas and the United States gained in population at the expense of the rural areas but this did not apply to Smith County since the county lost far more than the towns gained (see Table 5). From 1900 to 1940, the county population decreased approximately 5,802 inhabitants or 35.4% of its total inhabitants. At the same time, the population in four towns gained and in two decreased, but the total gain for the towns was less than 6%. Reports from the 1950's indicate that this decline is leveling off again. Perhaps a modern agricultural economy and the present land yields can support the existing population. What effect the building of Kirwin Dam and introducing irrigation will have is yet to be seen (see Chapter V).

There were several ways in which these thousands of homeseekers who streamed into the county between 1870 and 1878 (the 1878 census showed an increase of 8,249 in the eight years) could gain title to the land on which they settled. This was the golden age of the Homestead Law, passed May 20, 1862, and put into operation in January, 1863.[17] It was well understood and well advertised before Smith County became actively involved seven years later. It allowed every citizen, twenty-one years old or head of a family, the right to homestead on surveyed lands to the extent of one quarter section (160 acres) at $1.25 per acre.

Beginning in 1870 there were a series of acts passed modifying the original Homestead Law and making it easier to get title. These acts

---

[17] Statutes at Large, 1862-1863, Vol. 12, pp. 392-393.

Table 5. Population in each town and township by decades from
1880 to 1950 and 1959 in Smith County, Kansas.*

Town or Township	1880	1890	1900	1910	1920	1930	1940	1950	1959
Banner		483	539	446	423	368	238	121	106
Beaver	1362	429	496	476	433	397	287	223	176
Blaine		668	750	597	636	482	377	260	166
Cedar	1449	807	566	470	449	394	298	229	174
Centre	1827	496	464	492	465	427	345	273	218
C. Plains		574	511	440	407	355	195	133	96
Cora		605	577	470	463	341	258	163	142
Dor		403	309	290	300	227	136	102	99
Garfield		369	392	424	343	293	183	134	103
German	1200	491	443	429	391	360	226	152	93
Harlan		666	490	568	588	522	409	295	228
Harvey	1431	721	751	676	463	353	327	255	191
Houston	1819	470	466	400	420	366	282	181	119
Lane		628	672	689	414	362	299	203	174
Lincoln	1488	501	434	481	392	341	300	220	195
Logan		597	601	554	523	390	356	280	189
Martin		663	685	588	306	392	282	161	117
Oak	1673	795	852	735	554	468	434	325	236
Pawnee	1634	526	475	459	459	420	240	208	147
Pleasant		621	543	506	449	413	299	218	151
Swan		539	512	368	379	318	161	151	132
Valley		483	499	430	396	368	279	197	177
Washington		536	482	476	430	347	243	191	140
Webster		545	510	477	404	312	241	178	139
White Rock		615	654	661	455	386	240	202	169
Athol					330	270	218	203	146
Cedar					144	126	145	86	77
Gaylord	233	314	338	322	346	297	243	231	275
Kensington			310	550	595	537	577	635	620
Lebanon		301	590	734	824	689	675	610	612
Smith Center	254	767	1061	1426	1635	1632	1670	2026	2410
Totals	13885	15613	16384	15365	14985	13543	10582	8846	8016

* Reports of the Kansas State Board of Agriculture and U. S. Census Records.

undoubtedly stimulated the western migration to Kansas, including Smith County. For instance, an amendment of April 4, 1872 allowed the period of military service to be deducted from time of residence except the applicant was obligated to have at least one year of residence on the land.[18] If the claim was sold before proved up, it vested no title to the purchaser. Abandonment had to be reported to the government and approved by the commissioner of the general land office, then the purchaser made entry as if it were the original one, although he gained the benefit of previous improvements. This is one reason why it is so difficult to trace records on homesteads.

Any person planting an osage or hawthorn fence, or who would build a stone fence four and one-half feet high around any field within ten years of the passage of the Kansas law of 1869 was to receive an annual bounty from the state of $2 for every forty rods so planted, cultivated and kept up.[19] Any person planting trees on one acre or more of prairie land within ten years after passage of the Kansas tree culture act (1869)[20] and was successful in growing and cultivating them for three years or in planting and protecting one-half mile or more of forest trees in an approved manner along any public highway for three years was paid an annual bounty out of the county treasury.

This was undoubtedly the beginning of the so-called "hedge-rows" found on one or the other side of practically every mile-line road in Smith County. (The author was a girl there and has vivid recollections of those miles of trees along the roads.) Modern farming, the drouth in the '30's, and the

---

[18] 42nd Congress, Session II, Statutes at Large, Vol. 17, Ch. 85, p. 49.
[19] General Statutes of Kansas, 1868, Ch. 40, Art. IV, Sec. 2-3, pp. 495-496, approved Feb. 20, 1867.
[20] General Statutes of Kansas, 1868, Ch. 112, Sec. 1-4, pp. 1094-1095.

grasshoppers have accounted for the near-disappearance of what once was a common sight in the county. Traces of the old stone fences could still be found in the Solomon Valley in the 1940's, but they too are fast disappearing. They had never been plentiful due to the lack of stone and the expense of construction.

In Smith County a large number of timber claims were planted. The Timber Culture Act of 1873[21] was later modified to require only ten acres of timber for title, and many Smith County homesteaders followed this plan. Many early settlers cannot be dated for their time of settlement by homestead records due to their use of the pre-emption act of 1841 in obtaining public land.[22]

In a humorous vein, Smith County settlers held that Uncle Sam was really betting the settler a quarter section of public land against $16.00 ($6.00 filing fee, $10.00 registration fee) that he could not stick on the land for five years. Most of the Smith County settlers won the bet. The Federal Land Office was opened January 16, 1871, at Concordia, and there were more entries made there in a comparable time than at any other land office in the United States.[23]

---

[21] 42nd Congress, 3rd Session, U. S. Statutes, 1872-1873, Vol. 17, Ch. 277, p. 605-606, passed March 3, 1873.

[22] This gave the individual actually thirty-three months from the date of settlement before proof and payment had to be made. It required him to make a declaratory statement within three months from the date of settlement (many did not in the early days of slow transportation and no formal law enforcement), then make proof and payment within thirty months after filing the declaratory notice. Statutes at Large, Vol. 5, Ch. 16, p. 457, Sept. 4, 1847.

[23] F. G. Adams, op. cit. p. 81. Federal Land Office, Concordia, Jan. 16, 1871 to Apr. 1, 1873, 9,540 homestead entries, 5,894 pre-emption filings, 2,000 final proofs. By Aug. 5, 1872, Smith County settlers were taking their land office business to Cawker City. Here there were 1,010 homestead entries, 1,974 pre-emption claims, and 487 soldier filings by April 1, 1873.

Notices like the following could be found in nearly every issue of the
early papers:

> Land office at Kirwin, Kansas, No. 11921, August 16, 1886.
> Notice is hereby given that the following named settler has filed
> notice of his intention to make final proof in support of his claim
> and that said proof will be made before the probate court, or Dis-
> trict Court at Smith Center, Kansas, on September 25, 1886, viz:
> T. A. Campbell, D. S. 19673 for the South half of the southeast
> quarter of section 26, township 2, Range 11. He names the follow-
> ing witnesses to prove his continuous residence upon and cultivation
> of said land, viz: D. M. Adams, Wesley Young, Ed George, J. B. Justice
> of Salem, Kansas.
>   - John Bissell, Register[24]

These laws seem, in the twentieth century, unbelievably liberal, but
for many of the homesteaders the $16.00 was a fortune. If there was one thing
they had in common, it was the lack of money. A. R. Barnes had to borrow six
dollars to pay his filing on the first homestead on Beaver Creek. L. T. Reese
told the story of meeting L. C. Uhl, who later became well-known in the county
and state in his law practice, walking into the county with his belongings,
consisting of a law book, tied up in a red bandana handkerchief. From his
own account, it is said Joel Burrow walked to the county barefooted from the
end of the railroad line at Clay Center. He had one pair of shoes but wanted
to save them. He later became President of the First National Bank at Smith
Center and President of the Central National Bank of Topeka. George McNeice,
in later years a successful newspaper editor, said that "had it been a matter
of life and death to him, he could not get sufficient cash together for months
at a time to buy a postage stamp. Things got so bad he had to buy calico to
make trousers and go barefoot."[25]

---

[24] Elmer Stump, "History of White Rock Township," Unpublished manuscript
at State Historical Library. Above notice was copied from an old copy of the
Salem Argus.

[25] C. Clyde Myers, "A Town That Bloomed, Then Faded," p. 387.

One settler gave this description of life on the frontier. It might fit all of the Kansas counties on the edge of settlement at that time as well as Smith County.

> We were all poor alike. The men and women did their own work because they had nothing to pay for help. If one man had a job he couldn't do alone, like harvesting or thrashing /sig/ he changed work with his neighbors. If a family got to the bottom of the meal barrel, they could not go out and earn a few dollars. There was nobody able to hire and pay wages. Everybody was in a struggle for subsistence. I don't mean to say there was an absolute dead level of equality. There were some slight lines of social demarcation drawn. For instance, Uncle Dave Fowler, on Flat Rock Creek, lived in a five-room house with a roof of sawed shingles; he actually had a team of American horses. He was a "bloated Plutocrat."[26]

The lack of money did not seem to be considered a hardship in the same class with cold, hunger, fear of Indians, famine and sickness, and above all, the terrible loneliness of the frontier. Settlers welcomed every opportunity to get together, from log-raising for a new house or barn to a funeral or social gathering. Social activity was most desired in the fall when the harvest work was done.

> In those days there were no social cleavages -- everyone was the social equal of everyone else as long as he behaved himself. They got together at dances and social gatherings, debating societies, and revival meetings; spelling bees and singing schools were organized in all the country schoolhouses.[27]

And of course, for the men, hunting was the favorite sport. Hardships and poverty were appalling, but through it all there was wholesome enjoyment by people hungering for human fellowship.

---

[26] Henry Staack, op. cit., p. 41-42.
[27] A. L. Headley, op. cit.

Mrs. Cora Ream, a pioneer daughter in Smith County, writes in her "Frontier Memories" that

> in those days folks had time to be friendly. There was
> not as much to detract the people's minds. Homes were more
> stable and people were happier though they had much hardship
> to endure. Really, people were so busy keeping the souls and
> bodies together, they had no time to think of much else. It
> was the desire of every man to own a home and every woman to
> care for it. The home was the foundation stone on which they
> were built.[28]

Nowhere did this friendliness prove stronger than in the time of trouble, such as a fire or a death. It seemed nothing short of miraculous the way news spread, considering the lack of communication and the distance between settlers. The news of a death usually reached the neighboring families the same day, and each one learning it sent out several of the older children to tell nearby settlers.

> They came with food and offers of help. Material to work
> with was scarce, but there was no scarcity of hands to help the
> grieving ones. In the covered wagons in which they had come there
> had been only room enough for the necessities, but these people
> were ready to share those necessities with the unfortunate neighbor
> for whom they felt such deep sympathy.[29]

They learned early to get along with what was available and appreciated small things that may not seem understandable in the twentieth century. Virginia Harlan Barr wrote of her experience one Christmas when they were snowed in and she, then a small child, wanted some Christmas activity. Her aunt, Lulu Harlan, although a girl not much older, made Virginia a rag doll with buffalo hair, and they exchanged small china animals that each had brought with her. Mrs. Barr treasured hers for many years.[30]

---

28 Mrs. Cora Ream was a daughter of Mrs. William Skinner who taught school in Gaylord in 1872. Her "Frontier Memories" is a valuable manuscript of the people and incidents of early Smith County.

29 Margaret Nelson, op. cit., p. 153.

30 Virginia Harlan Barr, "Reminiscences of Early Days in Kansas," Unpublished manuscript at the State Historical Library, 1938.

Food was a major consideration for the settler. Grocery stores were part of the general merchandise store by necessity. The main staples purchased there were sugar and tea or occasionally beans. In the drouth or grasshopper years, or due to scarcity of money, even sugar and tea were omitted. In the worst grasshopper year, 1874, for some reason the grasshoppers left the cane fields nearly untoubhed. That winter people were called "sorghum-lappers" because many subsisted on sorghum and bread, mostly cornbread. They managed to purchase enough corn to grind. Grist mills, sawmills, and sorghum presses were the first industries to locate in the county. At one time there were four large water Flouring Mills along the Solomon River; namely, Wilson and Son, Excelsior Mills, Keeler and Son, and Bougman and Talley.

Fall brought a flurry of activity on the homesteads to prepare for the long winter. September brought a rush to get the hay in. All of it had to be mowed with the scythe, hauled in and stacked close to the stables. Fireguards had to be plowed, the cane had to be stripped and taken to the mill for the year's supply of sorghum. Each farm hummed with industry, for each family was dependent on their own resources. There was the additional problem of lighting. There was no coal oil within a hundred miles, so there was no chance to use lamps. Every bit of grease used for candles was carefully preserved from wild animals that were killed, because there were too few domestic animals. Wood ashes were saved to make lye, which was added to the waste fat and cracklings to make soap. It was also used in the making of hominy, another staple of diet along with mush. Every housewife raised her hops in the garden and with cornmeal made her own yeast cakes. The hops were dried and stored in the cupboard. There were no jars for canning. All fruits and vegetables, even the wild plums and grapes, were dried. Occasionally a few glasses of jelly could be made if the family were fortunate enough to buy some sugar. They were carefully covered and put away to be used only in case of sickness or for very important company. Jams and butters were made with sorghum. Another luxury was coffee. It was purchased green, browned in a bread pan in a slow oven but stirred every few minutes. When the grain cracked brittle between the teeth, a lump of butter was put in the pan and blended thoroughly to give it a glaze and richer flavor. It was someone's duty to grind it in the mill before each meal. Pumpkin was cut in rings and dried to be used for pie. Large stone jars were filled with pumpkin butter made with sorghum if there was a surplus. The homesteaders did not lack vitamins either after they were established. Sauerkraut juice was in every cellar in the barrel of stored kraut. Carrots and beets, covered with damp sand, kept nicely as did heads of cabbage and sacks of onions, and the potato bin was full. White flour was precious and hoarded; griddle cakes were made of shorts and eaten with sorghum; gravy was a common item on the menu. Thus the soil provided the vegetables and the prairie the game for meat for the settler who had to be self-sufficient to exist.[31]

From manuscripts written by early settlers,[32] from personal interviews with and letters received from children of these settlers, the conclusion can be drawn that the majority solved the problem of a home by first building dug-outs. Many of these have been described as windowless, so small that the table was set outdoors between meals, and yet housed families of six, eight, or even

---

[31] From Mrs. Margaret Nelson's book, op. cit.; conversations with Mrs. Hattie Baker, the author's grandparents, and other early Smith County settlers or their descendants.

[32] Mrs. Cora Ream, op. cit.; Virginia Harlan Barr, op. cit.; A. L. Headley, op. cit.; Frank Barnes, op. cit.

fifteen until a better abode could be built. There are many records of
schools, churches, even funerals and weddings, being held in these dugouts.
These were followed in popularity by the sod house which usually seemed like
a palace in comparison. The walls were built of plowed sod, the roof usually
poles covered with sod. Needless to say, they were not too water tight when
it rained. John Lenau, a settler southeast of Cedarville, began constructing
a light-weight plow in his blacksmith shop that would break the sod better
than the heavy plows brought from the East. They became popularly termed
"grasshopper plows." He could make about one hundred a winter.

Some fortunate individuals were able to build frame or log houses.
Frame houses were few because the only lumber available was the native sawed
lumber, usually cottonwood, that warped in the hot sun. Lumber freighted in
by ox team came from various railroad points such as Waterville, Hastings,
Nebraska, or even Marysville. Of course these points became closer as the
railroad moved across the state. Few log houses except along the streams
were built due to the scarcity of trees. The existing trees were not large
enough or lacked uniform size to make their use practical.

The southern part of Smith County was fortunate in having plenty of
native limestone rock available, large enough to quarry and soft enough to
cut with the hand tools available. Many of the business buildings, homes,
school, and churches of Harlan were constructed from stone. Thus the pioneer
settlers made use of materials at hand on the prairies much as the Pilgrims
did on the coast. In his poem, "The Homes of Kansas," Miller pictures the
types of homes constructed as settlement advanced.

The Homes of Kansas[33]

The cabin homes of Kansas!
How modestly they stood
Along the sunny hillsides
Or nestled in the wood.
They sheltered men and women
Brave-hearted pioneers;
Each one became a landmark
Of Freedom's trial years.

The sod-house of Kansas!
Though built of Mother Earth,
Within their walls so humble
Are souls of sterling worth.
Though poverty and struggle
May be the builder's lot,
The sod house is a castle
Where failure enters not.

The dug-out homes of Kansas!
The lowliest of all,
They hold the homestead title
As firm as marble hall.
Those dwellers in the caverns
Beneath the storms and snows,
Shall make the desert places
To blossom as the rose.

The splendid homes of Kansas!
How proudly now they stand,
Amid the fields and orchards,
All o'er the smiling land.
They rose up where the cabins
Once marked the virgin soil,
And are the fitting emblems
Of patient years of toil.

God bless the homes of Kansas!
From poorest to the best;
The cabin of the border,
The sod-house of the West;
The dugout, low and lonely,
The mansion grand and great;
The hands that laid their hearthstones
Have built a mighty state.
          - Sol Miller
           Editor of Troy Chief

---

[33] Copied from John and Susan Simmonds, compiled by Frank W. Simmonds, 1940.

CHAPTER V

BOOM OR BUST[1]

Smith County was based economically upon agricultural production from
the time the plow turned the first furrow in the prairie sod. Climatic
hazards such as drouths, blizzards, and periods of excess moisture directly
affected the trend of social, economic, and political conditions in the county.
Also of utmost importance were price trends in the country as a whole because
the main markets for the agricultural products were outside the county. Apparently unrelated incidents had a direct effect. For instance, railroads
made marketing easier and gave an impetus to more intensive agriculture.
Principally speaking, when the majority of determinants was favorable, it
was "boom"; when they were unfavorable, it was "bust". Over the period of
approximately ninety years, separate consideration of each factor would be
impossible. Thus, some consideration will be given to the major factors,
showing their effect upon the trends of economic and social conditions in
the county through the decades.

Looking over the broad expanse of prairie sod, the pioneer settlers
must have had something of an element of prophecy within their souls. They
certainly must have had faith that the prairies would be made to yield in
abundance in order to find the courage and determination to face the combined
perils of the frontier and climate. Records show that their faith was justi-
fied, even from the first crop literally scratched into the virgin soil.

---

[1] All statistics in this chapter not otherwise specified were obtained
from the Kansas State Board of Agricultural Reports and Federal Census
Reports, 1872-1957.

Because the buffalo grass roots were so entwined and tough, the sod could not be worked down after it was plowed, so the farmer walked along and dropped the corn seed in the sod furrow. Eventually as the grass rotted, the ground became a field. In 1871-1872 sod corn made exceptionally good crops, and these first settlers' enthusiasm ran high. M. W. George on White Rock Creek raised 50 bushel of corn to the acre; James Bailey sowed 5 acres of wheat and raised 30 bushel per acre.[2] In the late summer, after the grass had cured from the summer heat, a prairie fire, thought by the pioneers to be started by the Indians south of the Republican River, swept all of Smith County. Most livestock and the few possessions of the settlers were saved by fireguards either previously plowed or hastily put in at the time, but it cut down on the game for winter food and feed for the stock as prairie grazing was depended on for the cattle, oxen and horses.

The winter of 1872-73 had been dry and mild with a few blustery, cold days, and most of what snow there was had blown into the draws. Easter Sunday, April 13, 1873, had dawned unusually warm and sultry. About four in the afternoon the wind suddenly began to blow from the northwest, becoming in a few hours "a veritable hurricane." There was heavy rain for about two hours, then the temperature began to fall, and the rain changed to sleet, then to snow. After the storm was over the country looked like one glistening sheet of snow and ice, the ravines were leveled, drifts were piled ten and fifteen feet deep — to the eaves of buildings. For ten days the town of Smith Center was without groceries. The country was searched for cornmeal and side meat

2 F. G. Adams, The Homestead Guide, p. 231.

for the hungry.[3] More than three fourths of all the livestock in the country perished, buried deep under snow in ditches and ravines, and some loss of life was reported.

A story of one of the more fortunate families is given in the diary of the Simmonds family:

> When the storm abated, my father, Angus, and Grandfather, John, went out to see what had become of their oxen and cows. They found the stable destroyed, and livestock nowhere to be seen. Thinking of course that the cattle had drifted along with the storm, they followed Dry Creek south for about three quarters of a mile, and when they reached what had formerly been a deep ravine in the bed of the creek, they found it levelled with drifted snow. There they saw just the tips of the long horns protruding through the solidly frozen snow crust. They surmised that the cattle were dead and went to bring shovels to dig them out so that the hides might be saved. When they dug through far enough they found the oxen and cows all alive, even the calves.... They had crowded for shelter under a precipitous bank, where the snow had drifted over them, literally burying them. A hard crust had frozen over the top, and the cattle stamping about in the snow underneath had formed a protecting cavern. Their good fortune, however, was not shared by the other members of the family or neighbors; most of them lost practically all of their livestock — a tragedy in that pioneer country.[4]

As S. D. Flora, federal meteorologist, pointed out in his report on Kansas weather, it was not so much the severity of the storm that caused the hardship and stock loss as the unpreparedness of the settlers, due to recent arrival, of proper stock accommodations, food, or even homes.[5]

As if to make up for the freak storm, there was heavy rainfall during the summer of 1873, and excellent crops were raised. Several tried spring wheat that spring, even though the seed was $2.50 a bushel. They sowed it

---

[3] Mrs. Florence Uhl, from a manuscript prepared and read for Civic League (Club), Smith Center, Kansas, November, 1925.

[4] Frank W. Simmonds, op. cit., p. 123.

[5] S. D. Flora, Climate of Kansas, p. 253.

broadcast, then carefully harrowed it in. David Nelson and Gus Barnes (in Martin Township) each planted an acre. It had to be cut with an old-fashioned scythe and cradle, and then each sheaf caught up and tied by hand, and the grain beaten out by hand. The yield in each case was about 30 bushels which was taken to Hastings, Nebraska, 75 miles away to be traded for white flour.[6]

It was about this time or a year or two later that Frederick Wagner and William Drno on Cedar Creek were each able to prepare and plant about ten acres of wheat. The following spring they went to Hastings and brought home the first threshing machine. It was a small box-like contraption that set on the running gears of a wagon. Two hundred bushels was a big day's run for this thresher but they were kept busy until late in the fall threshing for themselves and the neighbors.[7]

By 1874, many of the earlier settlers had much of their land broken up and planted, and later settlers were quickly improving their farms. Crop prospects were never better. The corn was just in roasting ear stage and an abundant crop of wheat was almost ready for harvest. On July 26 there was not a cloud in the sky; it was still and warm. About the middle of the afternoon the sky became hazy and speedily darkened until the chickens went to roost. Then with a whizzing, whirring sound the grasshoppers began to drop to earth in hordes. They were on and in everything. The ground was covered in some places to depths of three and four inches. They dropped into wells in such numbers the water was unfit to drink. The fish in the creeks died in the fouled water. They seemed to like anything with perspiration on, and attacked hoe and pitchfork handles, the harness on the horses, and even straw

6 Margaret Nelson, op. cit., p. 181.
7 Ibid., pp. 196-197.

hats were reported eaten. Dave Nelson on Beaver Creek had a new Peter Schuettler wagon with shiny green paint, but it was an unpainted box when they finished. In only a few hours they had cleaned up everything green and growing except the sorghum. They swarmed into the houses and ate clothing. They ate the fruit and leaves off the trees, leaving peach pits hanging on bare limbs. They ate the pith out of the center of the cornstalks.

Mrs. Nelson reports some of the homesteaders became hysterical and wept, others felt it was a plague and prayed, others cursed, but the grasshoppers continued their devastation. After about forty hours they rose and left a denuded country behind. Too late to plant another crop, the settlers faced virtual starvation. Many immediately packed up and left, some never to return, but some came back the next spring in time to plant again. The Kansas State Board of Agriculture reported of Smith County that "it is thought half of the people will need assistance. Many have left and more are going."[8] Others had no one to go to or worse yet, nothing to go on. It was reported that 1,500 needed food and 1,150 needed winter clothing by fall.

"Governor Osborn listed the counties most seriously affected included Norton, Osborne, Smith and Phillips. Most of the people in these counties had been poor upon arrival and they were still unprepared to face a disaster of such magnitude.[9]

Governor Osborn called an emergency session of the legislature, the first special session ever called, and it passed measures authorizing the counties to issue bonds for relief, but these were later declared invalid, so they

---

8 Kansas State Board of Agriculture Annual Report, 1874, p. 32.
9 James C. Carey, "People, Problems, Prohibition, Politicos, and Politics, 1870-1890," John Bright, ed., Kansas: The First Century, V. 1, p. 379.

accomplished little. An appeal was made to eastern states for aid and 124 carloads of food and clothing were received besides cash, but it is said much of this never reached the counties most seriously affected.[10]

Mrs. Nelson said that Dr. Higley and R. K. Smith, at their own expense, started east and appealed for aid in each town and city. The plan worked, and food and clothing began to arrive by freight wagons directly to Smith County.[11]

In the spring of 1875 the eggs laid by the grasshoppers the previous year began to hatch. Discouragement among the settlers was complete, but those with seeming abundance of faith began spring planting. Before crops were large enough to be materially injured, the 'hoppers took wing and left. The Kansas State Board of Agriculture reported some unusual crops tried in Smith County that year. Farmers raised 99 bushels of castor beans, 302 pounds of cotton, 357 bushels of flaxseed, 250 pounds of hemp, 2,337 pounds of tobacco, in addition to regular field crops. There were 41,593 acres of taxable land (this meant that it was "proved up" or title received). As can be seen from the accompanying map (see Fig. 9), there still was considerable land to be homesteaded; and most of the settlement followed the river or creeks except around Smith Center.

March 1, 1876 saw 38,031 acres ready to be seeded and the numbers of live-stock were increasing with 2,040 horses, 4,516 cattle and 3,392 hogs reported.

---

10 Charles C. Howes, This Place Called Kansas, pp. 165-170; material was also used, in addition to personal accounts, from: Frank W. Simmonds, op. cit., pp. 41; Alfred E. Gledhill, "Among We Sens," Unpublished manuscript at the Kansas State Historical Library. "Among We Sens" means "Among Ourselves."

11 Margaret Nelson, op. cit., pp. 201-212.

83

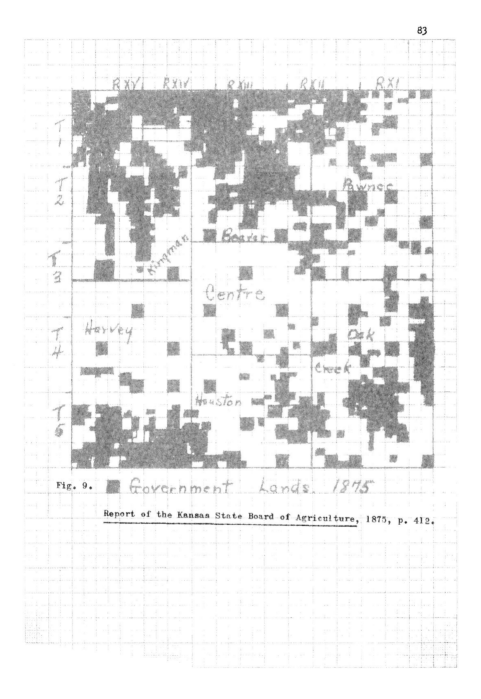

Fig. 9. ■ Government Lands, 1875

Report of the Kansas State Board of Agriculture, 1875, p. 412.

Wellman stated in his speech that spring wheat averaged 12-15 bushels per
acre, corn 50-60, potatoes 150-250 with single potatoes exhibited that weighed
2 and 3 pounds, cabbages averaged three feet in circumference and cabbage exhibits at the fair had been as large as 5 feet. Pumpkins and squash weighed
at 100 pounds, watermelons, 50-60 pounds and cornstalks were 15 feet in
height.[12]

By 1878, much of the land was settled and towns, schools, and churches
were being established. By March, 1878, there were 82,751 acres of taxable
or deeded land in the county, double the figure of three years earlier.
Another year added 210 tracts of 160 acres each or 33,600 more deeded acres
making a grand total of 116,351 acres or nearly one fifth of all the land in
the county.[13] There were flour mills at Cedarville, Gaylord, and Eagle Rapids.
Two plow factories were operating at Gaylord and Smith Center. With 97 school
districts and 2,864 children in school, 41 regular school houses, and as nearly as can be found 38 organized churches, the county was well on the way to
establishment. Money was still scarce and payment in kind not unusual. Mrs.
Ben Orr Williams, who was educated at the State Teachers' College, Oregon,
Missouri, came to Smith County in 1878 in a covered wagon. She taught school
and her first salary was $3.50 per month, sometimes paid in duck eggs or corn.

What was optimistically reported in local newspapers and speeches[14] as
the "best thing that happened to the county" occurred in September, 1879 when
a branch of the Union Pacific railroad came up the valley. Gaylord was the
terminus until the spring of 1880. Population grew rapidly; people came for

12 Rev. W. M. Wellman, op. cit., (speech, no page).

13 Smith County Pioneer, April 4, 1878.

14 Collection of clippings on Smith County at Kansas State Historical
Library, Vol. I.

fifty miles for supplies.

The events of the decade from 1880 to 1890 seemed similar to what is known in the twentieth century. There were good years and bad, but the people were getting established so they could weather out the bad with the hope that the future would be better. New settlers kept arriving to replace those who became discouraged or for other reasons no longer called Smith County home. In 1882 the county declined in population (2,000) then steadily gained to the biggest population ever known in 1900, that of 16,384.

Dust storms were reported as bad in 1880, with a "terrible" one in May, and more in September. At this time, however, they were being reported all over the west and central part of the state. They were again severe in 1882, although no complete crop failures were reported for these years.

June 20, 1881, a tornado hit Gaylord on Monday night and carried away the new church they were building on a "good stone foundation with six bolts two feet into the walls" but nothing was salvaged except the foundation.[15] Government land eligible to homestead was down to 820 acres, but there was 7,200 acres of common school land, average price $3.25 per acre.[16] Apparently land prices were good because the minimum on school land was set at $3.00 per acre and usually the minimum was current price.

In 1872, all listed crops including prairie pasture was 5,310 acres, and by 1882 it had increased to 341,304 acres. From January to May, 1882, Smith County farmers shipped more than 300 hogs and 300 cattle from Red Cloud,

---

[15] Smith County Pioneer, June 24, 1881.
[16] Kansas State Board of Agriculture Report, 1883, p. 466.

Nebraska. One sale of 113 cattle, averaging 1,548 pounds, brought $12,500. Money seemed to be increasingly plentiful as Pratt and Kelley, who had homesteaded about 1871, built the Gaylord Rolling Water Flour Mills at a cost of $13,000 in 1882-1883.

The year 1886 proved to be a prosperous one, although it began with a storm. What was later called the "Great Blizzard of 1886" is described by S. D. Flora thus:

> At the time of the great blizzard of January 7, 1886, housing in the western counties /including Smith/ was poorly constructed and often of a temporary nature, fences were few and far between and there were little facilities for feeding and sheltering livestock. /This sounds more like Smith County when the blizzard of 1873 hit./ January, 1886 was one of the coldest months, if not the coldest, on record in the state, with heavy snowfall that seems to have covered the ground almost continually. This in itself would have caused much suffering and loss of livestock under conditions then existing.... A cold wave with heavy snow that caused drifts ten feet deep began on New Year's Eve and continued through January 1, which made it almost impossible to replenish the scanty supplies available. Lack of proper nourishment was already weakening livestock when the blizzard struck on January 6. In describing this storm, a section of the 'Annals of Kansas,' by the State Historical Society has this to say: ... "rain turned to snow accompanied by high winds and below-zero temperatures. Scores of settlers living in impermanent houses and cowboys and travelers, bewildered when landmarks were obliterated, were frozen to death. It was estimated that 80% of the cattle in the path of the storm perished and those which survived were 'walking skeletons'." Another report by the Kansas State Historical Society, Vol. XII, 1911-1912 read as follows:
>
> "Record for January, 1886 show 50-100 persons frozen to death and cattle by tens of thousands destroyed in the two weeks of zero weather." As there were few, if any, fences cattle drifted with the wind until they reached an obstruction or some kind of shelter in draws. There they piled up and were frozen.... Records show but three passenger trains entered Denver from the east during the entire month of January, 1886.[17]

---

17 S. D. Flora, op. cit., p. 253-254.

P. H. Hammond, livestock dealer in 1886, was paying $5 per hundred-weight for hogs, wheat 47¢ per bushel, rye 28¢, oats 15¢, and corn 18¢. T. H. Iden shipped a carload of the "finest hogs ever sent from this station[18] /Gaylord/ to Kansas City. The load averaged 350 pounds and netted £4.90 per hundred — seemingly a good price.

The year of 1887 damned with railroad excitement! The Rock Island Railroad split the county from east to west through Smith Center; new towns were established, Kensington and Lebanon became railroad points and Gaylord, Harlan, and Cedar took a slump. The price of farm lands rose sharply; quarter sections sold at an unheard of $20.00 per acre. Wheat was 40-60¢; corn 10-20¢ per bushel; eggs 6-12¢ a dozen; steak in the butchershops 10¢ a pound or three pounds for 25¢; pork 2¢ less; potatoes 50¢ a bushel.[19]

The Old Settlers' Souvenir Booklet in 1912 in reporting about the nineties said, "There were probably more crop failures during these ten years, or mortgages foreclosed, and more emigration from Smith County, much of it to Oklahoma, than ever occurred before or will again." /Written before the 1930's./ It went on to point out that the 1890's were a long stretch of "dreary years of pinching poverty and general discontent."[20] It was hot and dry all the spring of 1890. Hundreds of fields of corn never reached tasseling stage before they were dried up by hot winds. The year 1891 produced a fair crop, then 1892 was a bumper crop but the price was low. Corn was the main crop (see Table 7), and 10¢ a bushel corn hurt the economy of the whole county, based on agriculture as it was. The year 1893 was listed as a

---

18 Gaylord Herald, 1886.
19 Old Settlers' Association Souvenir, 1912.
20 Ibid.

"scorcher" followed by an almost total crop failure. February, 1894, a
snow and dust storm raged for three days. Drifts were three feet deep;
livestock was lost. It was one of the three times Lebanon was cut off by
snowdrifts — the other two times in 1912 and 1916. Passenger trains were
held up three days to a week in town before the huge drifts were opened.
Then in the summer a tornado hit the south part of Lebanon, destroying some
buildings, but not killing anyone. In 1895 the dust storms were "bad" all
year. There was some improvement in 1896, and 1897-1898 were more nearly
average although each year was dry and hot and some farmers had failures
or near failures.

In 1880, 92.5% of the farmers owned their farms and 7.43% rented; in
1890, 72.9% owned and 27% rented with mortgages beginning to be recorded
on many farms.[21] Many original settlers were becoming landlords. It was
during this decade that the great Populist wave swept the country. Crop
failures and resultant hard times had changed the Farmers' Alliances or
Farmer's Mutual Benefit Associations, supposedly non-political groups,
into complaint groups that gradually grew into the People's Party or Populist Party. Economy became the watchword of these groups and many local
complaints about high prices, the new method of buying wheat by test which
was thought to be a trick to take advantage of the farmer, and the practices
in the county courthouses gradually spread to state and national platforms.
William Jennings Bryan, Sockless Jerry Simpson, Mary Ellen Lease, and others
proclaimed Wall Street a double-headed monster strangling the country. They
wanted an end to monopoly and tariffs, loan sharks, exorbitant freight rates,

[21] U. S. Census, 1880, p. 298; U. S. Census, 1890, p. 259.

and they favored regulation of industry and political reform.

Kansas rode the crest of the Populist wave which in 1892 swept a large Populist majority into the state legislature. Five of the ten Populist candidates elected to the National Congress that fall were from Kansas, this being one half of the Kansas delegation in Congress. Smith County was a banner county in the Populist movement with a six to eight hundred majority in the vote in the county year after year. Col. Joe Wright, editor of the Cora Union, was candidate for Lieutenant-Governor one year, and George Smith, a noted Populist from German Township and active business man of Kensington, served in both branches of the legislature.

A. L. Headley wrote that "it would be difficult for anyone not living at that period to visualize the huge outdoor mass meetings attended by thousands of farmers.... These meetings approached religious revivals in fervor and ardor."[22] William Miller of Lebanon vicinity, his son and two daughters organized a quartette and parodied popular songs as "Goodby, my lover, goodby." They sang,

> "The ship of state must round the bend,
> Goodby, old party, goodby!
> It was loaded down with G. O. P. men,
> Goodby, old party, goodby...."

Their services were in constant demand all over Smith and neighboring counties.[23]

---

[22] A. L. Headley, unpublished manuscript, Kansas State Historical Library.

[23] Etta Beardslee, Lebanon's Golden Jubilee, 1887-1937.

By 1899 the worst of the depression had begun to lessen.

George Evans, principal of the Cedar schools reports that city is enjoying a building boom. The bank is in a new brick building, the mill, idle for months, is again in operation and many of the property owners are putting in new sidewalks. The Missouri Pacific officials claim that more business is done at Cedar than any place between Downs and Edmond.

Corn up in Beaver Township is making 30-50 bushels to the acre on farms owned by John Morrison, George Stalling, and Frank Biehn.[24]

With the return of better times the Populist Party lost its support. People were tired of reform and economy. By 1904 Populism had faded even in Kansas. That year saw a record number of Socialist votes in the state, which indicated where disgruntled party members turned. There is no evidence that this movement ever won much support in Smith County. There was a leaflet printed by M. L. Lockwood at Lebanon October 15, 1908, called The Important Question in which he expressed the opinion that it would be a calamity if the Socialists took over the government.

In 1900 the heading in the Pioneer over the picture of E. W. Agnew said,

Our New Sheriff. The First Republican to be Elected in Smith County in the last ten years. There is considerable boasting in this issue of the Pioneer over the Republicans cutting into the Populist ranks in the election and over the majorities of Populist candidates being cut from around 900 a few years before to about 100.[25]

There was one movement that spread over Smith County in 1901 and more or less persists and that was prohibition. Many people held strict views on

24 Sixty Years Ago items in the Smith County Pioneer, Nov. 26, 1959.

25 Smith County Pioneer, January 11, 1900. Smith County voters have always been predominantly Republican except the years of Populist majorities over Kansas, and during the "dust storm" years of the early thirties when economic conditions again led the shift to the Democratic Party. The county officers were so consistently Republican that Jules Jarvis, probate judge for twenty-four years and the only Democrat elected year after year, put a special "thank you" in the paper one year to the voters for ignoring the party he belonged to and voting for him personally.

the prohibition movement even before it became a state issue. Smith County residents boast that there never was a licensed saloon within the borders of the county. In 1901 the Kansas State Temperance Union urged a general uprising in an anti-liquor crusade. Fifty Smith Center citizens massed together and gave "jointkeepers twenty-four hours to get out of town."[26]

In 1901 the weather was again the dominating feature in the county. There was a drouth in the summer. Prolonged and excessively high temperatures during July averaged hotter than ever before recorded. These records held until 1934. The 1901 drouth apparently was not too damaging financially because in 1902 twenty-two of the twenty-five townships and three fourths of the school districts were free of debt. Also receipts at that time for the Rock Island Railroad Station were $90,000, and deposits in the banks were one third of a million dollars with $265,000 in the First National Bank at Smith Center.[27] The first decade in the 1900's was profitable in Smith County. This is reflected in the number of owner-operated farms. The Federal census of 1910 showed there were 2,535 farms in Smith County, with 1,607 or 63 per cent operated by owners and 921 operated by tenants. Owner farms free from mortgage numbered 920. Prices received for farm products were high. Under the date line February 17, 1910 the Pioneer wrote: "Hogs sold for $8.90 a hundred in Kansas City Monday, the highest price ever paid in that city. Hogs sold in Smith Center Tuesday for $8.25."

The State Weather Bureau reported that a period of decided deficiency in rainfall began in 1910 and continued until 1918, except 1915, one of the

---

26 Kansas State Historical Society, Annals of Kansas, p. 335.
27 Office of County Clerk, Smith Center, Kansas; financial statements of the banks of the county, as published in the county papers, 1902.

wettest years on state-wide record.[28] There were also unusually heavy snow-
falls in the spring of 1912. Trains had not run through Lebanon or Smith
Center for some time, then another blizzard hit March 13-14 with high winds
drifting the snow. Drifts fifteen to twenty feet deep were piled in the
Rock Island Railway cut east of the station. When the snowplow came through
March 16, a crowd was there to see it. In the crowd was twelve year old
Harry Agnew, who became separated from the others, was buried under the snow
and suffocated.[29]

The fifteen years from 1900 to 1915 saw the introduction of a commercial
fruit and cider industry and the first known irrigation in Smith County by
J. B. Polka who had settled on a farm two miles north and two miles east of
Smith Center in 1891. In 1894 he had planted nine acres of the farm to apple
trees and in 1904 five more acres were planted. Mr. Polka's inventions helped
overcome the climatic hazards and increase production. In the spring during
blossom time it was necessary to have orchard heaters in the Smith County
climate. Polka drew his own specifications and had 1,200 constructed. These
were placed at two rod intervals through the orchard. An unusual windmill was
built for additional watering. Burl Armstrong helped make the base — a
building eight feet wide, eight feet high, and sixteen feet long with a small
tower on top and a wooden wheel mounted on top of the tower, all made on the
farm. The water was carried over the orchard by a tile system. This is the
first known irrigation in Smith County. The average apple yield was two to
three thousand bushels. The largest crop, in 1915, was about five thousand
bushels. Some of the apples were made into cider in a mill on the farm which

28 S. D. Flora, op. cit., p. 1.
29 Mrs. Hattie Baker Collection.

could press fourteen bushels at once. Most of the orchard was killed out during the drought of the 1930's.[30]

The years 1915-1919 meant prosperity to Smith County if one may judge from the newspapers. From Gaylord: A quarter homesteaded for $216 in 1872 was worth $16,000. (October 2, 1915.) From the Topeka Journal:

> To live and do business in the banner corn county of the state for 1915 is an honor. In round figures the farmers of Smith County raised about eight million bushels. There is an estimated 50,000 bushels of corn in the three elevators besides the cribs due to shortage of grain cars. E. C. Wolfe who operates one elevator has 25,000 bushels of corn and 15,000 of wheat in sight and no cars.[31]

The same article also listed the aggregate deposits of the two banks at $391,853. There had been 150 autos sold in 1915 and except for the shortage more would have been sold. A. E. Crosby had started a garage in August and already sold fifty Fords.

The year 1920 saw a reduction in the corn acreage harvested and prices declining but the cost of farm machinery, wages, and freight rates increasing steadily.

1919 wheat harvested 130,264 acres; corn 138,592 acres

1920 wheat harvested 89,867 acres; corn 100,123 acres

---

[30] Summarized from material prepared by Mrs. Hattie Baker and obtained by her from a son, Ed Polka, Riverton, Nebraska. J. B. Polka lived on this place until his death in 1928 and Mrs. Polka until her death in 1949. They reared nine children, two of which still live in Smith County. After the parents' death the farm was sold to Harry Reese, son of Trube Reese who homesteaded one mile west of the Polka land. In 1910 Mr. Polka started a herd of registered Aberdeen Angus cattle, probably the first registered Angus in the county. He used as his farm name "Applewood Angus Farm" and a son, Ed, uses the same name at Riverton, Nebraska in 1959. In 1911, J. B. Polka purchased what was believed to be the first tractor in Smith County. It was a Rumly Oil Pull 25-45 horsepower and was used for threshing.

[31] Topeka Journal, January 29, 1916.

A depression in values of farm products continued in 1921 but 1924 was a banner corn crop year and twice the acres of wheat in 1923 produced over three times the crop. In 1927 the state harvested more acres in field crops than ever in history and Smith County was no exception. Some average prices for 1927 in the county were wheat $1.17, corn 64¢, potatoes 89¢.[32]

Beginning with the thirties are years that will rank in Smith County history with the Grasshopper Year of 1874. It was a period of constantly decreasing returns in farming. One of the best wheat crops in history in 1930 dropped to the poorest in 1932. Prices spiraled downward in spite of declining yields.

Table 6. Comparative average prices in Smith County, 1930-1932.

Crop	1930	1931	1932
Wheat	$ .63	$ .34	$ .29
Corn	.64	.29	.15
Potatoes per cwt.	.87	.61	.32
Hogs per cwt.	8.00	3.40	2.40
Beef cattle per cwt.	7.40	4.90	2.40

The great drouth or family of drouths began the latter part of June, 1930 with a period of almost two months of excessively hot dry days. One of the driest years on record was 1933 and July set all records over the state for hottest days. In 1934 there was intensive drouth, record breaking

[32] Biennial Reports of the Kansas State Board of Agriculture, 1920-1928.

heat and frequent dust storms, but 1935 topped them all.

The dust storms began in the spring of 1935 that led to the name of "Dust Bowl" for Kansas and Smith County was affected. Many days the telephoned warning would come ahead, "The dirt is coming!" Schools would be hastily dismissed; people would close up houses and businesses. Smith Countians will always remember the chickens going to roost at ten in the morning because it was dark as night, of fathers rushing to school to get the students and sometimes not making it home in the car because the dirt got too thick to see to drive, of washing the chickens' nostrils because they were clogged with dirt, helping put adhesive tape around all the windows to try to shut out the dirt, but still it would lay in ripples across the floor after the storm, of seeing the top of fence posts or maybe the lever of a piece of machinery sticking out of the dirt drifts.[33]

In April, 1935 dust was carried in the upper air currents to the Atlantic seaboard. Dust storms continued intermittently in the spring of 1935 and other seasons of 1936 to 1939 inclusive.

As if dirt storms were not enough, excessively heavy rains fell in May and June, 1935, causing floods. Then there was excessive heat in July and August, a wet fall and early winter. Early in 1936, dirt came again! The story was about the same in 1937, only now aggravated by grasshoppers. They stripped whole cornfields when they came in on the wind from the southwest in June, ate the wheat as soon as it sprouted in the fall and again in the spring. Poisoned mash was scattered on the wheat fields in hopes of

[33] This is a personal recollection of the author who was in school at this time.

stopping them. By now the empty farmsteads over the country were making it look forlorn, and the papers hardly had room for news between the sale advertisements.

The year 1938 was unfavorable for crops; there were more acres of wheat but fewer bushels produced. Corn was a little better although there were fewer acres harvested.[34] Thus each of the ten summers ending with 1940 averaged above normal in temperature with those of 1930 and 1934 especially hot — years that no one who lived in Smith County, Kansas will ever forget.

Charles Easterly, Fort Hays State College, made an intensive study of land ownership in Smith County for 1900-1940 and found some very interesting trends. The number of farms in Smith County decreased from 2,834 in 1900 to 1,963 in 1940, or a 30.7 per cent decrease. The population decrease was 35.4 per cent in the same period. The greatest decrease in both farms and population was from 1930 to 1940. Up to 1920 farms from 100 to 174 acres were the largest group; since then it was the 260-499 acres group; the number of 500-999 acre farms increased from 75 to 202; and the 1,000 acre farms or over increased from one in 1910 to 19 in 1940. The average size farm increased 40.5 per cent. The number of farms decreased but so did the number of owners from 1,445 to 608, part owners from 506 to 421, and the number of tenants increased from 799 to 1,061 in 1930, but dropped to 932 in 1940. This increase in tenancy can best be explained when the records of deeds and mortgages are studied. The number of warranty and quit claim deeds decreased, but the number of sheriff's deeds increased enormously since 1930; in fact, 800 per cent in ten years from 1930 to 1940.

---

[34] Biennial Report of the Kansas State Board of Agriculture, 1937-1938.

In 1940 there were over five times as many deeds or seven times as much acreage granted to life insurance companies, federal land banks, banks, mortgage companies, etc. as there were in 1900:

Warranty deeds to companies,
    banks, etc., 1940, 19 for 3,460 acres.

Sheriff's deeds, 1940, 60 for 10,737 acres.

There were 17,460 acres deeded in different ways to insurance companies, mortgage companies, banks, etc. in 1940, although the first record of large tracts being so deeded were in 1937. Easterly suggests if such practice continues during the next forty years, practically all the land in Smith County will belong to companies, and especially the Federal Land Bank, to whom most of the deeds were granted. In 1940 alone the Federal Land Bank and Federal Farm Mortgage Corporation secured deeds to 10,077 acres. There were 67 foreclosures in 1938. However, a decade like the thirties may never hit the farmers again.[35]

The forties and fifties dulled the bad memories and restored some faith among the people. The years 1941-1942 saw a return to more normal rainfall beginning to restore subsoil moisture. The largest wheat crop on record and the best corn crop since 1932 was raised in 1942. The value of wheat harvested doubled from 1941 to 1942. In the year 1944 agriculture production and prices reached an all time level. During 1945 and 1946 there was an attempted adjustment from war to peace. The big wheat crop in 1946 was made on 4,000 fewer acres but had a greater money value due to high prices. Wheat production was low in 1949 — 770,000 bushels but in 1950 a record breaking

[35] Charles C. Easterly, "The Trend of Farm Population and Land Ownership in Smith County, Kansas, 1900-1940," pp. 22-69. Unpublished M.S. Thesis, Ft. Hays Kansas State College, 1941.

1,771,000 bushels were raised and livestock production was high in the county.[36] Also attempts were made at artificial rainmaking, and television antennaes became common as did home freezers with the expansion of Rural Electrification Associations. Self-propelled combines rolled into the fields and airplane spraying for weeds helped wheat production. Irrigation projects on the major waterways became topics of the day.

Due to the severe drouth in the thirties, the first interest was manifested in a proposed irrigation project on the Solomon River. So the preliminary meetings were held in 1932. By November 15, 1945 the required number of signers was secured and petition filed with the Chief Engineer of the Water Resources Board. It was granted April 20, 1948. On June 29, 1950 a charter created the Kirwin Irrigation District No. 1, the first district in the state of Kansas for irrigation. The district officers were G. W. Caldwell, Harlan; Perry L. Sweat, Smith Center; Floyd Freeborn, Gaylord. The disastrous flood of 1951 led to an appeal for the dam and the first appropriations were made in 1952.[37]

The town of Kirwin near the new dam was named for Col. Kirwan, Commander of Camp Kirwin, established for protection of the settlers from the Indians. The United States Land Office was located there from 1875 to 1893.[38]

The dam is planned to provide irrigation for 11,500 acres of the river valley (see Fig. 10) most of which is in Smith County.[39] What effect it will

---

[36] All statistics for the 1940's taken from the Biennial Reports of the Kansas State Board of Agriculture, 1941-1950.

[37] "First Efforts to Build Dam at Kirwin Dates Back to 1932," Phillips County Review, June 9, 1955.

[38] Kirwin Dam Dedication, June 10, 1955, compiled by the Phillips County Review, Phillipsburg. At the dam dedication, June 10, 1955, the direct descendants of Col. Kirwan, nine year old James, and Nancy, seven, were honored guests. They were the great-great grandchildren of Col. Kirwan.

[39] Kansas State Board of Agriculture Biennial Report, 1956-1957, p. 6; all statistics in this chapter not otherwise specified were obtained from the Kansas State Board of Agriculture Reports and Federal Census Reports, 1872-1957.

have on the historically important settlements of Gaylord, Harlan, and Cedar remains to be seen. Undoubtedly it will increase total production and bring new money into the county.

During the year 1955 farm prices averaged only 84 per cent of parity — the lowest in fifteen years and on a continual decline. Dry weather in 1953 continued into 1954 and while not serious, it caused crops below average and hurt many farmers. Smith County followed the national and state trend to larger and fewer farms due to advanced mechanization, increasing costs of production, and lowered farm income, but this also caused a decrease in tenant operation. There was 30,000 acres less wheat harvested in Smith County in 1955 and a drop of 41,000 acres in corn, meaning a big drop in cash income of nearly $6,000,000 for the county. "The rains came in 1957, bringing at least temporary relief to a thirsty Kansas agriculture that had been parched by the driest five-year period in history.[40] Farm product prices in 1957 equalled the lowest levels since 1940 and prices paid by the farmers were near an all-time peak.

What the future has in store for this High Plains county with no other apparent resources except the soil and the whim of the climate will have to be consigned to the faith that the homesteaders seemed to find in their "Home on the Range."

---

[40] "$19,500,000 Kirwin Dam Dedicated in Western Kansas," To the Stars, Kansas Industrial Development Commission, July-August, 1955, Vol. 10, No. 4, p. 24-25.

Table 7. Farm statistics for Smith County, Kansas, 1873-1956.**
All numbers are in thousands, after 1878.

Year	Wheat acres	Corn acres	Cattle	Hogs	Horses
1873	259	7,173	1,230	536	695
1874	52	15,231	2,915	2,984	1,421
1876	743	19,052			
1878	5,132	24,521	4,272	14,078	3,452
1880	23	77			
1882	5	74	6	20	5
1884	15	77	10	32	6
1886	16	94	16	56	8
1888	5	77	18	30	10
1890	7	2	22	52	13
1892	35	113	20	34	12
1894	58	140	13	37	12
1896	26	189	10	37	12
1898	34	196	19	75	12
1900	51	179	31	70	12
1902	119	144	24		12
1904	67	166	28	61	12
1906	64	175	30	74	14
1908	76	166	17	55	15
1910	69	172	24	43	15
1912	82	170	17	44	16
1914	94	160	21	40	17
1916	74	192	29	39	17
1918	83	168	24	27	16
1920	90	160	27	27	15
1922	76	154	26	45	13
1924	79	164	26	50	12
1926	69	191	21	30	12
1928	82	184	16	38	10
1930	85	190	25	37	11
1932	71	187	27	44	10
1934	53	158	40	32	9
1936	75	171	18	12	7
1938	172	53	13	10	6

Table 7. (Concl.)

Year	Wheat acres	Corn acres	Cattle	Hogs	Horses
1940	68	36	14	15	6
1942	100	85	23	12	5
1944	83	140	30	56	6
1946	113	97	36	23	6
1948	115	84	34	23	5
1950	123	73	32	25	3
1952	141	74	44	26	2
1954	105	66	45	14	1
1956	100	25	42	13	1 >

** Kansas State Board of Agriculture Reports, 1873-1956.

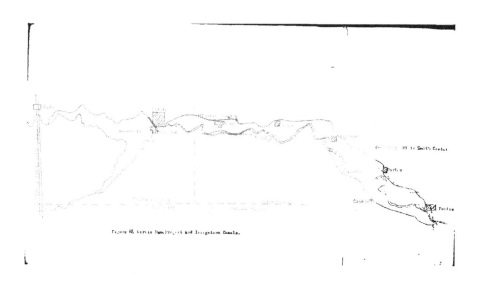

Figure 40, Harlan Dam Project and Irrigation Canals.

EXPLANATION OF PLATE III

Fig. 1. Dust cloud rolling in, 1935.

Fig. 2. Dust storm in Smith County, 1935.

Fig. 3. Rock Island snowplow which buried Henry Agnew while
opening drifts at the city limits of Smith Center,
March 16, 1912.

Fig. 4. Pile of wheat on the pavement in front of the high
school in Smith Center, 1937. Approximately 100,000
bu. in pile.

Fig. 5. Irrigation canal from Kirwin Dam, southeast Smith County.

PLATE III

Fig. 1   Fig. 2

Fig. 3   Fig. 4

Fig. 5

CHAPTER VI

COUNTY SIDE-LIGHTS

During the ninety years since the first settlers began to arrive in
Smith County, many changes have been wrought. The image has changed from
Indians, buffalo, and grasalands to prairie schooners and ox-teams; then
as though on a moving screen are seen dugouts and sodhouses, the breaking
plows of homesteaders, puffing trains, schools, churches, businesses, lusty
politics, fields of grain, trucks, streetlights, television antennaes, stream-
lined trains, and mechanized farms in swift progression. Through the generations that saw these changes are found names of people, occasions and places
that have become institutions, incidents of fun and fellowship, of sentiment
and tradition. These varied names or incidents are not related to each other
except through the ties to a geographical area or through the interested and
interesting people of Smith County, yet they have a place in the history of
the county. That it would be impossible to mention all the names — if they
could all be found — of the people who settled, even the early pioneers, or
of the noteworthy incidents happening every year, can readily be seen. Only
a few topics can be given to show a trend of the times or record some outstanding events or mention a few persons who contributed more than average.
Such descriptions are frequently representative of other Smith County families.

Newspapers

In the same category with schools, churches, roads and mail, newspapers
are ranked as a badge of civilization. Available copies of the first Smith
County newspapers show that local news consisted mainly of opinions on elections,
politics and personalities concerned with politics. Men, campaigning for

105

township offices rated more space in the columns than state candidates do
in the twentieth century and a candidate for county office was front page
news for months. There was apparently little attention given to libel for the
newspapers entered into controversies of the day and pulled no punches, whether
discussing politics or personalities.

The Smith County Pioneer, the first paper in the county, was first published at Cedarville, supposedly under a cottonwood tree, by Mark Kelley on
October 30, 1872. It informed the people of the action of the county commissioners in dividing the county into townships in preparation for the first
election. It was distributed by riders to locations having grist mills, sorghum presses, or centrally located claims to be circulated to the residents of
the county. It was declared to be the "most westerly located newspaper published in Kansas" at the time. The Cedarville Town Company purchased the
Pioneer in 1873 to press their campaign for county seat. In the next few
months it was edited successively by Mark Kelley, Lew Plummer, and W. D.
Jenkins. In the fall of the same year, it was sold to Levi Morrill, who
moved the equipment to Smith Center, since it was definitely decided on as
the county seat. In October, 1874, he sold it to Will D. Jenkins, Jr. who
in 1878 changed the name to the Smith County Kansas Pioneer. When he took
it over, the circulation was 140 copies and he increased it to a "bonafide
subscription list of 1,300 cash paying subscribers."[1] He sold it to W. H.
Nelson and J. N. Beacom who shortened the name to Kansas Pioneer. In 1887
Nelson and Beacom dissolved partnership. Beacom continued the Kansas Weekly

---

[1] Smith County Pioneer, April 4, 1878; duplicate of Smith County Pioneer,
Oct. 30, 1872 reprinted in Smith County Pioneer, Sept. 8, 1932; address given
by A. L. Headley on the "History of Pioneer Newspapers" at The Old Settlers'
Assoc. annual meeting, 1959; Levi Morrill was half brother of S. N. Morrill,
Governor of Kansas, 1895-1897. See page 47.

Pioneer and Nelson published the Daily Pioneer from November 1, 1887 to some time in 1888. In the meantime, the Smith County Record, founded February 3, 1882 by E. M. Burr at Smith Center, was on March 7, 1884, purchased and named the Smith County Bulletin by J. Q. Royce, then consolidated in 1890 with the Pioneer under the name of Pioneer-Bulletin, Beacom and Nelson, editors and publishers. In 1893 the paper was renamed the Smith County Pioneer with W. H. Nelson as editor and publisher.

Around 1890 the Farmers Alliance was organized and it soon formed the nucleus of the Peoples Party or Populists. A group of Smith County Populists banded together to publish a newspaper to promote their ideas. M. L. Lockwood, who had a little printing plant with a hand press on North Main, in Smith Center, put out the first issue of the Smith County Journal on August 16, 1890. Ben T. Baker, veteran publisher (see Representative Smith Countians, p. 183), was made manager the next year. Later Scott Rice and Baker bought out the other interests and were owners of the Journal for several years. Baker managed and published the paper while Rice continued as an attorney and served in the legislature. A few years later Baker and Rice built a two-story structure, the first floor for the printing plant and the upstairs for law offices. When Baker died in 1917, Clyde Wolfe, an employee, ran the paper for a year or so, then Tell Peterson and Jim Murphy of Russell owned the Journal for a short time. Mrs. Ben Baker had to reclaim it both times and finally took over publication herself until 1920 when the Journal was sold to Jones and Busenbark. In 1923 they sold it to the Pioneer and the Smith County

Journal ended its career.[2]

Smith Center had several other papers at different times. They were the
Democratic Messenger, later called the Smith County Messenger, September 6,
1900 to 1910; the Independent, December 22, 1879 to 1880; the Kansas Free
Press, October 3, 1879 to 1881; the Light of Liberty for Smith Center and
Lebanon, September 1891 to 1895. That these were published mainly to es-
pouse some political cause can be inferred from the names.

In the meantime, other newspapers in other communities in the county
were being established, often in competition to each other over some point
of policy or politics. Usually, they disbanded or consolidated when the
issue was settled. However, each of these papers, though often short-
lived, had a tremendously important place in preserving for posterity the
week by weak history of the people of this county. These reports may have
seemed unimportant to the contemporaries, but at a time when means of communication were meagre, local news was not recorded in the city dailies.

The Gaylord Herald was established September 4, 1879 by J. W. McBride.
It was sold to Webb McNall in 1880 and soon after to L. C. Headley, who with
his family moved to Gaylord in 1879. He continued publication until he moved

[2] The Populists who organized the Journal is uncertain. Mrs. Scott Rice
remembers her husband was one and the History of Kansas Newspapers, published
by the Kansas Historical Society, gives M. L. Lockwood and J. A. Wright as publishers, which is not surprising as they were in newspaper business over the
country for years. Mrs. Baker remembers the hand press used was bought from
Lockwood so he may have published for the Populist group after the sale. Due
to discrepancies in accounts in the History of Kansas Newspapers and accounts
written by residents, Mrs. Baker, A. L. Headley (newspaper man in Smith County
for over sixty years), Walter Boyd (with over sixty-six years continuous experience) and others were consulted. All the above information on the Smith
Center papers and on the following papers has been compiled from Kansas State
Historical Society, History of Kansas Newspapers, A. L. Headley, address,
"History of Pioneer Newspapers," and letters from the veteran newspaper editors
cited, unless otherwise specified.

to Ponca City, Oklahoma. After twenty-two years of publication it was sold
to the Pioneer in 1901 and A. L. Headley, editor of the Pioneer moved the old
press and files to Smith Center. Also acquired by the Pioneer in 1901 was the
Bellaire News, founded in 1900 by Till Vinsonhaler. A. L. Headley founded the
Gaylord Sentinel, July 24, 1902. George P. Leary was publishing it in 1916
with fourteen years of news service to its credit. It was discontinued February, 1925. The Harlan Advance was started in the spring of 1882, principally to advance the interests of Gould College, but it outgrew the inten-
tions of its founder and became a four-sheet paper under the management of
W. D. Lane. Harlan had several other attempts at printing papers such as
the Harlan Advocate, established June 1885 and discontinued in 1887; the
Harlan Chief was printed from November 29, 1883 to 1885; and the Harlan
Enterprise saw light for one year, November 24, 1887 to 1888.

The small northern township town of Cora had a paper during the same
period, the Cora Union, printed February 11, 1886 to 1887. Reamsville, also
in the northern part of the county had two papers, the Dispatch, February 14,
1884 to 1885, and the People's Friend, October 20, 1887 to 1888. Cedarville
had other papers after the Pioneer was moved out; namely, the Cedarville
Telephone, May 17 to December 27, 1883; the Cedarville Review, January 31,
1884 to 1885; the Cedarville Globe which had the town's longest continuous
publication, from July 11, 1886 to 1890; and the Cedarville Enterprise from
April 13, 1911 to 1912. In 1887 there were seven papers being published in
the county: Smith County Bulletin, Kansas Pioneer, and Bazoo at Smith Center,
Gaylord Herald, Harlan Advocate, Cedarville Globe, and Cora Union.

Lebanon, Athol and Kensington all had papers beginning around 1900 because
their towns were not started until after the railroad came through the county
in 1887. The Athol Record was established November 12, 1908 by W. A. Williamson,

and Ed Bronough was editor in 1915. It put out a "Souvenir Edition" in 1909
with a valuable and informative history of the churches, school, businesses
and people for the first twenty years in Athol. The Record, owned by H. P.
Beason, moved to Smith Center in 1933. In 1946 Beason and W. E. Lee purchased
the Pioneer and consolidated the Review and the Pioneer into one paper, the
Smith County Pioneer.

Lebanon's papers are really descendants of the Salem papers, because they
were moved to Lebanon when much of Salem migrated there after the railroad
missed Salem. The Salem Argus was begun March 1, 1881, by George Reed. It
had a press run by horsepower, very modern for the day. George McNeice, a
long-time newspaper editor and politician in Smith County, took it over and
edited it until it closed, but the name was later taken for the Lebanon paper.
McNeice edited a paper in Gaylord before going to Lebanon to run the Argus.
M. L. Lockwood was another editor who began in Salem September 2, 1885 with
the Friend and published it until 1887. The Lebanon Criterion was the first
newspaper in New Lebanon, one source giving the founder as Byron Thompson,
another as Joe Wright. It was founded in 1887, the same year that Lebanon
began. In 1889 Joe Wright and M. L. Lockwood merged and began publication
of the Lebanon Journal. In 1903 the Lebanon Criterion and Journal merged
and the name was changed to the Lebanon Times with George Tew, editor, and
L. M. Linton, publisher. Webb McNall of Gaylord began the Lebanon Argus
with George McNeice as publisher in 1898. The Lebanon Journal was sold to
A. L. Headley who changed the name to the Criterion again. In 1905, Joe
Wright and his sons Harve and Will consolidated the three papers as the
Lebanon Times. It began to be published semi-weekly, January 1918, then
returned to a weekly, August 1921, under Melvin Hibbs, publisher and owner.
In 1923 it was sold to Frank A. Hart. In 1960 the editors were Clyde L.
and Mildred I. Goodman.

The Kensington Mirror was founded May 10, 1883 by W. H. Nelson and J. N. Beacom, with O. L. (Tink) Reed, as first editor. Jas. W. Boyd was the first employee in the office and he and Allen Sanford soon bought the business. During this partnership thirteen-year-old Walter Boyd started working there in 1894. In 1903 he purchased the business and has since continuously owned and operated it (1960) with a record of sixty-six years of service in a Kensington business firm and is the oldest continuous newspaper editor in Smith County.[3]

The Smith County Pioneer published a "Sixtieth Anniversary" issue September 8, 1932 with interesting historical material for the entire county in the paper. It reprinted a duplicate of the first Pioneer as nearly as modern type would reprint it. It was headed:

The Pioneer
Cedarville, Kansas.   October 30, 1872
Mark J. Kelley, Ed.

This issue stated that the Pioneer had made its appearance 6,120 times, and a copy of each issue laid end to end would form an unbroken belt around the world, or that the bound volumes stacked would make a pile twenty feet high. In 1960 there were three remaining newspapers in the county, the Kensington Mirror, the Smith County Pioneer, and the Lebanon Times, but with improved means of communication and transportation they cover the entire county quite adequately and continue reporting the news "as they see it without fear or favor."[4]

---

[3] Walter Boyd, personal letter to the author.

[4] It is to this "grass-roots" source that the historian of today gratefully refers for facts of yesteryear. The Kansas State Historical Society has preserved and bound a copy of every issue of every paper published in Kansas since 1875 as nearly as possible. Next to the Library of Congress it has the largest newspaper collection in the country and is an invaluable source for the Kansas student or layman who cares to consult it.

Post Offices and Ghost Towns

According to the official postal records there have been fifty-two post offices in Smith County. Six were established before organization of the county, namely, Gaylord, Cedarville, Dresden, Germantown, Porter's Ranch, and Cora, all established in 1871. The greatest number at any one time was thirty-one in 1883. The last one established was Thornburg and it operated for two years. Several offices were in operation for only a few months as can be seen from the accompanying table.[5]

A most precious thing to the settlers on the far-flung frontier, isolated as they were from contacts with others, was a letter from "back East" or "back home". Sometimes letters were passed around and read until they were literally in shreds. The United States postal service was the basis of this communication, but on the frontier the delivery of mail depended on a great deal of volunteer and neighborly cooperation. The United States Government was willing to authorize a post office almost anywhere, if the postmaster or deputy would carry the mail for three months without cost from some point to which service had already been established. Thereafter the post office must exist on its own revenues. If that was not sufficient, the settlers must make up the difference or they lost the post office. The pay for a postmaster in Smith County was apparently $12.00 a year. Most of the early postmasters were also country storekeepers, and this was a convenient arrangement. The store was the natural gathering place for the settlers, and the possibility of mail made a good drawing card for the store. Some of the early post offices were serviced with riders making regular trips

---

[5] Information from accompanying table from U. S. Post Office Department, Washington, D. C.

from one to three times a week, but there is no record of pay or who paid them. Others depended on weekly freight wagons; fortunate indeed was the station on a stage route which received mail on regular schedule. These places were feeder stations for the more isolated places that received their mail when someone "went to town" or "went to the store." Anyone at a post office picked up the mail for all the neighbors on the way home or in his immediate area, often riding or walking out of his way to deliver a letter; his pay -- the joy that the receipt of such a rare gift brought.

The introduction of the rural free delivery in the early nineteen hundreds led to the discontinuance of the small country post offices and introduction of the automobile led to means of faster travel and the demand for more and better roads. Today many of these little villages are truly "ghost towns" and no physical traces exist in the mid-twentieth century. Only nine of the post offices in Smith County are in existence in 1960.

Gaylord was the first one established, June 2, 1871, with W. D. (Bill) Street the postmaster. Bill was a picturesque frontiersman. Legend has it that he was a professional buffalo hunter, that he rode up the river on a cow pony bringing a muzzle-loading buffalo rifle, liked the looks of the country, so made a dugout on the banks of the Beaver where it joined the Solomon. His venture into business was made when he erected a shanty from native cottonwood and sold a meagre stock of provisions to the settlers of the Solomon Valley. Firearms and firewater -- mostly the latter - provided his main sales. Finally mail was carried weekly by stagecoach between Cawker City and Kirwin. Street, by this time tired of his job, spent most of his time hunting buffalo. The mail was dumped on the shanty floor and patrons sorted out their own, until one day a postal inspector dropped in. Bill lost his job! There were too many settlers for good hunting by then so he went west to Decatur County where he must have become more civilized because he once represented the county in the state legislature.[6]

George R. Parker came to Gaylord from Cawker City, built the first real store and succeeded Street as postmaster. When the railroad reached Gaylord, September 1879, S. D. Cummings hauled mail on his stage line from Smith Center to Gaylord.

Cedarville, the next permanent post office was established one month after Gaylord, July 3, 1871, with John Johnston who ran the store as post-master. The same stage to Kirwin would go to "Cedar" so they had mail weekly. Johnston put the mail in a box and let each one sort out his own until the inspector came along; then he had to swear in all the patrons as deputies so they could continue to sort out whatever mail they could deliver.[7] The name was officially changed to "Cedar" May 19, 1906.

The Smith Centre post office was established January 8, 1873 with Wates M. George the first postmaster. Mr. and Mrs. George had moved into the first building in Smith Centre. This building, constructed of rough cottonwood boards from the sawmill near Salem, was used for a hotel as well as post office. However, Wates George reported in early postal records that the first mail in Smith Centre was brought in a gunny sack from Salem, May 1872.[8] The word had been given out about the day the mail would arrive and settlers had gathered, eagerly hoping for mail from home.

[6] Mrs. Margaret Nelson, Home on the Range, p. 45; Mrs. Dick Gedney, article in Smith County Review, Sept. 3, 1936.

[7] A. L. Headley, manuscript, op. cit.

[8] Smith County Pioneer, March 17, 1898; T. L. Reese, articles in Smith County Review, Fall, 1936.

Smith Centre had a unique distinction of being a town with a post office in the middle of its main thoroughfare for awhile. During a building rush in 1888-1889 the lot on which the little frame building housing the post office was located was sold to the Opera House Company. L. T. Reese, who had been postmaster since 1885 and was handling seven star routes out of the Smith Center distributing office, asked for permission to move the office. His instructions were to move it out into the street and await further orders. Lack of agreement between the merchants of North and South Main street over a new location caused much delay. In the meantime the building was inter-fering with traffic as well as being in the way of the bricklayers on the Opera House. The postmaster had the post office mounted on wheels and moved it to the center of the intersection of Main and Kansas Avenue, had it jacked up on blocks four feet above the ground and there it stood by the town well for more than a year. Finally, the order came to locate the post office "on South Main street, outside the railroad limit, which is eighty rods from the baggage room door." It was established on the west side of Main, block 21, and remained there until 1952 when it was moved three doors north.[9]

The location of Athol post office was established next. It was first named Corvallis, February 19, 1875, with Andrew J. Allen as postmaster. The name was changed to "Athol" February 9, 1888, when that town began to grow due to the arrival of the Rock Island railroad, December 1887. Mrs. Laura Cameron was honored in November, 1936 on the completion of thirty years of service as mail carrier on a rural route out of Athol. She was one of the five regular women rural carriers in Kansas and one of fifteen in the United

[9] Mrs. Hattie Baker, op. cit.

States. Mrs. Cameron was fifteen when she made the first trip over the route, May 18, 1906, using a team and buggy.[10]

Lebanon post office was established February 16, 1876, with Benjamin B. Ray as postmaster, but it was located in what is now called "Old Lebanon", four miles southeast of the present location. When the railroad came through in 1879, it missed the towns of Salem and Lebanon, so a new location was laid out adjoining the railroad and "New Lebanon" established. Business establishments and residences, including the post office, were moved from both Lebanon and Salem to the new location.

Harlan post office was established just 15 days after Smith Centre under the name of Thompson, on January 23, 1872, with Samuel C. Thompson the first postmaster. The name was changed to Harlan, September 11, 1877. There is the story that the post office at Harlan was really the outgrowth of two others. It is said the first one to serve the settlers in the area was in the home of Sylvanus Hammond, and was called Dresden. Dates from the official records for Dresden are: established December 1, 1871, discontinued September 18, 1877. Then the Keelers, father Truman and sons James and Castle, came and erected a flour mill, store and blacksmith shop on the Solomon River. The post office was opened here, March 20, 1877 with Truman Keeler as postmaster under the name Eagle Rapids. Meanwhile a new town was being laid out two miles farther northwest, and eventually the big Keeler store was moved there, and the post office went too. This was Harlan, so named September 11, 1877. Eagle Rapids was discontinued December 22, 1877.[11]

---

[10] Progress in Kansas, Official Publication of the Kansas Chamber of Commerce, November, 1936.

[11] From a personal letter of Oscar Crouse, Harlan Township, to the author.

Kensington was organized and the post office established January 7, 1888, when the Rock Island railroad built west of Smith Centre. Lewis M. Uhl was the first postmaster.

Bellaire was similarly established as a railroad station and the post office opened March 6, 1888, with Thomas M. Decker the first postmaster.

Claudell, the ninth and last post office established that is still in existence in Smith County, began November 18, 1898 with Orrin S. Harris as postmaster.

Very little information is available about the ghost town post offices of yesteryear, except they served their purpose — and a very important one it was to the early settlers. The few incidents found give a picture no doubt characteristic of them all. Dave Nelson, one of the first settlers on Beaver Creek in 1871, gave the following account of postal matters:

> Our settlement was a long way from town in ox-team and lumber wagon days, and getting mail to and from the post office was a big problem. The Gaylord post office was established, but mail was still a long way from us in the north part of the county. Gus Barnes applied for commission as postmaster of the Ballard post office which was to be situated on the quarter joining him on the south, and received his commission March 28, 1872. There several had laid out a townsite which they called Ballard in honor of the surveyor who had located all of us on our claims, but there was never a building put on the town site. Gus would walk to Gaylord for the mail and we would call at his house for it or if Gus would get a chance he would send it to us by anyone going our way. If it should happen that he would be away from home, he would take the mail over to a neighbor's, the Ellis family. Gus didn't profit much from his post office job ($12.00 a year) and on October 26, 1874, he resigned.[12]

The next post office in the area was at Bowdenville where John Bowden had homesteaded in section 10 (now Pleasant Township) on Middle Beaver Creek

---

[12] Manuscript of Reminiscences of Early Days in Martin Township by Dave Nelson to his daughter-in-law, Margaret Nelson and loaned by her to the author.

and had a saw mill, grist mill, and sorghum mill at a beaver dam which he used for waterpower. The mill area was a popular gathering place. The post office was commissioned January 10, 1876, but for some reason Bowden resigned October 24, 1878. This office was moved to a log store that John Barracks and his son had built on his claim about three miles farther north (section 34, Martin Township) where it was named Beaver. Barracks closed out his stock of goods in 1880 but kept the post office until November 10, 1882.

Earlier Dave Reams had opened a store in a small sod building in what was jokingly called "Sod Town" because nearly all of the buildings were of sod. The post office was moved there November 10, 1882 and the name changed to Reamsville. This office closed January 31, 1941.

Dispatch post office was established October 29, 1891 in the general store of Peter Dolphan on Oak Creek. Bert Dolphan was star route carrier between Dispatch and Cawker City, bringing the mail three times a week. The White Oak area received their mail from Salem which was serviced by the tri-weekly stage until the railroad reached Burr Oak, then the mail was brought to Salem daily.

The Twelve Mile settlement (Garfield Township) was eighteen miles from Cawker City, the nearest post office. The postmaster at "Cawker" labeled a box "Twelve Mile" and put all the mail for settlers from the county line north in the box. When anyone came to town he took all the accumulated mail and distributed it as best he could. Like the dugouts and soddies, these haphazard methods sufficed for the time, but in the winter of 1873-74 a meeting was called at which a petition was signed for a local post office with Joseph Gledhill, postmaster. It was established June 24, 1874. The patrons of the office had to arrange to get the mail to the office themselves, bearing the expense of so doing. Each one paid a small amount and a carrier was hired to go to Bethany (now Portis) once a week for the mail. It was on a stage route from Concordia to Kirwin. Millard Thomas made the trip each Saturday on foot, but soon resigned because his salary of twenty cents a week did not pay for shoes. T. J. Tompkins carried the mail for a year until Twelve Mile was put on a star route from Smith Center to "Cawker" along with Crystal Plains (James Clough, postmaster), Rotterdam (John Walters, postmaster), Orange (Leonard Baertsch, postmaster), and Oasis (Ad Kennedy, postmaster).

The first contractor on the star route was Billy Jenkins, editor of Kansas Pioneer. His first trip over the route was his honeymoon with his bride in a canary yellow lawn dress and he in the conventional black wedding clothes. The trip was made to Cawker City on Friday and back on Saturday, but sometimes subscribers worked out their subscriptions to the paper by driving two or three times. As the railroad came up the valley, the route for Twelve Mile deliveries was changed from Downs to Smith Centre. After repeated resignations by Joseph Gledhill due to illness in the family, the post office at Twelve Mile was discontinued February 28, 1894.[13]

Transportation in Smith County

Transportation pertinent to the development of Smith County may be divided into three phases: stage lines, railroads, state highways. Smith County was not settled when the Leavenworth and Pike's Peak Express Company stage line ran through the county in 1859. The first stage lines in the county after settlement carried mail and passengers from railroad terminals to the new frontier

---

[13] Condensed from an article by Alfred Gledhill, loaned to the author by F. H. Gledhill.

Table 8. Post offices of Smith County, in order of establishment.*

Name	Date established	First postmaster	Date discontinued
Gaylord	June 2, 1871	W. D. Street	
Cedarville	July 3, 1871 (Changed to Cedar May 19, 1906)	John Johnston	
Dresden	Dec. 1, 1871	Sylvanus Hammond	Sept. 18, 1877
Germantown	Dec. 18, 1871	Frederick Wagner	June 30, 1893
Porter's Ranch	Dec. 28, 1871 (Changed to Stuart May 31, 1881)	William H. Porter	Dec. 31, 1903
Cora	Dec. 11, 1871	Julius Nelson	Feb. 29, 1904
Smith	Feb. 27, 1872 (Changed to Valley Forge June 3, 1873)	Orlando Denison	Apr. 25, 1876
Ballard	March 28, 1872	Agustus Barnes	Oct. 26, 1874
Oriole	June 19, 1872 (Changed to Sherwood Dec. 5, 1882)	Thomas M. Straw	Dec. 31, 1903
Covington	Aug. 5, 1872	Ommel A. Burk	Oct. 15, 1890
Darrel	Oct. 23, 1872	William Hobbs	Apr. 16, 1873
Smith Centre	Jan. 8, 1873	Wates M. George	
Thompson	Jan. 23, 1873 (Changed to Harlan Sept. 11, 1877)	Samuel Thompson	
Stone Mound	Jan. 30, 1873	George Smith	May 21, 1886
Crystal Plains	Oct. 2, 1873	John B. Nickel	Oct. 27, 1888
Judson	June 24, 1874	Hyman J. Trevett	Dec. 31, 1901
Twelve Mile	June 24, 1874	Joseph Gledhill	Feb. 28, 1894
Union	Dec. 21, 1874	Ebenezer Fox	Aug. 26, 1878
Corvallis	Feb. 19, 1875 (Changed to Athol Feb. 9, 1888)	Andrew J. Allen	
Bowdenville	Jan. 10, 1876 (Changed to Beaver Oct. 24, 1878; to Reamsville Nov. 10, 1882)	John Bowden	Jan. 31, 1941
Lebanon	Feb. 16, 1876	Benjamin B. Ray	
Clifford	March 14, 1876	William Meadows	March 26, 1888
Custer	July 26, 1876	Latimer M. Dyke	March 31, 1894
Ohio	Dec. 5, 1876	Orrel H. Straw	Sept. 30, 1901
Eagle Rapids	March 20, 1877	Truman Keeler	Dec. 22, 1877
Cad	Jan. 23, 1878	Elias S. Mobley	March 18, 1878
Sweet Home	Feb. 6, 1878	George M. Shafer	Nov. 11, 1887
Camarge (Long Den)	Aug. 11, 1874	John L. Cook	March 11, 1885
Eminence	May 7, 1879	William H. Pounds	Sept. 27, 1881

Table 8. (Concl.)

Name	:	Date established	:	* First postmaster	:	Date discontinued
Andrew		Nov. 30, 1880		Edmond Palmer		July 14, 1884
Anderson		Feb. 28, 1881 (re-established Aug. 27, 1890)		James Smith		Aug. 22, 1893 Dec. 15, 1902
Lookout		Apr. 19, 1881		Samuel B. King		Aug. 1, 1881
Tyner		Sept. 5, 1881		Benjamin Russell		March 31, 1904
Troublesome		June 12, 1882		John Martin		Jan. 30, 1894
Hardilee		Aug. 3, 1882		Isaac N. Deppen		Sept. 30, 1901
Plexus		Feb. 8, 1883		Eli W. Beebe		June 26, 1883
Light		Feb. 8, 1883		Winslow Fuller		July 20, 1883
Orange		March 22, 1883		Leonard Baertsch		March 8, 1887
Womer		Oct. 1, 1883		Joseph Cheetham		Feb. 28, 1905
Jacksonville		Aug. 11, 1884		Robert F. Boyd		Dec. 30, 1899
Uhl		March 24, 1886		James D. Mollison		Aug. 31, 1891
Kensington		January 7, 1888		Lewis M. Uhl		
Bellaire		March 6, 1888		Thomas M. Decker		
New Hope		(Phillips Co.), Aug. 20, 1884; (Smith Co.), March 9, 1891		James Wherry Benjamin F. Moss		Apr. 30, 1894
Oasis		Aug. 11, 1891 (re-established Dec. 20, 1900)		William Mason		Sept. 9, 1896 Jan. 31, 1902
Dispatch		Oct. 29, 1891		Peter Dolphin		July 14, 1904
Oakvale		May 28, 1895		Sanford Vinsonhaler		Dec. 14, 1903
Claudell		Nov. 18, 1898		Orrin S. Harris		
Humer		March 30, 1899		William F. Mathes		Dec. 31, 1903
Posyville		Feb. 6, 1901		John F. O'Neill		Aug. 15, 1903
Reach		Dec. 24, 1901		William G. Smith		Dec. 31, 1903
Thornburg		Oct. 27, 1902		Josiah H. Wilson		Feb. 29, 1904

* U. S. Post Office Department, Washington, D. C.

Early post offices and ghost towns.

1.	Carmarge	29.	Smith Center
2.	Alexus	30.	Bellaire
3.	Ohio	31.	Stone Mound
4.	Tyner	32.	Custer
5.	Beaver	33.	Lebanon
6.	Reamsville	34.	Old Lebanon
7.	Eminence	35.	Sweet Home
8.	Thornburg	36.	Andrew
9.	Anderson	37.	New Hope
10.	Womer	38.	Claudell
11.	Judson	39.	Cedarville
12.	Sherwood	40.	Hammer
13.	Oriole	41.	Copenhagen
14.	Hardilee	42.	Oasis
15.	Germantown	43.	Crystal Plains
16.	Jacksonville	44.	Stuart or Porter's Ranch
17.	Bowdenville	45.	Light
18.	Uhl	46.	Posyville (Webster, section
19.	Troublesome	47.	Gaylord
20.	Cora	48.	Harlan
21.	Reach	49.	Eagle Rapids
22.	Covington	50.	Dresden
23.	Kensington	51.	Twelve Mile
24.	Clifford	52.	Orange
25.	Union	53.	Rotterdam
26.	Ballard	54.	Dispatch
27.	Athol	55.	Good Hope or New Hope (Swan)
28.	Corvallis	56.	Oakvale (Crystal Plains)
		57.	Coyote
		58.	Smith (Valley Forge)

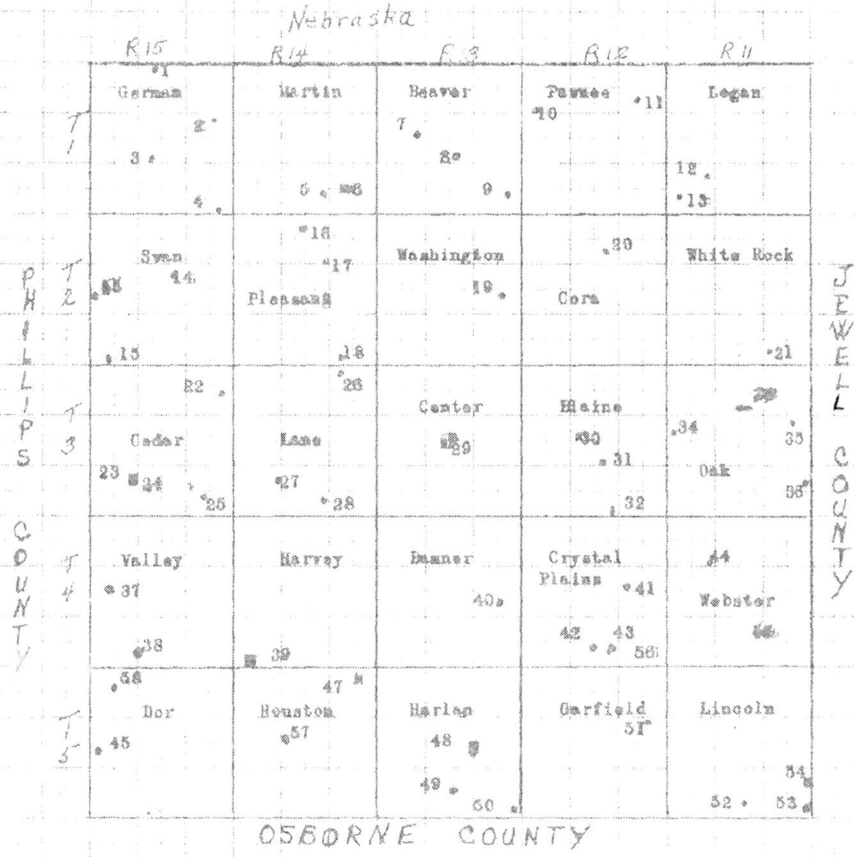

Nebraska

	R 15	R 14	R 13	R 12	R 11
T 1	German °1 / 2° / 3. / 4.	Martin / 5. 6	Beaver T. / 8° / 9.	Pawnee °10 / °11	Logan / 12. / °13
T 2	Swan °44 / °13 / .15 / 22.	°16 / °17 / Pleasant / .18 / °23	Washington / 19.	°20 / Cora	White Rock / °21
T 3	Cedar / 23 24 / °25	Lane / °27 / °28	Center 29	Blaine °30 / .31 / .32	.34 / Oak / 35. / 36.
T 4	Valley °37 / °38 / .56	Harvey / 39	Danner / 40.	Crystal Plains °41 / 42 .43 / 56.	Webster / 44.
T 5	Dor / .45	Houston °57 / 47	Harlan / 48 / 49. / 60.	Garfield 51	Lincoln / 54. / 52. 53

OSBORNE COUNTY

Some not located: Darrel, Ced, Lookout.

Figure 31. Location of early post offices and ghost towns as nearly as can be ascertained from existing evidence.

towns. The first official stage line was established in the spring of 1871, and made weekly trips between Cawker City and Kirwin in Phillips County. The first mail stop was at New Arcadia (now Downs), Bethany (now Portis), Dresden (now Garfield Township), Thompson (west of present Harlan), Gaylord, Cedarville, and Kirwin. After 1873 a stage line came into the county from some point east, presumably Concordia, to Jewell City, then Salem, then Smith Center. An early advertisement describing stage departures stated:

U. S. Stage Line, J. R. Burrow, Prop.

Stages leave Smith Center on Monday, Wednesday, and Friday. Make connections at Red Cloud for Hastings and other points on the B. & M. Will carry passengers and express.

The importance of the railroad to the settlement of Kansas cannot be over emphasized, but it had a somewhat different connotation in Smith County. The trains came _after_ the county was well on the way to settlement so it escaped the overnight building, the tough characters and crudeness often associated with many fly-by-night and terminal towns that grew up along the railroad. The people in the county were settled, "solid" citizens before the railroads came, and the towns that grew up along the tracks such as Kensington, Bellaire, and Lebanon were mainly settled from earlier towns that had been built previously.

The Central Branch of the Union Pacific had built from Atchison on the Missouri River one hundred miles directly westward. In 1873 the western terminus was Waterville, Marshall County. Plans were made to send one branch north to the Republican Valley, one southwesterly to the Solomon. That the news created excitement in Smith County is understandable for settlers who were accustomed to a two weeks trip with wagons to rail points at Waterville or Hastings to get supplies, lumber, and store merchandise. There are many early accounts of these overland trips.

After the St. Joseph and Denver City Railroad was built from St. Joseph on the Missouri River to Hanover on the Little Blue in Washington County, through Fairbury to a connection with the B. and M. railroad at Hastings, daily stages from Marysville and Hanover carried passengers and mail to all parts of the Republican and Solomon Valleys.[14]

The Central Branch of the Union Pacific received a grant of 245,166 acres of land based on the Pacific Railway Act of July 1, 1862.[15] The ready and swift sale of this land and the onrush of settlers to the west led to an extension of the line in 1878-1879 up the Solomon Valley. It reached Gaylord in September 1879. It was customary for the railway company to urge each township through which it built to vote bonds for its construction. About half of the track in Smith County would be through Houston Township with the towns of Gaylord and Harlan, the other half through Harvey Township with Cedarville. Houston folks voted bonds, but the settlers in Harvey Township and Cedarville vigorously opposed them. Due to intense local disagreement, an election was held. Sections 4, 5, and 6 in Houston Township voted with Cedarville; sections 34, 35 and 36 in Harvey Township voted with Houston. These sections changed townships due to this disagreement. The abstracter's maps today show these two townships as the only ones of the twenty-five that are not six miles square (see Fig. 8, Chapter III). Railroad construction was held up at Gaylord until spring, then in retaliation the railroad company, while it constructed the railroad through Cedarville, refused to build a station there or to stop the trains until several years later.

---

[14] F. G. Adams, op. cit., pp. 123-135.
[15] A. Bower Sagesar, "The Rails Go Westward," Kansas, the First Century, John D. Bright, Ch. X, p. 227.

By 1885 the business interests in Salem, Lebanon, and Smith Center were
agitating for a railroad through their area. Surveys were made to the county
from several different routes in 1886-1888, but no offers were made to build.
Finally the Chicago, Kansas and Nebraska Company proposed a branch line
through the county if Oak, Center and Lane Townships would each raise certain amounts in bonds. Center Township voted the bonds quickly, but the
other two townships refused. Finally Salem and Lebanon areas raised the
amounts on their own initiative. Construction started west from Fairbury,
Nebraska, but rumors flew faster than the ties. Reports that new surveys
were made from Lebanon ten miles east of Smith Center to the southwest and
one to the northwest, but the railroad was giving out no information. Finally, after a summer of nervous strain and flying rumors, the railroad pushed
straight west at a point two miles east and two north of Lebanon. On October
27, 1887, Smith County Bulletin reported:

> The railroad company has all of the townsites in Smith
> County located and named except the one in Blaine Township.
> /Bellaire/ The town in Oak is well known already and is
> called New Lebanon. The town in Lane is called Athol and
> the Cedar Township town is called Kensington.

Salem and Lebanon both were missed by about two miles. Needless to say, this
rang a death knell for these two towns. Salem, a large town of over 500 population, began to shrink in two months time as houses, businesses, and all
sort of buildings were on the road being moved to the new location laid out
on the railroad by the company and named Lebanon. The residents of "Old"
Lebanon, although deeply disappointed, decided to join too and began the move.
Other residents came from Cora, Stuart, and surrounding settlements until
Lebanon soon was a bustling town. On the 11th day of November, 1887 at 7:20
P.M. the railroad reached Smith Centre. The men worked one hour and twenty

minutes overtime to drop the last rail over the town cite line so they might
join the huge celebration prepared for the event. Mabel Corn, fourteen-year-
old daughter of Attorney A. M. Corn and the first white child born in Smith
Centre, was selected to drive the first spike. Preparations were made for a
huge bonfire. Mr. Slade, the city baker, had been employed to bake 500 loaves
of bread and cook two two-year-old heifers for the "feed" which he did to per-
fection. Capt. McDowall had a large order for oysters and crackers; Trube
Reese was in charge of the beer supply, and had sent Bill Perry to a Franklin,
Nebraska brewery to get sixteen eight-gallon kegs of beer and Henry Alborn had
ordered 200 tincups. There were 250 men in the construction gang and the
lighting of the Goddess of Liberty pole -- a forty foot pole wrapped with old
rags and saturated with tar and turpentine -- was the signal to "Let them
come!" It was a celebration that few forgot!

A corresponding gala celebration was held for the fifty year Rock Island
Jubilee, September 23, 1937. Mrs. Mabel Corn LeMasters, Toledo, Ohio, was
present to drive the symbolic golden spike. Registrants who had been present
in 1887 numbered 124. John Pollock, who was head of the construction gang
on the railroad in 1887 and handed Mabel the spike, came back from Almena and
again handed her the one she drove in 1937.[16]

Smith County, located as it was between the main river valleys, did not
have many early long-distance trails. However, the size and location of the
county enabled it to have one of the first twentieth century "highways" in
Kansas. There were three roads running across Kansas from east to west by

[16] Smith County Review, September 16, 1937. Mabel Corn LeMasters'
husband was an engineer on the New York Central Railroad. She died April 4,
1957, at the age of 82 years. Her sister, Bertha Corn Masters was the only
member of the first graduating class of Smith Centre High School, 1891.

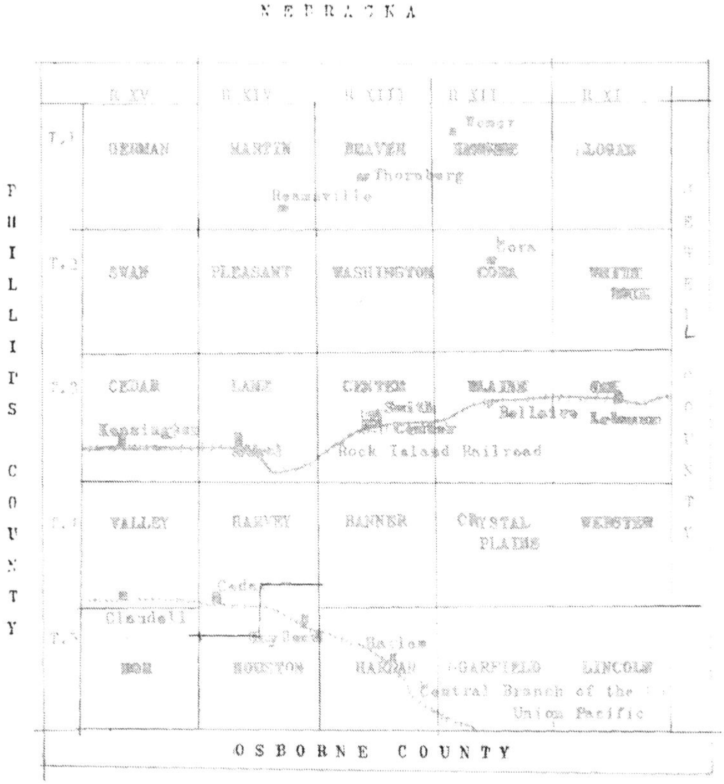

128

NEBRASKA

Figure 12. Townships and railroad routes in Smith County, Kansas

1912.

All of these roads were given fancy names by the organizations which had promoted them, and every organization was trying
to sell its particular highway to the public. There was the
Santa Fe Central Kansas Boulevard which ran through Marion,
Great Bend, and Ness City; the Golden Belt Route, which ran
from Kansas City through Junction City, Wakeeney, and Goodland;
and an unnamed northern route later called the Rock Island Highway which ran from St. Joseph, Missouri, through Marysville,
Norton, and Goodland.17

Newspapers called the first Rock Island Highway a "wagon route" across

Kansas from St. Joseph to Denver. What was to become US 36 was organized at

Belleville, Kansas, March 21, 1913. An organization was created to mark an

east-west route across the northern tier of counties and to form a direct

route between St. Joseph and Denver, Colorado. The Topeka Daily Capital

March 22, 1913, made the statement that "one of the most active bunch of

good road boosters in Kansas met at Belleville and organized another wagon

route across Kansas." The Capital might more truthfully have said the group

had organized another "paper road" across Kansas — for that was what most

roads were in those days. However, agreement was reached on a tentative route

which for many miles paralleled the Rock Island Railroad from which it took

its name. Later the road was merged into the Pike's Peak Ocean-to-Ocean

Highway and when the Federal markers were adopted it was given marker number

36.

The members meeting at Belleville voted to log and map the route. They

authorized the secretary to raise funds to finance the project and take charge

of the tour. At that time no one at the meeting had traveled the entire route,

knew where it was, nor knew the mileage. The plan followed township roads the

---

17 Kansas City Star, August 11, 1912.

130

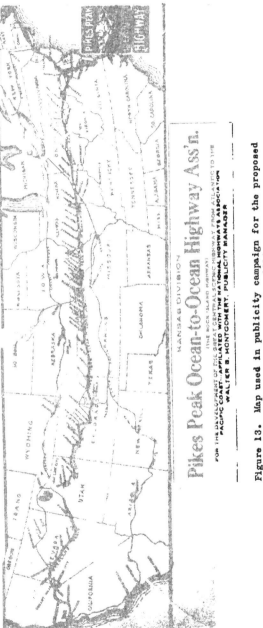

Figure 13. Map used in publicity campaign for the proposed Ocean-to-Ocean Highway, 1913.

entire distance. The St. Joseph Commerce Club offered to finance one car, an Overland 79, owned and driven by Dr. Stevenson. The St. Joseph Auto Club financed the pilot car, a Kissell. The official party which started from the Robidoux Hotel on the morning of September 21, 1913, was composed of Governor George Hodges, D. E. Watkins, secretary of the Kansas Sunflower Auto Club, W. S. Gearhardt, engineer from Kansas State Agricultural College, a Blue Book representative, and officers of the highway association. They arrived in Denver four days later at two o'clock in the morning in the mud — but the highway was officially logged and mapped, placed in the Blue Book and started on its way to national fame — they hoped. Because Governor Hodges was in the party, schools were dismissed, flags flown, children lined the route to greet the governor, bands played. Mayor E. L. Johnson of Belleville drove his new Marmon car to Marysville to escort the party to Belleville for a night celebration. The group got stranded between Belleville and Marysville in the mud and did not arrive until the following morning. On the return trip the mayor's car got stalled and did not reach home for two days. Such was the condition of roads in Kansas in 1913! The Colorado Springs Chamber of Commerce wanted national highway connections and had the "Rock Island Highway" re-routed through their city. St. Joseph and Colorado Springs each contributed $5,000 a year to publicize the road, paint poles, erect markers, and get out maps and advertising folders. It was advertised thus:

The Rock Island Highway claims the shortest mileage between the Missouri River and the Rocky Mountains. The route is well marked with official red and white metallic markers, is graded practically the entire length, is highly improved, being a county road in every county, is systematically dragged after each rain. Thousands of cement bridges and culverts have been put in on the

route and, being located away from the rivers, it is entirely
free from sand stretches which annoy the motorist so much in
July and August.[18]

U. S. Highway 36 in 1960 is part of a major coast-to-coast highway that
is hard-surfaced all the way. Hard-surfaced No. 9 follows the Solomon River
east and west through Smith County. U. S. 281 connects with U. S. 36 at
Smith Center and goes south through Osborne. There are also many miles of
county roads, many of them surfaced with crushed native limestone rock. Each
township also patrols a road on every section line in most instances. Thus
Smith County is supplied with a system of well-improved roads.

Smith County Schools

The establishment of schools was one of the first interests of the early
settlers. Since it was an accepted and commonplace fact, little has been
written about the Smith County schools.

Apparently the first school in Smith County was taught in a dwelling
house by Mrs. J. D. Loucks at Cedarville in the spring of 1872. District
No. 1 was the first to be organized in the county and was formed in Cedarville in August 1872, and a school house was built at the cost of £1,700.
The location of the school house and other incidents aroused considerable
ill feeling and the district lost its schoolhouse twice by fire, alleged to
be the work of incendiaries. The school building was promptly rebuilt each
time, better and more expensive than the one previous.[19]

A vivid description of an early school near Cedar was made by Frank W.
Simmonds, a native of Smith County. He was born in a sod-roofed dugout on

18 Topeka Daily Capital, May 9, 1915.
19 A. L. Headley, op. cit.

his father's homestead near Cedar. He recalled that:

> After building their homes, the settlers immediately estab-
> lished school districts, the school houses being built of sod
> with dirt floor and sod thatched roof supported by a huge ridge
> pole. The desks were rude benches and terms of school were short,
> a three months term during the winter for the larger pupils and
> three months during the summer for the smaller pupils. The teacher
> usually boarded 'round and received a mere pittance for pay.

> ...our home district, the Silver Ridge school, was about three
> miles north of Cedarville. Here in a sod school house I attended
> school for several years; from forty to fifty pupils were in at-
> tendance. We sat on benches made of split logs with the flat sur-
> face up and supported by long pegs driven into the rounded side of
> the logs. The blackboard (used only by the teacher) consisted of
> boards nailed together and painted black. Water was carried from
> a neighbor's well three-quarters of a mile away. Water was dis-
> pensed from a large wooden water pail with a dipper. At certain
> intervals some pupils would be permitted to pass the water, carry-
> ing the pail up and down the aisles. As I recall it, I believe we
> younger pupils gained much of what we learned from listening to the
> older pupils recite. In arithmetic we ceaselessly drilled in ad-
> dition, subtraction and the multiplication tables. ...In reading
> we used first McGuffy's readers and later the Barnes readers....
> Some of the early teachers I recall were Maggie Clark, Marion Wilcot,
> N. H. Withington and many others. The teacher usually offered prayer
> on opening school each morning and we all joined in singing hymns.
> Among the favorites were "On Jordan's Stormy Banks I Stand" and
> "Beulah Land." The school houses were used as churches on Sunday.[20]

The first school at Gaylord was also established in 1872 and taught by

Mrs. Agnes L. Skinner. The schoolhouse was described as a little log shack

in the west part of town. In 1873 a frame schoolhouse was built, then in 1881

a four-room school was constructed, forty feet by forty feet, at the cost of

$3,555. The first term in the new school found 120 pupils taught by two teach-

ers.

Unusual "school lunch delicacies" brought to this early school were

pickled beaver tail, baked coon, and stewed skunk. Pie suppers relied on

---

[20] Frank W. Simmonds, New York City, in a letter of reminiscences to
Bert Headley, September 1, 1932. The school described was probably typical
of many of the schools in Smith County.

wild fruits, currants, plums, wild grapes, and pumpkin. An early school girl
said "pancakes should decorate the coat of arms for pioneers" as a staple of
the diet.[21]

Several school districts were organized in 1873: Germantown, August
1873; Lincoln Township, District 24, July 1873; and Oak Township, District
34, 1873. This did not mean that there were no schools elsewhere, for many
areas held subscription schools with each family paying according to the number of pupils enrolled, usually a dollar a month per child, and this was often
paid in corn, molasses, vegetables, or extra time of boarding.

The settlers on Beaver Creek organized a subscription school in 1872
with Sam Yarrick, one of the first homesteaders in 1871, as a teacher. This
had been his profession in Iowa. This school, the eighteenth subscription
school in the county, was held in a dugout, and the charge was one dollar
per month per pupil. This was followed by school in a sod schoolhouse on the
John Dyer homestead, taught two terms by Stella Higley, daughter of Dr. Higley,
author of the now famous song, "Home on the Range."[22] Often formal school
districts were not organized for some time as there were no taxes paid so no
income could be derived from organization. No formal education beyond eighth
grade was required of a teacher. Usually the main problem was to find someone
who had the time and willingness to teach. Often there were no two school
books alike in these early schools.

An important social event was the Friday night program at the school.
Children would present a program and the adults would have a debate, "spell-
down", or arithmetic match.

[21] Mrs. Cora Skinner Ream, in an article published in the Kansas City
Star, March 23, 1941.
[22] Margaret Nelson, op. cit., pp. 232-240.

The first school in District 7, Oriole, was held in a dugout with T. N. Wiley the teacher. The next teacher was Mrs. A. R. Wilson, who had come as a widow to homestead.

School district No. 4 was organized at Smith Centre in 1873 and the first building, of stone construction, was finished in time for the fall term in 1874. It was built two stories high with a tall bell tower. When an attempt was made to issue bonds for the new building, it was learned the required number of pupils was one short, so John Goodale, age twenty-eight was enrolled. Mrs. Cordelia Miles was the first teacher at a salary of $20 per month. For several years the stone schoolhouse was the only place in town large enough for public entertainment. Church services were held there on Sundays; shows, both home talent and traveling, and Masonic lodge meetings also made use of the building. Following the grasshopper plague, so many settlers moved away that only one room was used, then in 1878 so many arrived that soon both rooms were crowded, and by 1884 other buildings had to be rented until a bigger schoolhouse could be built. This trend was seen all over the county.

In 1874 there were 47 organized school districts in the county with the value of school property listed at $14,819.[23] The first county superintendent of schools was Edmund Hall who held the office from 1872 to 1874. He committed suicide in 1874 in the hotel by shooting himself, apparently due to political opposition and the printing in the Smith County Pioneer, that he was really Elmer Davis from Maine who had deserted his wife and children, fled his creditors and came to Smith County. He was also very unpopular with the teachers because, on the day of examinations, he had

[23] Report of Kansas State Board of Agriculture, 1876.

announced that he would issue no first grade certificates, although many had
been teaching in the East on such certificates previous to coming to Smith
County. School was held in what is now Banner township in a dugout until the
stone school house was built in 1881 by stone mason David Weltmer and neighbors.
It still stands and was used until 1947. When the Weltmer children attended
there were seventy-five pupils, sitting three in a seat, and only one teacher.
Eighteen grandchildren and two great-grandchildren of David Weltmer, besides
his own six children graduated from this stone school house.[24]

In 1875, Twelve Mile also had school in a dugout with Ellen Taylor of
Crystal Plains as the teacher. She received $8 a month and board. She piled
what books they had on the table at night and put a heavy stone on them to keep
the pack rats from carrying them off.

In 1876 it was reported that there were 77 organized districts in the
county. In the 1879-1880 Biennial Report of the State Board of Agriculture
gave 106 schoolhouses in the county, 61 log, 23 frame, 6 brick, and 16 stone,
so progress was being made in quality as well as quantity as there also was
listed 4,835 school population for the same years. Average salary given was
male, $21.15, female, $18.56 per month.

Harlan's first school building was a small one-room stone building which
was soon replaced with a four-room frame structure, but the upper two rooms
remained unfinished for some time. This community also had the unique position of having a college. There is much disagreement among sources on the beginning of Gould College. In 1881, a meeting was called, open to all citizens
of the community, and $3,000 was subscribed for the building. A. L. Bailey

---

[24] Personal letter to the author from Mrs. Mabel Hinshaw, granddaughter
of David Weltmer, homesteader in 1872.

donated six to eight acres of land for the campus for the privilege of naming
the college. David Weltmer and Mrs. Margaret Beauchamp were mentioned as pro-
ponents of the project. Fred Newell, who did some study on the history of
schools in Smith County in 1940, said that Isaac Williams, minister and Elder
of the United Brethren Church of Harlan was one of the chief backers, as was
W. S. Bradford of Mansfield, Ohio, who helped survey the townsite. Andreas'
History of Kansas said it was organized under the patronage of the United
Brethren Church with the Rev. A. W. Bishop, A.M., who had taught at Avalon
College in Missouri, as president. The charter reads as follows:

> We, the undersigned citizens of the state of Kansas, hereby
> associate ourselves together as a corporation to be called Gould
> College Association for the purpose of establishing and maintaining
> an Educational Literary, Scientific and Collegiate school to be
> located at Harlan, County of Smith and state of Kansas. Said school
> to be under the control of a Board of seven trustees to be elected
> from year to year by West Kansas Annual Conference of the Church of
> the United Brethren in Christ. The term of the existence of this
> association shall be perpetual. The trustees for the first year are A.L.
> Baily of Harlan, Kansas; J. W. Williams, Harlan; C. W. McKee, Elmira,
> Kansas; A. S. Poulson, Salem; J. Knight, Salem; J. H. Bonebrake, Lecomp-
> ton, Kansas; J. J. Durch, Cawker City, Kansas. It is date 25 day of
> October A.D. 1880.25

The Gould College building was erected in 1881-1882 from native limestone
from the hills near Harlan. It was about fifty by sixty feet, two stories
high, with a shingle roof topped by a flat deck about ten feet square, support-
ing a cupola housing a bell. This bell still rings (1960) from the tower of a
church building erected in Harlan in 1905. The first floor of the interior was
divided into three main rooms, the chapel or assembly room occupying all the
east half of the building with two rooms on the west wide. A hallway with
stairs to the second floor led to a girls' dormitory. Some of the rules for
Gould College sound amusing eighty years later, but reflected the social

25 "Corporations Charters, Secretary of State", Book 11, October 25,
1880, Archives, Kansas State Historical Society.

customs of the day. For instance:

    1. All students shall use no profane or unbecoming language; shall abstain from all games of chance, the carrying of arms, and the use of intoxicating liquors; they shall be kind and obliging to each other, and show due respect to their teachers.

    2. Students shall not engage in loud talking, running, jumping, or scuffling in the halls of the college, nor practice loafing about stores, the depot or other places of resort.

    3. Students shall not ride for pleasure on the Sabbath, and ladies shall not ride with gentlemen at anytime without previous permission from the Ladies' Principal.26

In the year 1882, there were four members of the faculty: A. W. Bishop, (Greek, Language, Mathematics); Miss E. C. Bishop, (Latin, German, French); V. M. Noble, (Music); and W. A. Ray, (Tutor of Common Branches). There was an enrollment of seventy-two students, forty-three men and twenty-six women. In 1884, there were five regular faculty members: V. M. Noble, president; G. W. Shannon, mathematics and language; Miss Newell, music; Miss May Webster, science and grammar; Todd Reed, penmanship, band, and business. The term of school was nine months divided into three sessions with a tuition fee of $15.00 for each session. From fifty to one hundred students were enrolled each session. Most of the courses ran over a two-year period and were designed for those wanting to go into teaching, banking, or business.

A. L. Bailey reportedly named the college for Jay Gould, owner of the branch line of the Union Pacific which was built up the Solomon Valley in 1879. It was hoped that he would endow the college, but the Gould interests sold out to the Missouri Pacific lines, and without more substantial backing than student fees and gratuities from friends the college was doomed to failure.

---

26 Mrs. Margaret A. Nelson, "Rules for Gould College," presented to the Kansas Historical Society, October 30, 1942.

However, it operated for a period of ten years, 1881-1891. The building was used for all religious services for sixteen years after the college closed or until 1905, when the new church was built and the college building torn down.[27]

C. U. Nichols, when county superintendent, published the first "Annual Report, Course of Study and Normal Announcement" for Smith County in 1895. Its specified purpose was to "provide plain, practical and progressive outline to unify the work of the teachers throughout the county" and to simplify classification and regulate promotion and graduation. He asked that each teacher follow it as conditions permitted. Some of the interesting provisions were: A pupil was to finish the first reader by the end of the second year, be able to pronounce all the words at sight, spell 90 per cent of them, and read with ease. The third and fourth year pupils studied reading, writing, spelling, arithmetic, and language. The seventh to ninth years added geography, history, and physiology. The instructions under the course of study for physiology were: "Complete and review a higher work in this subject. The outline of the work is here left to the judgment of the teacher; 'judge ye well'." An added admonition was "Do not make a hobby of anything!"

This report also gave a program for the Normal School or Institute that all teachers were expected to attend for one month in July and August. It listed 145 school districts and 4,974 pupils enrolled, 175 teachers in the

_____

[27] General information on Gould College not previously cited: A. T. Andreas, op. cit., p. 910; Fred Howell, "History and Development of Education in Smith County, Kansas," unpublished manuscript loaned the author by Mrs. Margaret Nelson; Oscar Crouse, unpublished manuscript written for the author for this work; Marilyn J. George, unpublished manuscript loaned at Kansas State University.

county in 1895.[28]

There is no definite record when the first high school districts were organized in Smith County. The first ones were apparently the outgrowth of the elementary schools in Smith Center, Lebanon, and Kensington, with more advanced work gradually added. There is a record that Smith Center had no graduating class in 1899 due to the additions to the course of study, offering four years of high school work and qualifying the student for entrance into the state colleges. This brought "boarding students" into town from all over the county for a four year high school. The high school moved into a separate building of its own in 1918 for the first time.

Smith Center organized the first four year high school in 1898 and the members of the first graduating class with four years work completed were: Emma Detwiler (Smith), Ida Allborn (Montgomery), Abbie Wentworth (Gift), Gertrude Cannon (Miller), Floss Barger (Brandt), Mattie Curry (Moorman), Althea Gift (Lattin), Bertha Cary (Fay), Alice Walker (McVicker), Charles Ashbaugh, Elsie Detwiler (Nelson), and Walter Cary. They graduated in 1900.[29]

Harlan was once more in the van in establishing the first Rural High School in Smith County. For this, the land was donated in the east part of town by James F. Nichols, one of Gould College's alumni who had continued his education at Emporia, and spent his life as a teacher. The Rural High School was in operation forty years, July 11, 1916 to the end of the 1946-1947 term, when the building was continued in use by the grade school. Other Rural High Schools organized in the county were Athol, August 25, 1919, Cedar, April 25, 1921, Gaylord, April 25, 1921. Only Gaylord had a rural high school in the

---

28 Copy available at the Kansas Historical Library.
29 Mrs. Hattie Baker, op. cit.

Table 9. County Superintendents in Smith County, 1872-1961.*

Date		Name
1872-1874		Edmund Hall
1875-1876		R. C. Ellis
1877-1878		Mrs. Flora Morse
1879-1880		J. W. Pearce
1881-1884		D. H. Fleming
1885-1887		Mrs. Millard
1888-1889		V. M. Noble
1890		Miss Livermore
1891-1894		J. W. Amis
1895-1899		C. U. Nichols
1900-1902		A. H. Peppen
1903-1907		Ed Breokens
1907-1913		John Haney
1913-1917		Miles Elson
1917-1923		William McMullen
1923-1925		Esse Miller
1925-1929		Orval Tracy
1929-1933		Lloyd Simmonds
1933-1935		Walter Moore
1935-1945		W. E. Lee
1945-1949		Gertrude M. Mecka
1949-1961		Floyd Kugler

* Kansas Educational Directories, Kansas Superintendent of Public Instruction, 1872-1960.

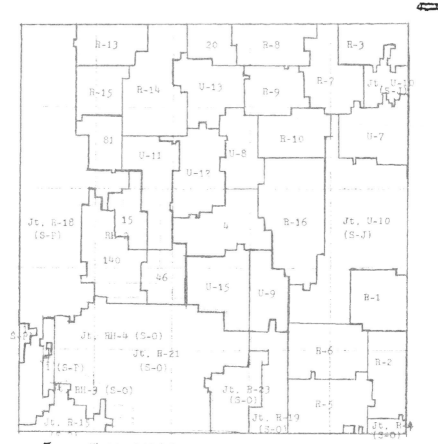

Figure 14. School Districts in Smith County, 1959-1960.

District No.	Name	District No.	Name
R-1	Stuart	4	Smith Center
R-2	Oak Creek	15	Pleasant View
R-3	Mt. Hope	20	Pleasant Hill
R-5	Twelve Mile	46	Corvallis
R-6	Barefoot Nation	81	Highland
R-7	Oriole	140	Athol
R-8	Woner	U-7	Independence
R-9	Lone Star	U-8	Dewey
R-10	Cora	U-9	Pleasant Dale
R-13	Pleasant View	Jt. U-10	Lebanon
R-14	Reamsville	U-11	Beaver Hill
R-15	Liberty	U-12	White Eagle
R-16	Belloire	U-13	Thornburg
Jt. R-18	Kensington	U-15	Rising Sun
Jt. R-21	Gaylord	Jt. RH-4	Gaylord
Jt. R-23	Harlan		

county in 1960, and Kensington, Lebanon, and Smith Center each maintained a high school.

In 1940 there were 133 school districts in the county with 109 in operation. Under the consolidation program, the number had been reduced in 1959-1960 to thirty-two operating districts, nineteen of them one-teacher districts (see Fig. 14). Statistics show that Smith Countians are far better than the national average in education which speaks well for their school system. The 1950 census showed for years of school completed for the 5,470 adults twenty-five years or older in the county, only ten, or less than .2 per cent of the total had no schooling; 2,265 had completed grade school; 1,425 had completed high school; 235 had three years of college; and 120 had college degrees.

Music and Books

S. M. Travis, who had ten years service as head musician on a U. S. destroyer, came to Smith County in April 1872 with his two brothers, and in October of that year organized the first band in the county. The ten-member band ordered their instruments from Chicago at the cost of $22.00 apiece, $200 for the instruments and $20 freight to Russell, Kansas, the nearest railway station at the time. Emery Travis went to Russell to get the instruments with a wagon and ox team, the trip taking him a week. The members of the band and instruments played were:

S. M. Travis, Cornet, leader and director	Andrew J. Allen, Bass Drum
Dan Travis, Cornet	Tom J. Burrow, Bass
L. T. (Trube) Reese, Alto	Wm. Garretson, Tenor
Wm. Roll, Alto	Hank Batchelor, Tuba
Emery Travis, Cornet	Wm. Hodson, Tenor

The first Smith Center band played for a big celebration when the town won the location of the county seat in 1873. A platform of rough cottonwood boards was

erected for a dance that night. The Kelley-Harlan orchestra that was later
the first to play the song, "Home on the Range", played for the dance. Settlers from all over the county attended the celebration.[30]

In the year 1880, the band was reorganized with only eight members this
time, and just one, L. T. Reese, who played in the original band. The other
members were R. D. Pritchard, cornet and leader; W. H. Nelson, cornet; Will
D. Jenkins, alto; Vern Webb, alto; Scotty Elliot, alto; Ed Edson, tuba; Ed C.
Stevens, bass drums; and Reese, alto. W. H. Nelson was publisher of the
Pioneer for several years and city postmaster at one time. Will D. Jenkins
bought and moved the first paper to Smith Center and was in newspaper work
in the county for years. Ed Stevens came to Smith County with his folks in
1872 and settled on a homestead north of town; later he was a merchant in
Smith Center for years. Vern Webb came with his parents and sister, Flora
(later Mrs. L. T. Reese) in a prairie schooner in November 1877.[31]

In the early 1900's a band known as "Smith Center Ladies Band" was
organized with Wardie Stone as leader. This group of twelve young ladies,
in their white shirtwaists, black skirts, and soft white felt hats, played
at the county fairs and other entertainments for several years. It included
Mabel and Blanche Boughman, Sadie, Nan, and Lina Owens, Mrs. George Hendricks,
Myrtle Jarvis, Kitty and Anna Harwood, Flora Bryan, and Ruth and Mabel Bowen.
Hendrick's Military Band, advertised as the "Leading Band in Northwest Kansas,"
was composed of twenty-eight members and director, George Hendricks. In the
late 80's it furnished music for many occasions.[32]

30 Mrs. Hattie Baker collection, op. cit.
31 Ibid.
32 Ibid.

Lebanon had an outstanding military band about 1906 that traveled to distant points to furnish music at events to which they had been invited. They had fancy uniforms and a brightly colored coach pulled by four horses for their excursions. Some of the sixteen members were Charlie Leonard, Bill Leonard, Charlie Adams, Will Weldon, Ross Tygart, Cliff Fogle, Jim Waldon, Albert Myers, George Jackson, and Bill Branton.

Music has always been appreciated in Smith County and each high school has trained instrumental and vocal groups. Municipal bands, vocal groups, and dance orchestras have also developed. It would appear not unusual that the state song of Kansas should also have originated there.

Public libraries have a certain mark of intellect and culture for a community and Smith County is to be commended on at least two groups who have very strenuously worked to organize libraries in their home towns. The Lebanon Library was organized November 7, 1900 and joined the State Federation of Women's Clubs, March 15, 1911. The charter members were Jennie and Mary Adams, Mary Arbuthnot, Maude and May Dykes, Ethel Felton, Sadie Lewis, Emma Moore, Sarah Peters, Lizzie Nichols, Lenora Skillin, Ida Tygart, and Bertha Winegar. They began the campaign with a waffle supper and bazaar that netted $100, then began a general solicitation for books. Mrs. H. A. Dykes took a special library course to catalog the books. Mrs. John Weddle, president for four years, was responsible for securing much of the funds. Chicken pie suppers, bazaars, home talent plays, anything to make money was used, and in 1905 they were able to erect a building 24 by 40 feet. In 1925 the city voted to accept the library and levy a tax for its support. The ladies were able to turn over a free public library with 1,923 books, ground and building as their contribution to the betterment of their town and community. Some

of the librarians were Mrs. Ethel Felton; Mrs. Nell Housel, thirty-three
years service; Mrs. Thelma Dilley; Mrs. Ula Lockie, five years assistant
and twenty-four years librarian. In 1958 there were 8,581 books besides
other materials. The money donated by the friends of C. J. Arbuthnot, long-
time Lebanon druggist, was used to buy a new bookcase to be used for Kansas
books and materials. The will of M. M.Grabosch in 1958 left to the library
250 books and eighty acres of land, the revenue to be used for the library.
This expressed the appreciation the people had for what thirteen civic-minded
women began in 1900.

From a small library of three hundred books, managed by a club of women
to a free reading library of 8,000 books is the story at Smith Center. Mrs.
Minnie Slagle of Smith Center presented a paper at the State Library Association in 1905 telling how to organize a library in a small town. The idea
originated in a reading club in 1897. The Woman's Harmony Library Club was
organized to conduct a public library for the use of Smith Center and vicinity.
A charter for ninety-nine years was received from the state April 28, 1897.
They asked the superintendent of schools, lawyers, doctors, ministers, and
some other qualified persons to make book lists; from these 360 volumes were
ordered. Each member donated a chair and other furniture. Three rows of
cigar boxes, eight boxes in a row were used for library cards. Reading cards
were sold for one dollar a year. Members held food sales to raise money toward a building fund, then a talent of twenty-five cents was given each member
who was to return it in three months with any profit and tell how it was made.
A minstrel show was so successful it had to be held two nights to accommodate
the crowds. Upstairs office rooms were used first, then the club purchased a
brick building on Main Street and hustled to raise the money to meet the $50.00

payments each month. A few years later L. M. Dundas, real estate business man, offered to trade a four room home and four lots for the brick building. It stood where the Community Hall that houses the library now stands (1960). February 1, 1922 the Library Club deeded to the city of Smith Center the lots and building with the provision that the new building would house the library and provide a librarian at the expense of the city. In 1923 there were approximately 5,000 bound volumes on the shelves. Miss Rose Hadden, a long time teacher in the county, was first city librarian. The fortieth anniversary of the library was observed by a tea with club women from the entire county in attendance on April 15, 1937. The highlight of the program was a review of the book, Sod and Stubble, written by Dr. John Ise. The review was excellently prepared by Mrs. R. A. Samuelson. The book was very appropriate because it was a story of pioneer days of the Ise family who lived just over the line in Osborne County. The charter members who began this worthy project were not available but the presidents through the years until the club was disbanded in 1922 were Mesdames W. H. Nelson, E. E. Dugan, B. W. Slagle, A. Haberly, B. T. Baker, W. E. Fleming, John Detwiler, L. T. Reese, Verne Barger, H. C. Smith, Ray Henderson, R. K. Sargent, Fred Uhl, Glenn Stoops, J.G. McDowell, E. S. Rice, J. D. Flaxbeard, Charles Uhl, and Frank Timmins.[33]

Infamous People and Incidents

Cattle Kate, alias Kate Maxwell, whose real name was Ella Watson, once lived in Pawnee Township, Smith County. The true facts of her later life and the incidents leading to her hanging at Sweet Water, Wyoming, July 20, 1889,

---

[33] Ibid.; Mrs. Minnie Slagle, "Organizing a Library," Topeka Daily Capital clipping, 1905.

have never been known, but that she did not deserve the death meted out to
her is the opinion of Judge C. Clyde Myers who has done a great deal of research on the subject. Clyde Myers, oldest of the Myers children, started to
Salem school in 1893. Also in school at the time were the sisters and brothers
of Ella Watson. He said they seemed nice enough, that they must have been in
the early teens at the time. Their father was a solemn-faced man who wore long
brown whiskers. Myers was too young to understand at the time, but he remembered there were whispers of something mysterious about the family — apparently the fact that the older sister had "gone bad." (Her father gave her age
as twenty-eight when hanged.) Her parents were called good folks, good neighbors, and good citizens.

As nearly as the story can be pieced together, Ella had gone to Red Cloud,
Nebraska, where she had teamed up with Jim Averill. No more is known of them
until they became known as homesteaders in the middle of the cattle kingdom at
Sweet Water, Wyoming. The situation at this time in Wyoming was not friendly
to homesteaders. Kate and Averill were warned to leave, but there never were
any rustling charges filed against them in the courts by any of the ranchers
led by A. J. Bothwell. However, on July 20, 1889 they were hanged by seven
ranchers. Charges were never proven against the ranchers as all the witnesses
either died or disappeared mysteriously. Mr. Myers, after extensive research
in Wyoming, thought many of the wild stories told about Cattle Kate and Jim
Averill were started after the hangings to justify the crime. They apparently
were victims of the cattleman-homesteader frontier.[34]

---

34 Judge C. Clyde Myers, "Cattle Kate", an unpublished original manuscript
with notes of sources, loaned the author for this work, March 1960. Ella Watson,
alias Cattle Kate, is featured in several published books some of which are
Powder River, Maxwell Burt, Farrar & Rinehart, New York, 1938; Calamity Jane
and Other Lady Wildcats, D. Aikman, Henry Holt and Co., 1927; Wyoming, Frontier
Style, Velma Linford, Old West Publishing Co., Denver; Banditti of the Plains,
A. S. Mercer, University of Oklahoma Press, Norman, 1954.

Another group of famous outlaws that had a connection with Smith County was the James-Younger gang who hid out in Oak Township, section 19, and possibly White Rock Township, sections 14 and 15, at times between 1878 and 1882. Walter Herndon, who lived there said there were re-occurring reports that two members of Quantrell's gang lived in the area. Both the James and Younger brothers were known members of Quantroll's border fighters, but in those days questions were not asked about the neighbors. Riley A. Holmes homesteaded the site of Old Lebanon. Before that he had been neighbors to the James family in Missouri and they and the Youngers stayed at his place. This apparently was a hide-out between crimes far from home, away from railroads and roads. Jesse James was later shot in the back, Frank was pardoned and lived out his life on a farm between St. Joseph and Kansas City; some of the Younger brothers were shot, others went to prison. Smith County residents had no direct quarrel with them.[35]

Another man they did have a quarrel with in 1903 was Tom Madison (or Madson) who committed a triple murder in Lebanon, one of the most gruesome and notorious murders in Kansas. Madison, a farmhand in the employ of Elmer Spurrier, became infatuated with Mrs. Eda Williamson who lived with her thirteen-year-old daughter and mother, Mrs. Eliza Payne, 57. When his attentions were spurned, he entered the house where they were asleep and, armed with the shank of a cultivator, beat them in the head and face until they were unrecognizable. Madison had returned to the Spurrier home about two a.m. it

---

[35] Ray Myers, article in Lebanon Times, February 18, 1960, also personal letter, map, and note to the author giving definite locations. This story was given Warren Herndon, who with his wife and family reside on the site of Old Lebanon. His father, Walter Herndon, homesteaded there in 1878, and told his son the outlaws' horses were kept in the pasture across from his place. Mrs. Josie Cox told Ray Myers, reporter who wrote the article, that she lived neighbors to the James family southeast of St. Joseph (Missouri) and had heard that they were in the area, but would not positively confirm it.

was known, but was gone in the morning, leaving behind a blood stained hat and blood on the tank where he had washed. A posse started out when the triple murder was found, but lost track of Madison in a cornfield near Red Cloud after tracing him to places where he had forced residents to feed him and let him change clothes. About two weeks later his body was found in a draw on a farm seven miles north of Red Cloud. A half empty box of rat poison and a gun were beside his body and he had a bullet hole in his head. Apparently he was a suicide.[36] Logan Township was a rather dangerous place in which to live in 1903 to judge by the incidents that fall. A farmer, John Anshutz, was shot by a highwayman while returning home one Sunday evening. He was robbed of $25.00, but the robber thought he had more money. He died the following Sunday. The robber was never found.[37]

In White Rock Township occurred a tragic example of mob rule in the early days. A group of horses were stolen from Bob Wilson near Salem. In 1872, stealing a man's horse usually stranded him far from assistance and was considered the worst crime of all. The man and a boy about sixteen were caught with the horses in Nebraska before they were sold. The culprits were brought back to Wilson's, given a trial and hung by the posse. They were buried one-half mile west on the C. C. Prevost farm. The "boy", identified as Guy Whitmore, died protesting his innocence. The man was identified by a woman in the crowd at Wilson's as Jake Hines. The bodies were later exhumed by three doctors for study and the "boy" was found to have the fully mature bones of an

---

[36] Red Cloud Chief, September 17, 1903, October 2, 1903; Elmer Spurrier, unpublished manuscript on Logan Township, Kansas State Historical Library.

[37] Red Cloud Chief, November 20, 1903; Smith County Pioneer, November 12, 1903; Elmer Spurrier, op. cit.

adult so his appearance must have been deceiving but this did not excuse mob
rule although conditions of the day may have.[38]

Another person to gain notoriety after leaving Smith County was Roscoe
(Fatty) Arbuckle, born in Logan Township. His uncle, Charley Arbuckle, homesteaded there in 1887. Roscoe was the son of William who came to Smith County
in 1876, and left in 1890 when the family moved to Idaho, then California.
Arbuckle, weight 266 pounds, height five feet, eight inches, had won fame in
comedy parts in the movies. On September 12, 1921, he was arraigned for the
murder of Virginia Rappe, motion picture actress, after a party in his rooms.
Three trials were held but he was finally acquitted of murder. Whatever the
truth was, he apparently was one person who had won success and was ruined by
it — and he gave his birthplace as Smith County on the police blotter.[39]

County Organizations and Celebrations

There undoubtedly have been many Smith County organizations through the
years that have served their purpose for fun and fellowship, education, politics, religious advancement or competition, but very few written accounts have
been left to record the part they took in the development of a county that
people are pleased to designate as "home".

The Smith County Agricultural Society was organized to promote the interests of agriculture, horticulture, stock raising, mechanical and other
interests related to agriculture. The constitution was adopted August 28,

[38] Found in many early day accounts of Salem, White Rock, and Old Lebanon.
These accounts are surprisingly free of discrepancies in this particular case.

[39] Topeka Daily Capital, September 15, 1921; Outlook, January 3, 1923;
Literary Digest, Jan. 13, 1923. The Outlook called his proposed reappearance
in movies as "An Affront to Public Decency."

1875. The committee in charge was W. J. Zimmerman, L. C. Uhl, G. H. Edson, and F. D. Morse. The purpose was to sponsor an agricultural show of farm products that later became popularly known as the "County Fair" and was a high-point event of each year.[40]

When the Civil War was over, Kansas received an unusually large number of veterans as settlers. The organization, the Grand Army of the Republic, commonly called the G.A.R., was organized with chapters in Kensington, Gaylord, Lebanon, Cedarville, and Smith Center. The percentage of potential members in Smith County is not known, but in the peak year in Kansas in 1890, there were only 20,000 members of the estimated 100,000 veterans in the state. There were 106 members in Smith County in 1894 (see Appendix, Table 1).

A typical activity of the G.A.R. is given in the reminiscences of Frank Simmonds about the organization at Cedarville:

> The G.A.R. Post was a dominant organization of which my grandfather W. H. Simmonds, and uncles, George and John, were ardent members. Decoration Day was always solemnly observed. The entire community met at the town school house for Decoration Day services. The children were formed into companies and marched about a mile and a half to the cemetery where we placed flowers on all graves, especially all soldiers' graves. There would be held periodically G.A.R. campfire meetings and patriotic addresses. Tales of the war would be retold around the campfires. It is little wonder that we youngsters came to look upon and regard all Civil War veterans with awe and reverence.[41]

---

[40] Kansas State Board of Agriculture, Annual Report, Vol. 2, p. 239.

[41] Frank Simmonds, op. cit., p. 15. A list of "Smith County Old Soldiers Registered at the Reunion" was published in Smith County Pioneer, Oct. 14, 1897. The author can remember as a girl taking part in "Decoration Day" services at Cedar with each child trying to see who could learn the longest and most effective reading to give. The high point was the year she was chosen to give the "Gettysburg Address." Putting flowers on the base of the statue of the "Old Soldier" was a solemn occasion, and grandfather's name always had to be found each year on the memorial tablet. The Memorial Hall in Topeka, in which is located the invaluable Kansas Historical Society Library and Museum, is a lasting memorial to all G.A.R. members in the state as it was built with money paid to Kansas from the Federal Government for damages sustained during the Civil War. It was dedicated May 26, 1914.

The Smith County Old Settlers' Homecoming Association was organized in Smith County, March 5, 1912, with nineteen townships represented. R. L. Logan was elected president, H. L. Simmons, vice-president, Charles S. Uhl, secretary-treasurer. Persons settling in the county prior to January 1, 1880, were made eligible to membership. The organization voted to have no dues. There was a vice-president appointed in each township. The first reunion and picnic was held September 25-26, 1912, in Smith Center. A souvenir booklet of thirty pages was printed with early history of the county, pictures of early settlers and street scenes in the towns, and a roster of names of settlers prior to 1880 listed by townships. As far as could be ascertained, there has been a reunion held every year since for the past forty-seven years, some of them elaborate enough to be termed celebrations. At the meeting in 1933, there were pioneers registered as in attendance who had come to the county from 1869 through the 80's.

The Smith County Pioneer, October 4, 1956, reported "one of the largest crowds in the history of the Old Settlers Association met for a dinner and program at the Community Hall." Art Polihan, whose parents came to the county in 1870, gave the main speech. Registrations for the day were 318.

Through the years some of those joyful occasions that are termed celebrations become more like institutions; others are special or occasional so may be better termed celebrations.

In the latter class was "Hub Day" that took place in August, 1952, one mile north and one mile west of Lebanon. Ten years work was to be done in one day on a Smith County farm when 1,000 men were to completely rebuild and renovate 240 acres of "some of the worst land in Kansas." (It was considered by conservation experts as one of the worst examples of erosion in the county.) At 12:01 a.m. fifty bulldozers, earthmovers, plows, ditchers, carpenters, electricians, and others went to work. A house was erected, a dairy barn and loafing shed built, a well dug, electricity installed, and eroded fields leveled and terraced. Mr. and Mrs. Enos Groves were the tenants. The Farmers Home Administration loaned Groves money for his part and landlords C. W. Diehl and Ray McCord spent several thousand dollars for their share. Helping with the planning were Paul Gilpin, Smith County Extension Agent; Wes Seyler, WIBW Farm Service Director; and Francis Willmuth, United States Soil Conservationist. This dramatic change for a run-down farm provided excellent publicity for a well balanced farming program.[42]

When Ray Myers, who has lived all his life in the Lebanon community, was contacted on the results of "Hub Day", he wrote:

> That "Day" was one of the largest things I ever saw. If you were not there, it cannot be imagined. Estimated 20,000 people and I would say not under that. It was next to impossible to go there and get out. Cars were running bumper to bumper. The density of the guests crushed in the house floor. Much of the time the crowd was too dense for work — and some was done later.
>
> Enos Groves and wife, first were the operators, keeping a Grade "A" Dairy farm. After several years, Jake Amen and wife took over and seemingly are making good. They still run the dairy. Because of the large pond built that "Day" there is much fishing as it was stocked as a state lake. The land is farmed on the basis of feed for the dairy cattle. Mr. and Mrs. Amen also run the Arbuthnot Drug Store in Lebanon.[43]

In October 1887, the new town of Lebanon was laid out by the Rock Island Railroad in the middle of a corn field on the Gus Tomlinson farm. Despite the fact that the only water available near at hand was the town well with its pump and tin cup, ninety days later three blocks on either side of the main street were lined with one and two story business buildings, many of them moved from Old Lebanon and Salem. The first celebration of the founding of

[42] Topeka Daily Capital, July 26, 1952.
[43] Personal letter from Ray Myers to the author, March 8, 1960.

the town was held October, 1888 with a barbecue, home talent play, races, contests and general good times for all. This celebration has continued until it has become an institution in Smith County. In August 1937, Lebanon celebrated its Fiftieth Anniversary. A free beef barbecue was served to 4,427, all of the store windows were filled with pioneer displays from various neighborhoods, various entertainment was provided but the thing most enjoyed was the greetings of old friends and the reminiscing that was the order of the day down the full length of Main Street. Nine people registered as attending all fifty anniversaries. They were Henry Flood, Arthur Smith, J. T. Felton, Mrs. Mary Good, Mrs. Lanah Adams, W. H. Hartman, J. A. Hartman, W. L. Hartman, and Hoyt Lull.[44]

Another celebration that has become an institution and is known statewide is the Armistice Day (now Veterans' Day) Barbecue celebrated at Kensington continuously since November 11, 1918 except for a three-year span during World War II. Kensington was another town established by the railroad as a station between Athol on the east and Agra (in Phillips County) on the west. It was settled in 1888 and incorporated in 1900. Kensington began a celebration on its first anniversary in August 1889. These celebrations were financed by donations from the business firms and the sale of space for concessions along Main Street, which was always roped off. During World War I this celebration was discontinued, but on the signing of the Armistice "the remnants of this traditional anniversary were pulled together" and a barbecue and celebration held. By 1919 many of the servicemen that had returned from the war had organized an American Legion Post, Marren Post No. 166, named for the first man

44 Etta Beardslee, Lebanon's Golden Jubilee, 1887-1937; Lebanon Times, August 1937.

killed in action from Kensington. The Legion took up a collection and had a
barbecue in 1919, mostly for the veterans and their families. However, it was
so popular that the next year it became a community affair. The merchants and
many others gave donations and the Legion sold numbers on a Ford Touring car.
The proceeds from this sale were used to buy a site for a building that is
still used (1960) by the Legionnaires and their Auxiliaries. By this time the
combined celebrations of Armistice Day-Free Barbecue-Homecoming-Anniversary
had outgrown what the veterans could handle with their increased burdens of
trying to establish homes, businesses, and families, and pay for the Veterans'
Building. They prevailed on the Kensington Chamber of Commerce to take over
the "Armistice Day Barbecue and Homecoming", as it was now called. Veterans'
Day in Kensington is held regardless of the weather -- duststorms, blizzards,
mud, or snow does not stop it. H. V. Dilsaver, Kensington businessman reports that:

> This year, 1959, we had three large vats for cooking 1,500
> pounds of choice beef, and five large kettles of beans, well-flavored
> and delicious, 12,000 buns which were generously filled with meat and
> served to an estimated crowd of 2,750 people. The Auxiliary had baked
> seventy-five pies at the Legion Hall and each member donated three
> more. People are served in four lines with one especially for children;
> coffee is served with cream donated by the farmers and dairymen of the
> community. The serving is done by volunteers from the trade territory
> of Kensington.

> The Veterans' part of the activities consists of arrangements for
> and sponsoring of the parade. Fred Bierman and myself have been man-
> agers of the parade for the past thirty-five years. We give prizes for
> the best school, church, 4-H Club floats as well as others. There are
> many entries from surrounding towns, and the parade has grown to such
> an extent that we have to assemble on vacant lots nearly three-quarters
> of a mile from the Barbecue grounds in the City Park. The high school
> bands from all the surrounding towns participate. The parade is always
> led with a color squad of the American Legion, followed by squads from
> neighboring posts and a National Guard squad. For the past two years
> the National Guard has had the military honor of "Raising the Flag and
> Sounding Taps for our Departed Comrades." Our local Saddle Club puts

on a horse show and there is a football game in the afternoon. At
the half, the American Legion Auxiliary gives away the prizes, including a handmade quilt, on which they have sold numbers for ten
cents each. This keeps them well financed for the year.[45]

The stories of how these celebrations have grown are as much a part of
the life and history of the county as are the growth of the schools, churches,
homes, and businesses in the memories of the residents.

The Usual and Unusual

A thriving type of pioneer business in Smith County communities were
the livery barnes. They were nothing unusual in pioneer days, and as necessary as service stations in the twentieth century, but in later years they
are almost forgotten. Each town had one or more and the owner was always a
prominent citizen. Here each traveler into town and many of the residents
left their horses for care and feed. Here also equippage such as buggies,
wagons or riding horses were for hire. The livery barns kept teams especially
for the doctors of the town. As more and more farmers hauled grain and produce to town, the tie-barn was added where often twenty-five or more teams
would be tied and fed at a time. Expert handlers were on duty at all times.

An unusual attraction in Smith County was an elevator to be seen in
Lebanon after 1896. It was built by D. H. Hyde, a devout Free Methodist.
On the roof and sides he had printed in large letters Bible quotations and
texts. The trains used to have to stop to permit the passengers who had purchased tickets for the express purpose to see the elevator. Pictures of it

---

[45] Written for this work by H. V. Dilsaver, Kensington, Kansas. He was
born in a sod house six miles northeast of Kensington in 1892, and has lived
in the same house in Kensington for the past thirty-five years. He missed the
first two Armistice Day celebrations because he never arrived home from service until December 1919.

were printed in Eastern papers and Europe. Later the Rock Island railroad, upon whose property the elevator stood, compelled Hyde to paint out all of the religious exhortations. The elevator in 1960 was owned and operated by the Lebanon Grain and Feed Company.

A typical practice in the twentieth century was so unusual in the late 1880's that it stirred up a storm of protest. W. W. Pennington, a big hog and cattle feeder near Lebanon, drove cattle in from the Panhandle to feed. They were light of bone, rangy, and had massive horns, which caused them to take up so much room at the feed bunks that he conceived the idea of sawing off the big horns. This stirred up such a storm of protest that some of the people threatened to notify the humane society and have him prosecuted. It was never done, however, and Pennington lived to see dehorning become a custom.[46]

According to records, there was apparently a span of twenty-nine years between the first homestead filed in the county and the last one, or thirty years if one counts from reports of the first claim to the last homestead filed. Records in the National Archives, Washington, D. C., gives the homestead entry of Josiah Crick in what is now Webster Township, on Oak Creek, dated October 29, 1870, as the first one filed. Emery Creaver of Banner Township claimed to be the last man ever to file a homestead in Smith County. He took out papers on a quarter section in Banner Township in 1899, and built a sod house 12 by 40 feet. He proved up the land in 1904.[47]

An unusual service was one that took place September 26, 1881. This was the Garfield Memorial Service held in Smith Center the same day that Garfield

---

[46] Ray Myers, unpublished manuscript and letter.
[47] County Clerk's records, Smith County, Kansas.

was buried at Cleveland. There was a procession formed at the courthouse
headed by the cornet bands and Masons and Odd Fellows Lodges. Music was
presented by the Misses Aldrich and speeches given by seven of the outstanding citizens of the county.[48]

Smith County is mainly agricultural, but it has had some industries,
both usual and unusual through the years. From the time of first settlement
grist mills, sawmills, and sorghum presses were established to answer the
needs of the settlers. These have been followed by the elevators and mills
in nearly every town in the county to care for the grain, supply feed and seed,
and to mill flour. The elevators gradually have provided more space for grain
storage, but most of the feed and flour is now shipped in from terminal cities.

There was once a flourishing woolen mill located on the Solomon River
about two miles southeast of Gaylord. It was the only one of its kind ever
built in this part of the country. For a few years it prospered, making
blankets and woolen goods, thus providing a market for the wool from the
sheep shearings from large flocks of sheep then grazing on the bluffs of
the Solomon Valley. It was operated by Phillips and O'Hara about 1886, but
one of the original builders of the mill was an Englishman by the name of
Abraham Jeffs. After a few years, homesteaders took the pastures, the sheep
flocks were moved farther west, and the mill degenerated into a feed mill and
finally disappeared. For many years discarded spindles could be picked up
along the river.[49]

[48] Mrs. Hattie Baker Collection, op. cit.
[49] A. L. Headley, "Water Power Mills on the Solomon River," manuscript
written for the Smith County Historical Society. Only known living relative
in the county is a granddaughter, Mrs. Cora Loofburrow, residing in Smith
Center (1960). Mrs. Clara Cook, now of Los Angeles, California and who is
96 years old, vividly remembers her girlhood days spent in the vicinity of
the mill.

In the twentieth century several new industries, which while not large, contribute to the economic development of the county. The chalk mining industry has promise of expansion for the future since it is the only place in the United States that chalk is mined commercially (see Chapter I). An unusual occupation and sport developed in this area is greyhound raising and racing. During the early 1930's a number of Smith County men spent many Sunday afternoons and holidays coursing the wild Jackrabbits prevalent in this area. As this sport developed in other areas of the country, particularly Florida, the breeding, raising, and training of greyhounds became a money-making business. Lafe Colo of Cedar constructed the first coursing park and was one of the pioneer breeders of the present day greyhound. Other men connected with the business and sport include Dr. Lee Alders, Clem Johnson, Roy Mahin, Melvin Eller, "Prof." Anderson and Herman Grauerholz.[50] Kensington is the site of two industries, the Ray Hainke Manufacturing Company for the Kensington Power Lawn Mower. Ray Hainke invented the rotary lawn mower in 1939, and for a short time during World War II he was the only lawn mower manufacturer in the United States. His highest employment was approximately forty-five men and the distribution was all over the United States. Ray Hainke died in 1952, but in 1960 there was still a small production of the mower.[51] Bill Hainke, brother of Ray, established the Hainke Foundry also at Kensington, which made various machine parts. It is now closed.

---

[50] Manuscript written for the Smith County Historical Society by "Prof." Anderson, Gaylord School Superintendent for years and one of the largest winners in this area. One year his winnings exceeded $35,000.

[51] Personal letter to the author from Robert Hainke, Kensington, Kansas, son of Ray Hainke, March 17, 1960.

Although the county was dotted with sod houses and schoolhouses, there was apparently only one sod house ever used as a dwelling on the townsite of Smith Centre. This "soddy" stood for about thirty years on the site later occupied by Bonecutter Chevrolet Garage. Col. L. P. Sherman built the sod house in either 1872 or 1873 as a storage place for thousands of hedge plants that he sold over the county to homesteaders to plant along roads for tree culture payments (see Chapter IV). In later years he quit that business and established the Sherman House, famous as a hotel in western Kansas for decades. The sod house then was occupied as a residence for many years. No one knows exactly when it was torn down.[52]

Gaylord was a town of distinctions. It never hesitated to take the lead, and after the railroad came, the town was the trade center as far west as fifty to seventy-five miles and always meant to help its customers to relax after weeks or months of isolation. This led to an election in 1895 that started out a joke and backfired when an entire body of city officials elected for this progressive pioneer village of about 800 people were women. The women had complained that the men officials had neglected the proper care of the streets, that they allowed noisy and offensive conduct so a "decent" woman could hardly walk down the street, and most of all, that out-of-the-way places were allowed to dispense certain liquids of greater potency than water, this being ten years after the passage of the Kansas dry law which prohibited the sale of anything of an intoxicating nature except by prescription. The men challenged the women to put up a slate of candidates which could do better. They did — an entire ballot of women, except the city treasurer, an office held by A. M. Lewellen

---

[52] Mrs. Hattie Baker Collection, op. cit. Trube Reese was Mrs. Baker's informant.

from the time the city was incorporated. The men were hilarious, but women could vote in municipal elections and the all-woman ticket was elected. They were Mrs. W. H. Haskell, mayor; Mrs. Joe Johnson, Mrs. Frank Mitchell, Mrs. H. S. White, Mrs. Wm. Wright, and Mrs. Adam Abercrombie, city council; Mrs. J. H. Foote, police judge; and Miss Florence Headley appointed city clerk. They permitted Dave Hart to continue as city marshal if he followed the orders of the mayor. The reform of the city fell far short of expectations; the liquid refreshments moved outside of the city limits. But the women did get the business men to keep the sidewalks clear of trash and snow and tobacco chewers had to spit in the gutters. The incident of the election of women city officials created considerable notoriety and there were pictures and stories printed in the metropolitan newspapers, some of which, like a Texas newspaper, were not very complimentary. But Gaylord apparently did not mind a good joke and the women served out their terms.[53]

Gaylord again "made" the city papers in 1950 as "the town that did not give up". In brief, the article stated that a town of 1,000 had shrunken to 250 but refused to say die. The difference between it and a town of comparative size was the ages of the active residents, many of whom were septuagenarians and octogenarians. Mrs. Alice Campbell, 84, did her own work. Her landlord, insurance salesman and oil lease dabbler, Frank Blackburn, was 81. Pearl Swank, 78, clerked in the general store; Bob McClain, 80, was the town

---

[53] "City of Gaylord, 1886-1936," ten page pamphlet at the Kansas State Historical Society Library; A. L. Headley, "Ladies Ruled City of Gaylord," article written for Smith County Historical Society; this was not the first instance of a "lady" city government in Kansas, however. Fourteen women held county offices in Kansas in 1886; the first woman mayor was Mrs. Dora Salter in Argonia, Sumner Co.; five women elected to city council at Syracuse, 1887. Kansas was the first state to grant municipal suffrage to women, 1887. (Annals of Kansas, Vol. 7).

carpenter; and W. D. Lloyd, 90, ran the Ford Garage.[54]

The State of Kansas found some lost land in Smith County in 1956 when
the highway department prepared to condemn a new right-of-way for US 36
a mile west of the east county line of Smith County. The appraisers, Ross
Cline, Eli Shively, and Arden Dierdorf, found a tract of land of .39 acres
to which there was no title. The State of Kansas tried unsuccessfully for
several weeks to clear the faulty title. Ray Myers, correspondent for several local newspapers, wrote an item for his column of the unusual circum-
stance. Mrs. Milton Rogers, Esbon, sent a copy of the story to her relatives
in Oregon, and it was disclosed that sometime in the 1870's a sod church called
Sweet Home had been built on the land owned by a family named Hollingsworth.
When his farm was sold he had reserved the .39 acres the church was on. The
church group had gradually died out or moved and the incident forgotten in the
realm of time, until the state wanted that particular land. Three descendants
of the Hollingsworth family, now living in Oregon, got $11.00 apiece for the
site of one of the earliest churches in Smith County. The Smith County Pioneer
later reported an interview with Charlie Sargent who stated he had attended
services in the old sod church which stood there and was called Shiloh (or
Shilow) Church in the eighties. He did not remember who built the church but
John Hollingsworth owned the land. A store was originally operated in a sod
building near the Sweet Home cemetery and called the Sweet Home store and post
office run by a Mr. Shafer. Mr. Sargent's grandfather, Washington N. Rogers,
bought the store and post office and moved it west of the Shiloh church in a
frame building. There was a blacksmith shop run by Ed Barber across the road
on the north side. Sargent could remember when dust several inches deep was

---

54 Kansas City Times, December 1, 1950.

between the two buildings from covered wagons going by. In 1879 his grand-
father moved the store one mile north and ran it until the railroad came.
One of the pastors of the old sod church, Andy Poulson, married Mr. and Mrs.
Sargent.[55]

An unusual geographic obtrusion in the approximately level plains of
Smith County is the high chalk bluff that rears above the range of hills
bordering the Solomon Valley and locally termed for many years as Harlan
Hill. It stands northwest of Harlan on US 281 and K9 highways and overlooks
the Solomon Valley for many miles each way. The land on which the hill is
located was homesteaded by the Calvin Harlans for whom the town of Harlan
was named, and is now owned by Mr. and Mrs. Guy Caldwell. They donated an
area on the extreme top of the hill to the Coronado Area Council of the Boy
Scouts of America. A Statue of Liberty replica was erected looking out over
the valley and a small park and picnic ground built surrounding it.[56]

Some Representative Smith Countians

There are hundreds and even thousands of individuals who have a distinc-
tive part in the development of a community, not to mention a county, so an
attempt to name over a period of ninety years the leading individuals in Smith
County who, through individual service, have been outstanding is as impossible
a task as naming the several thousand individuals and their contributions to
settlement of the county. One can only hope to give some representative

___

[55] Smith County Pioneer, January 17, 1957.

[56] Smith County Pioneer, November 26, 1959. The State Highway Department reported that in 1959 an estimated 2,000 people visited or picnicked
there during the year.

individuals that illustrate the outstanding inspiration and talent found among the citizens of Smith County and the few cited in no way reflects on the contributions of all the others.

It seems appropriate to start with a few homesteaders who became well known over the county and to proceed to those native sons and daughters who followed some profession that brought merit to their native birthplace. Three homesteaders whose interest was interlaced all their lives with Smith County were L. C. Uhl, L. T. (Trube) Reese, and John Goodale. Reese and Goodale had been working on the railroad in their native state of Illinois when they decided to come west. They fitted up a covered wagon and started for Kansas; at Jewell Center they met J. W. George who had been surveying Smith County and he advised them to come to the vicinity of what was to be Smith Centre. They learned the land office was at Concordia, so unloaded the wagon at Jewell and made the trip there to file on claims. Reese chose the northwest 160 acres in section 10 and Goodale the quarter adjoining on the west. (This later was in Center Township and the road straight north from Main Street in Smith Center ran between the two farms.) The men then drove to Gaylord and started north to try to locate their homesteads. They arrived April 24, 1872. After they located their homesteads Reese later described his as "so level a fellow could stand in the middle of it and see a jack rabbit in any corner." They planted corn with a spade that year and had a dugout built by fall in which they lived together for two years.

In August 1872, while enroute to Jewell for seed wheat with a four-horse team and wagon, Reese and Joe Davis, another homesteader, saw a speck on the prairie just east of the breaks of Oak Creek. At first they feared an Indian decoy, but found it to be a small, light-complexioned white man dressed in a

blue serge suit and white shirt, carrying a red bandana-tied package that
afterwards proved to be a law book. He introduced himself as Leonard Uhl
and asked if they knew anything about a townsite known as Smith Centre some-
where out West. He went home with them and the next morning chose as a homestead the SW$\frac{1}{4}$, Sec. 9 in Centre Township. Leonard C. Uhl was born in Hessia,
Germany and came to America at the age of two with his family, living in Indiana and Illinois where he grew to manhood. He taught school for two years in
Decatur, Illinois, then came to Falls City, Nebraska, where his brother, George,
was living. There he read law and was admitted to the bar in Nebraska, June
18, 1872, and soon afterward decided to go to Kansas. In the spring of 1873
he had Reese and Goodale build him a sodhouse on his claim, then began to
practice law in Smith Centre. In his possession he had the one law book he
carried to the county. It was "Spaulding's Treaties." L. C. Uhl purchased an
eighty acre homestead relinquishment on the west of Smith Center townsite and
built a home in which he spent the rest of his life. He went back to Illinois
in 1875 and married his sweetheart, Miss Nancy Widick. They were parents of
two sons, L. C. Uhl, Jr. and Fred H. Uhl. His especial enjoyment in later
years were the trips he and his wife took, especially one to his native Germany in 1905, and the Shrine Pilgrimage to Manila. He came to the county
with $5.00, became a noted lawyer and abstracter, and after sixty years of
residence passed away June 4, 1932.[57]

John Goodale built a sod house on his farm and he and Laura Ann Logan
were married December 12, 1875. She had come to Centre Township in 1873. She
always said they made a good living by hard work and using the word "Economy"
for their guide. The Goodales moved to town in 1895, and Mrs. Goodale built

---

[57] Mrs. Hattie Baker Collection, op. cit.

a small church of her faith, "The Church of God", near her home. Her group worshipped there for many years until in 1946, when a large church was built in the northeast part of town. He died May 22, 1915 and she passed away September 29, 1953 at the age of 96 years.[58]

Trube Reese lived in Center Township for seventy-eight years. His long life was one of adventure. He saw the first stake that designated the townsite of Smith Centre, the first nail driven in the first building, helped dig the first grave in Fairview Cemetery, saw bands of Indians, herds of buffalo and deer, and helped many newcomers to get located. He had a keen memory of all of these things and even in the last years of his life, he enjoyed writing stories of his experiences or telling them to the children who loved to gather on the porch of his home on West Court Street. In 1879 he had married Miss Florence Webb at the homestead of her parents. They had come to Smith County in 1877. He was postmaster for several years, then went into the real estate business and stock buying. He was a member of the first band, belonged to the Masonic fraternity for seventy years, charter member of the Chamber of Commerce, honorary member of the Rotary Club, and member of the Congregational Church. He became known far and wide over the county as a friend to everyone. Mr. and Mrs. Reese celebrated their fiftieth wedding anniversary in 1929 with all their seven children and families at home. Mrs. Reese died in 1946 at the age of eighty-four, but for the first time in the history of Smith Center a person lived to be one hundred years of age and this was to be the privilege of Leonidas Troubador Reese. Two days of celebration was held and more than 500 friends signed the guest book. The high school

---

[58] Ibid.

band serenaded him and he insisted on greeting each of the sixty-five members personally. They knew of his life time interest in music. It was he who had first read the words of the poem, "My Western Home," and urged Dr. Higley to get Dan Kelley to write some music for what later became "Home on the Range." And so "Trube" Reese, as he was known to everyone, born at Abington, Illinois, September 12, 1850, died November 29, 1950, at the age of 100 years.[59]

Another future Smith Countian who walked into the county was Joel Randall Burrow. Burrow was born in Marion County, Illinois in 1853, a collateral descendant of John Quincy Adams. He came to Kansas on the railroad to Clay Center, the end of the line. He made his way to Jewell County with a wagon train, then walked barefooted to a point near Salem where he got a job. He had shoes but wanted to save them. Burrow once told Clyde Myers that he landed at White Rock with $7.50 in his pocket, but later loaned his brother-in-law $7 of that and started his fortune on the remaining 50¢. His brother-in-law, Martin Hall, was a merchant in Salem, then moved to Bellaire when the railroad went through and continued there the remainder of his life or into the 1920's. Later he secured the star mail route from Cora to Scandia, then moved to Smith Center where he soon had contracts to handle all the star routes. He handled these routes from 1873 to 1881, during which time he became well acquainted with the country and people. He prospered and purchased a hotel, livery stable, and store. He was asked to sign a note for a friend so he could borrow $100. Burrow asked how much interest he was to pay. The answer was what amounted to about 25 per cent. He made the loan himself, charging 18 per cent. The security was a three-legged cow, a buffalo calf, some horses and rattlesnakes since the friend was Andy Shaffer, who exhibited

59 Ibid.

the animals for a small sum. After this he started going farmers' notes. In 1874, so the story goes, he had accumulated checks to the amount of $400, and sent them by a young man of the vicinity to Hastings to be cashed, but this friend went to Kearney, filled up on corn whiskey, and when later found was in the army. This was one of his few bad investments. In 1880 he sold out his other interests and he and George White organized the People's Bank. George White had come to Smith County in 1873, opened a law office, and was county attorney in 1874-1875. On August 6, 1886, he organized the First National Bank with a capital of $50,000. A brick and stone structure was built in 1889. In 1901 he organized the First National Bank in Lebanon with Johnny Mossman as cashier. He later sold it to Andrew Lull. Early in the 1900's he formed the First State Bank at Athol with F. Fleming as cashier. The Athol bank merged with the parent bank at Smith Center about 1932, as also did the Bellaire Bank which had been established by Burrow about the same time. At one time he was president of the First National Bank, Smith Center, First State Bank of Athol, First State Bank of Bellaire, First State Bank of Portis, Osage County Bank, Osage City, First State Bank of Cawker City, and the Central National Bank of Topeka, Central Trust Company of Topeka, and Home Investment Company of Smith Center. He was Secretary of the State of Kansas from 1903-1907; served as Chairman of the Shawnee County Liberty Loan Committee during the first World War; and was delegate to the Republican National Convention in 1900. It is said he arrived in the county with fifty cents, homesteaded adjoining Smith Center, 1873, and died in Topeka in 1930, a financier.

Webb McNall was another homesteader who had a varied and colorful career. He was born in New York, came to Iowa with his parents. There he married Miss Annie Humberger in 1868 and they came to Gaylord and homesteaded in September 1872. He was one of the first township officers of Houston Township, and at

different times constable and deputy sheriff in Smith County, and editor of
the Gaylord Herald. In 1876-77 he was doorkeeper of the House of Representatives, later Commissioner of Insurance for Kansas, and in 1879 he was admitted
to practice law in the districts of Kansas. He became a successful lawyer on
railroad cases. He worked in the Kirwin Land Office from October 1889 to April
1892.

In the early days the McNalls lived at Gaylord in the old log school house.
Their daughter, Cora May, born March 25, 1872, was the first child born in Gaylord. Her death, November 1874, was also the first. Her mother had stepped
outside on an errand leaving the children eating breakfast. When two-year-old
Cora apparently decided to make some toast, she fell into the fire and died of
burns. Several years later Webb came home from Congress to deliver the July
4th oration at the celebration. Mrs. McNall started to the picnic grounds with
a team and buggy; her mother was in the back seat. The horses became frightened at the bridge over Beaver Creek, backed off the bridge and killed Mrs.
Humburger. Mrs. Ream, a neighbor of the McNall's wrote: "Webb McNall was in
a class by himself — a man of mighty ambition and purpose, and who through
all the struggles and all but overwhelming obstacles of his time, made for
himself a place in the worthwhile things of Kansas history."[60]

The Simmonds families were homesteaders that came to the Cedarville area
and helped the county to grow and mature. William Simmonds and wife with six
children had lived in successive places on the new frontier until they finally
settled at Buchanan, Iowa. Here Robert was killed in an accident. John, George,
and Susan Elizabeth were all married, Harriet and Angus were with their father.

[60] Mrs. Cora Ream, op. cit.

John had been in correspondence with Major John Morrison, with whom he had served in the Civil War. Morrison was one of the founders of Cedarville. Due to this the father, William, his sons, John, George, son-in-law, Nelson Goddard (wife, Susan), a widowed step-daughter of the Goddards, Sarah Jane Leighton, all with their families, came to Smith County and filed on homesteads in the Cedarville area in 1872. Harriet and Angus were too young to file. William originally homesteaded on the NE¼ Sec. 20, T4, R14, by pre-emption April 1872. He received the title at the Kirwin Land Office March 4, 1880. The final papers showed his age to be 61, all children married, wife deceased, natural-ized citizen. He had built a stone house and stable, had sixty acres under cultivation, planted fruit trees and hedge. His witnesses were neighbors D. H. Crosby and John Wolcott. In August, 1898, a tornado carried the house away and carried him more than a mile but miraculously did not kill him. He was eighty-one at the time. He died April, 1902 at the age of eighty-five. One of his sons, Angus M. Simmonds, homesteaded the SW¼ Sec. 17, T4, R14, January 15, 1876. When he received his title he gave his age as 29, with wife and three children. He had a stone house 14 feet by 16 feet, board floors, board and sod roof; forty acres of land broken. His witnesses were Dan H. Crosby, Asa Crosby, John Wolcott, and William Lyall, neighbors. His wife was Christiana Tillman, who had come to Marysville, Kansas when six years old and married Angus in 1876. One of their children, Frank, is included in this section under educators. Angus died at his home in Athol, 1927. John Simmonds, another son, with his wife and small daughter, Rosalie Simmonds (Cole), farmed his homestead, was Deputy Sheriff several terms, and had a livery barn and feed business. He died at Cedar in 1911 as also did George. Both were Civil War veterans. Susan Elizabeth, wife of Nelson Goddard, died at Kensington, 1925. Harriet married James Phillips at Cedarville, then homesteaded north of Angus in Harvey Township in 1873. Their home burned down in 1882. They were the only ones not to live their lives out in Smith County. They decided to go farther west after the fire and moved from one place to another until she died at Montrose, Colorado.[61]

The above mentioned Daniel Henderson Crosby came to the Cedar community in the fall of 1871 and took a homestead. He was born in Delaware County, New York, grew to manhood in Wisconsin where his folks had moved when he was twelve, and came to Smith County at the age of twenty-four. Although too young to enlist in the Civil War, and rejected twice on that account, he had several birthdays in quick succession and enlisted in 1864 in the Wisconsin Infantry which made a name for itself in history. In September 1878, he married Sarah Young, also daughter of pioneer parents who came to Cedarville in a covered wagon in 1876 with eleven children and settled on a farm south of Cedarville. John C. Harlan, for whom Harlan was named, and whose son later won fame by substantiating the claim of Smith County as the origin of "Home on the Range," was the probate judge who married them. (See license in Appendix.) They had one son, William, and one daughter, Lilly. The first town officers of Cedarville were G. H. Hunt, trustee; D. H. Crosby, Clerk; and Chas. E. Newman, Justice. About 1901, the Crosbys moved to Kensington where he opened a hotel that employed a number of people and became noted for the meals served in its dining room. In the Cedar cemetery, D. H. Crosby and N. P. Draper erected in May, 1921, a large monument in memory of their G. A. R. comrades who had passed on. It became a part of the Memorial Day program each year to decorate at the base and sound "Taps" for the veterans that had died. (See G. A. R. history.) Mrs. Crosby died May,

---

61 Frank W. Simmonds, op. cit., from geneology throughout the book.

1915, and Dan December 31, 1922.[62]

John D. Mahin and his family came to Smith County from Iowa in September 1878. This included five children, Isaac, Frank, Hubert, Caz, and a daughter, Salina. John traded a team of horses to a minister named Daney for the re-linquishment of his claim south of Cedarville. He later gave land on the northeast corner for the Glen Rock school where two of his sons, Isaac and Frank, later taught. Ike (Isaac), Frank, and Dooley all excelled at baseball in the days when it was a rough game. Dooley had a chance to go to the Chicago White Sox for a try-out but "felt Chicago was too far from Cedarville." Isaac and Frank studied law as well as taught school and were admitted to the bar. For many years they were prominent practicing attorneys, both in Smith Center and throughout the state. Salina Mahin married Alonzo Teeple, a pioneer teacher and later attorney. For many years he served as Probate Judge at Man-kato, Kansas and after his death, Salina finished his term and continued in that capacity for several years. Two of the great granddaughters taught school in the school for which their ancestor had donated the land; namely, Darcy, granddaughter of Isaac, and Ilene, granddaughter of Hubert.[63]

Mrs. Elsa Rice, a widow, and her five sons, William, E. R. (Eliott), T. M. (Mad), J. H. (Harve), and E. S. (Scott) arrived in Smith County in October, 1873. She took a homestead five miles northwest of Athol and as her sons became of age they too homesteaded until in 1912 the homes of the five brothers included 2,640 acres of highly improved farms. During all their lives the brothers were in daily touch with each other and each made his home in the county. The mother passed away in 1890, a true pioneer. In October,

---

62 The above pioneer homesteaders were the author's grandparents and William her father, thus her interest in Cedar, Kensington, and in Smith Center where she lived until married.

63 A history of the Mahin family written for the Smith County Historical Society and loaned to the author.

the family had a clan gathering at the old homestead owned then by one of the
sons, Mad, to celebrate the fortieth anniversary of the family arrival in the
county and the wedding of the youngest brother, Scott. There were a few less
than 100 members in the family by then. Late in November 1926, they had a
dinner in Smith Center at which time the brothers' average age was 73 years —
Will, Athol, 80 years; Mad, Athol, 76; Eliott, Kensington, 73; Harve, Smith
Center, 71; and Scott, Smith Center, 66 years old. The Smith County papers
stated that they all were hale and hearty and willing to work, and Will was
one of the few original homesteaders still living on his land. Scott Rice
died July 16, 1937. Scott studied law and was a graduate from the University
of Kansas in 1888. He then entered law practice at Smith Center where he had
remained. Some of his positions were Assistant Secretary of State, County
Attorney of Smith County, and Mayor of Smith Center. Harve died in 1936 at
the age of 80 years, Will in 1937 at the age of 91 years, Scott in 1937 at
the age of 77, Mad in 1940 at the age of 90, and Eliott in 1942 at the age
of 89. Thus ended the lives of five pioneer brothers who had a prominent part
in the making of the history of Smith County.[64]

Two judges may be mentioned for their services in the legal field. Jules
Jarvis was known far and wide throughout the county to adults and children
alike. He was born in Mahaska County, Iowa, in 1850 and came to Smith County
in 1886 where he was in the mercantile business. He was appointed deputy
sheriff, then elected sheriff for four years. From 1894 to 1898 he was
Deputy U. S. Marshal. He was elected probate judge in 1903 and although a

64 Smith County Journal, October 22, 1914; Smith County paper, December
2, 1926; July 22, 1937. Clippings loaned by Mrs. Jess Rice, Athol. Mrs.
Rice, whose husband is a son of Will Rice, and her brother-in-law, H. V.
Dilsaver of Kensington, contributed much information and help for this work.

Democrat, he held the office for twenty-four consecutive years "in the face
of repeated Republican landslides." He died in office in 1932.[65]

C. Clyde Myers had a dual acclaim -- one as judge, one as a writer. He
was born on the Tom Ricard homestead three miles northwest of Esbon, Jewell
County, the oldest of six children. He attended Salem school, and graduated
from Lebanon High School in 1907. He taught school in Smith County from
1907-1910. In 1910 he entered Washburn Law School, graduated in 1913, was
admitted to practice July 3, 1913. He started law practice at Lebanon; in
1913 he entered a partnership with Judge William Mitchell, Mankato; in 1914
he was elected county attorney of Jewell County and served four years. July
1920 he went to Kansas City, Kansas, as Assistant United States Attorney, then
stayed in Kansas City to practice law. In 1924 he served as Probate Judge of
Wyandotte County, 1927-28 as Assistant County Attorney. Since 1945 he has been
judge of one of the city courts of Kansas City. He says probably the best work
he has ever done was as Government Appeal Agent during World War I, a job for
which he was paid nothing and received more ill will than anything else. He
passed on claims for exemptions and made recommendations to the government.
Politically he has always been Democratic. Since 1922 he has been on a ballot
or holding office or both. His sister, Moda, started teaching school at sixteen after graduating from Lebanon High School. She later attended Colorado
Teachers College, University of Hawaii, Alaska University at Fairbanks, Old
Heidelberg University in Austria, and taught in Kansas City since 1925. Another sister, Ethel, became Girl Scout Executive at Middletown, Ohio. His
brother, Ray, and sister, Mattie (Mrs. Earl Pixler) live at Lebanon and a

---

[65] Smith County Pioneer, July 28, 1932.

brother, Fred, in California. He married Grace Swartz in 1933 and they have three daughters. He had done much writing for his own pleasure — "perhaps a million words of fiction, both short stories and book length ones" and another million words of Masonic philosophy that has been published all over the world. He had polio when about a year old. He says he probably would have been practically cured with today's methods, but was left with a permanent disability below the hips. He takes the attitude that it was probably good for him as it formed a challenge for him to hold his own with others. His philosophy in life and as a judge is "Call them as you see them!"[66]

Law and politics traditionally go hand in hand and names always win a great deal of publicity in either one. But too, they contribute an important part to the development of any area because law is a necessary attitude of civilization and as such must come with the first settlers. Many of the early lawyers have been mentioned through this history; mention of another one who is familiar to many people in the state was Hal E. Harlan. He was born on a farm near Harlan, Kansas in 1886, so Smith County can claim him as a native son although he moved with his parent to Downs in 1903. He graduated from the Downs High School in 1906, University of Kansas, and in 1912 was admitted to the bar. He opened a law office in Manhattan, was city attorney from 1916 to 1917, and in later years County Attorney of Riley County for four years, later was Chairman of the Republican Central Committee. In 1929 he was elected to the legislature as representative and during his second term served as speaker. In 1932 he was elected Senator from the 21st district, then held two terms

---

66 Biographical sketch of the Myers family and some historical notes on Smith County — Salem, Lebanon; personal manuscripts written by Judge C. Clyde Myers and loaned to the author for this work; letters from Ray Myers, Lebanon.

again in 1945 and 1947. In 1950 he married Miss Irene Knittle, private
secretary to Rep. Albert Cole. In 1947 Harlan was president of the Kansas
Chamber of Commerce and in 1950 the director. He died March 23, 1957 at the
age of 70 years.[67]

"P.M.A. State Chairman Farms on Week Ends" was a good introduction to
Emmet Womer, whose father homesteaded the land in 1870 that he farmed near
Womer, a community that was built around a town and post office of early days,
and named for his grandfather. His mother, Margaret Mitchell, was of Scottish
ancestry and came with her family to a homestead on the Kansas-Nebraska line
north of what was to be Womer in 1871. The Mitchells and Womers homesteaded
much of this area. His folks built the house in 1897 that still stands on the
farm — one large enough for the family of eight children. His father donated
the land for the United Brethren Church on the corner of his farm. All the
settlers in this area had to go to Riverton to get mail until the post office
was established in 1883. A sod post office was built in 1892, and Emmet,
although a boy at the time, helped on the job as did his father, Wes, and
brother, Mel (see pictures). Emmet graduated from Kansas Wesleyan University
and started farming. He was on the Kansas Production and Marketing Administration Board at Manhattan for seventeen years and chairman for three years. During that time he was a "desk man week-days, and dirt farmer on weekends" as
he gave personal attention to his 2,000 acre farm, the nucleus of which was
the homestead of his father. His wife, the former Grace Harlan, remembers
the day her uncle played for the first time "Home on the Range." Mr. and Mrs.
Womer have the unique experience of having a town named for a grandfather of
each of them — Womer and Harlan, both in Smith County. They have two children,

---

[67] Who's Who in the Kansas Legislature, 1929, 1932, 1947.

Sylvester and Hilda Jeane. Mr. Womer, now retired, still keeps an interest
in the farm and spends much of his time assisting in the work of the Smith
County Historical Society of which he was one of the organizers and the first
President.[68]

A doctor who is practically an institution and known in every part of
the county is Victor E. Watts. He was born in Unionville, Missouri on November 26, 1878 and came to Smith County December 1892. He attended common
schools, then Salina Normal University, then taught country school three
years — the first one at a salary of twenty-five dollars a month. This perhaps explains his continued interest in better schools throughout the years.
He has served many years on the school board. He then owned and managed a
country store at Cora for one year, and the next year entered Medical College
at Washburn (later affiliated with Kansas University), graduating in 1907. He
began practice at Womer in northern Smith County, moved to Smith Center in
1913 and has been there since. His main interest has been in obstetrics and
podiatrics or care of children. He estimates he has delivered approximately
2,500 babies. He has been elected Coroner of the county several times and
has been County Health Officer for decades. He was the first person to be
recognized by the local Rotary Club for "Service above self to his fellow
man" and that this is his motto is illustrated by his own words: "I do not
feel I have done anymore in life than is required of everyone. To me life is
service — service to my fellow man in whatever walk of life I found him....
A man is born, he lives, he dies, and the world forgets. Life is wonderful

68 Topeka Daily Capital, January 29, 1950; Smith County Pioneer,
December 12, 1949; Margaret Mitchell Womer, "That You May Know," a biography
dictated December 1935 and published for the children and grandchildren;
interviews in the Womer home in January and April.

just to be able to help; that has been my aim as I have lived."[69]

To writers goes most of the credit for the history that is preserved for later generations because writing outlives the span of generations. As Eugene Ware, Kansas author, says, "When all are gone, the book alone remains." The history of a local area is composed of the little things written by those on the scene or the record of things passed down by word of mouth. This could be called "grass-roots reporting" and a true "grass-roots" reporter is Ray Myers of Lebanon. He actually started writing the history of Smith County thirty years ago with his "Echoes of Old Salem" and "Early History in Kansas," and has continued to do so ever since in his column "Salem Ray" which he has written for more than half a century for the Lebanon Times, Smith County Pioneer, Red Cloud Chief, and Burr Oak and Mankato papers. He has had stories appear in the Saturday Evening Post, Topeka Daily Capital, and other city papers. He guesses his column is now "more than a mile long." Elmer Stump, a neighbor and friend, says of him, "He is a community man, church leader, and good farmer. He writes about his neighbors, down to earth, human interest stories." The Rev. Robert Goldsworth, pastor over northwest Kansas for fifty years once stated, "I have preached more than half a century. Counting my membership, Ray reaches more people every week, some 18,000, than I have in all my years in the ministry. His messages carry about the same ideas -- better people, good citizenship." One time some friends, unknown to Ray, entered some of his columns from the Smith County Pioneer in the news contest at the Hutchinson State Fair. He received third place for the state. This is what the judges wrote:

> Country correspondence -- Your Salem correspondent, Ray
> Myers, has won third place for the Pioneer in the 1957 Kansas
> Newspaper Contest. Mr. Myers tells his news as he sees it,
> hears it, lives it. He is a rare type of journalist of which
> there are too few. He is original, to the heart, and man to

---

[69] Victor E. Watts, personal letter to the author, April, 1960.

man in his writings and tellings. Please accept our congratulations to Mr. Myers, and his newspaper, the Smith County Pioneer.

A. L Headley, editor of the Smith County Pioneer, wrote of Myers:

> Salem, one of the ghost towns of the White Rock Valley, which once flourished to the northeast of Lebanon, has an unique distinction. It never has lost its identity. That fact is due almost exclusively to the versatile pen of Ray Myers. Myers has written a column from the Salem community for the Pioneer and other papers for more than one third of a century, rarely missing a week.[70]

A poet doctor other than the famous Dr. Higley, was Dr. M. F. Leary, who had arrived in Gaylord in 1879. He was the author of several poems, but the one entitled "The Ghost of Beaver Creek" was published in 1886. It so well pictures the difficulties and discouragement met by the settlers in the drouth years of the eighties when many left Kansas, yet it has a note of jest that expressed the determination of those who stayed.

The Ghost of Beaver Creek[71]

Where the water of the Beaver-Beaver Creek surpassing fair
Loiters sparkling in the sunlight (when there's any water there),
There is a legend and a story of a youth who, long ago,
Planted corn down in the valley, where no ear of corn would grow;
And as night her sable tresses spreads o'er Beaver's hills and dale,
Children gathering 'round their mothers shudder at the ghostly tale.

Early, early in the springtime, as the flowers came forth anew,
Blithe was he, with cheeks of roses, hair of gold and eyes of blue.
Light his heart and quick his footsteps on that pleasant spring day morn,
As he planted swiftly and deftly ripened grains of golden corn.
Then he laid aside his planters, harrows, plows, machinery, all
He had bought with note and mortgage coming due in early fall.

Straight and stately grew the cornstalks in their robes of brightest green,
And the neighbors vowed such "promise" ne'er before by man was seen.
And he tended well his treasure, cutting weed and sunflower strong
While his hymns of joy and gladness loud resounded all day long.
And he reckoned oft his profits and great wealth of shiny gold,
Safely loaned on monthly interest, when the corn was picked and sold.

---

70 Elmer Stump, "Ray Myers — Historian," an unpublished manuscript written for the Smith County Historical Society. The author might add that Mr. Myers, through interviews and many letters, and contacts with people in Smith County for the author has been of invaluable assistance in this work.

71 Dr. M. F. Leary, "The Ghost of Beaver Creek," Gaylord Herald, Summer, 1886.

But July's fierce suns fell on it, parching tassel, stalk and ground,
And the promised rains from heaven came, but always "went around";
And the chinch bugs — hungry fellows — hunting fields and pastures new,
Hurried fast into that cornfield, climbed each stalk and bored it through;
Then the hot winds from the Southland rushing past with fiery breath,
Till the stalk and leaf and tassel burned and blackened unto death.

And the youth with golden tresses, as that corn crop faded fast,
Hollow eyes and tottering footsteps told his fondest hopes were blast;
Gaunt and wasted grew his body, thinner, thinner every day,
Till one night in a Kansas wind it is said he blew away;
Nor was seen he more to wander where the Beaver's waters flow,
Though machine man with his mortgage hunted for him high and low.

But when midnight's hour approaches and shrill north winds folks alarm
There is seen a ghostly figure, ghostly basket on its arm,
Passing through the quivering cornstalks, uttering many a sigh and moan,
Seeking vainly for some ear — corn — but no nubbin there had grown.
And 'tis said by those who have seen it, that the spectre so forlorn
Is the youth who died on Beaver — starved to death while growing corn.

Leonard Prowant graduated from Smith Center High School with the class of

1917. He is a writer and publisher. Two of his books are Stanzas for Kansas

and a beautiful story called Christ Comes at Christmas Time. One poem par-

ticularly relating to Smith County is "Up Lebanon Way," a part of which is

included:

> Up Lebanon way, where I was born,
> They raise pigs, chickens, cows and corn;
> Things depend entirely upon the farm,
> And crop failures are viewed with some alarm.
> Industrial cities consider with scorn
> Rural centers like where I was born.
>
> Up Lebanon way, where I was born,
> They raise something besides stock and corn;
> I say it, and I have money to bet
> There live the finest people yet!
> Cosmopolitan friendship looks mighty forlorn
> Beside real friendship like where I was born.
>
> Up Lebanon way, where I was born,
> They raise pigs, chickens, cows, and corn;
> And to come right out and speak real plain,
> I admit it with pride and not with shame.
> I have to smother a feeling of scorn
> When city folks sneer at where I was born![72]

---

72 Leonard Prowant, Stanzas for Kansas, p. 48.

Robert Henry Reed, better known in Smith County as "Bob Reed", was an editor of the well known magazine, The Country Gentlemen, for twenty years before his retirement. His grandfather, Judge H. H. Reed, lived on a homestead about four miles north of Smith Center. Bob's father, O. L. (Tink) Reed, was born there and moved to Smith Center when his father was elected Probate Judge. Tink worked on newspapers here, then was publisher of the Kensington Mirror for a time, and later became owner and publisher of the Almena Plaindealer. Bob was employed in the Kansas City Star office for a short time, then was with the Saturday Evening Post before becoming editor of the Country Gentlemen. Recently he accepted a position from President Eisenhower as attache in the country of Netherlands in an advisory capacity.

A. L. (Bert) Headley, who was editor of the Smith County Pioneer for more than forty years has helped record more history than anyone will be able to include in one book, as he has been in the newspaper business approximately half the life of Smith County. Mr. Headley was born in a sod house on a homestead and began to help in a printing office when "so young it was necessary to stand on a box to reach the type case in the old handset days." He gradually progressed through the period of his more than sixty years experience to editor of the Smith County Pioneer for the last forty of those years. He was always an ardent politician (as were most editors starting in the 80's and 90's) and served as Republican delegate from the Sixth District when Herbert Hoover and Charles Curtis were nominated and served on publicity for Alf Landon when he was candidate for governor and later for president. He also served as publicity director for Frank Carlson in his six campaigns for congressman, press secretary during his two terms as governor and on publicity committee during his campaign for United States Senator. He was press secretary for Governor Ed Arn; and for many years had been chairman or secretary of the Smith County Republican Central Committee. He is now retired at Smith

Center and actively aiding the Smith County Historical Society (1960).

Two more people who have made a splendid contribution to preserving history through newspaper work are Mr. and Mrs. Benjamin T. Baker. Mr. Baker had a record with newspaper work of nearly forty years at the time of his premature death from cancer at the age of fifty-three, twenty-six of which had been in Smith Center. Mrs. Baker has been active in newspaper work since 1917 when her husband died and helped him out before that so her interest stretched over much of the span of Smith County history. B. T. Baker was born in Washington, Iowa and when a young lad came to Kansas and lived on a farm in Osborne County for a few years, then moved to Cawker City where the parents operated a hotel. While attending school Ben worked in the newspaper office of the Cawker City Ledger. Later he took a full time job with the Downs News until he was offered a better position in Colorado. A year later the paper in Colorado was sold and he came back to Smith Center to take charge of the Smith County Journal, a newly organized paper. He and Miss Hattie Cummings of Smith Center were married March 17, 1898 and lived in Smith Center until his death. Some clippings best illustrate Ben's status in his work:

> The Smith County Journal started last week on its 20th year. The editor of the Record can well remember back in the forepart of the 90's when the Journal was printed on a Washington hand press (the boss of this shop doing the inking act). The Journal has grown since those days and is now one of the best equipped shops in northwest Kansas. The editor of this paper worked for seven years on that paper and we owe about all we know about the printing trade to the present editor of that paper, Ben Baker, one of the best printers in the state.

> The Smith County Journal began its twenty-third year last week. With the exception of a year in its early history it has been all that time under the management of Ben T. Baker, a former Cawker boy, who began as a typo in the Record office. Ben has stuck steadily to his business and has made a success of it; he has recently erected an office building and promises other substantial improvements.[73]

---

[73] Athol Record, Aug. 8, 1910, Alf Williamson, Editor; Ibid., Aug. 5, 1913.

"Hattie", as she is known to everyone, was born at Indianola, Iowa and came to Smith Center when she was four years old or about 1880. She graduated from Smith Center High School in 1893. After her husband's death, she managed the Smith County Journal until the newspaper was sold in 1923. She stayed with the new owners until the newspaper was again sold to the Pioneer, then when H. P. Beason moved his Athol Record to Smith Center in 1933, she became one of the staff on it. She "went with the deal," as she laughingly put it, when Beason and W. E. Lee purchased the Pioneer in 1946 and consolidated the Review and Pioneer. In September 1949, Mrs. Baker suffered a hip fracture and has not returned to regular newspaper work except for writing at home. This work has largely become a matter of historical items about Smith County of which she is well qualified to write. She has a wonderful memory, a talent for exactness and detail, and a love for research and her subject that makes her collection a joy to read.[74]

A veteran newspaper editor in Smith County who deserves mention is Walter Boyd of the Kensington Mirror. Mr. Boyd states that his brother acquired the paper and he, Walter, began working there in 1894, at the age of thirteen years. In 1908 he purchased the business and has since continuously owned and conducted it. This makes his record sixty-six years service with the Kensington Mirror and fifty-two years as owner. Such a record is history in itself![75]

---

[74] Facts for these biographies were furnished by Mrs. Hattie Baker at the author's request though, like so many talented people, she felt her life nothing to write about. Much of the material used in this work was due to Mrs. Baker's "Collection" or to her on-the-scene research for the author, or to the wealth of reminiscences she recounted in visits.

[75] Walter Boyd, in personal letter to author, March 28, 1960.

A writer of note from Smith County is Mrs. Margaret A. (Dannels) Nelson.
She had several articles published, then became known for her book, Home on
the Range, published in 1948. Her foreword to the book best introduced it
when she wrote:

> Unlike stories of western fiction, which are filled with
> hair-raising tales of wild carousing in open saloons, cattle
> stealing, and two-gun men, the history of Home on the Range is
> a story of devotion and love. It is the story of courageous
> people who migrated into the prairie country to build them-
> selves a home, people who came into conflict with colossal
> forces of Nature which were fraught with perils, and which
> meant death if they should weaken. Few of these brave souls
> remain. One by one they have passed on, following the trail
> which leads home, and a carpet of short buffalo grass has
> gradually covered their last resting places. To their memory
> I dedicate this book.

Among the writers a place would be reserved for Dr. Brewster Higley
and Dan Kelley, writers of the words and music for "Home on the Range,"
the song that made people in the United States know there was a Smith County
in the heart of the nation. However, these writers are given a starred place
in the next chapter with the history of the song they created.

Not too far from the field of writing are the artistic accomplishments
in the field of drawing, painting, sculptoring, cartooning, and music.
Florence McVicker Squires was born in Smith Center and graduated from Smith
Center High School in 1926. She is a commercial artist and has had work pub-
lished in Pictorial Review, Ladies Home Journal, and Vogue. Her mother, Alice
Walker McVicker, also graduated from Smith Center High School, class of 1900.

Christy Hobbs, a graduate of Smith Center High School in 1927, is a cartoonist and draws "Billy Dug." Another famed cartoonist, Albert T. Reid, once
lived in Smith Center and attended school. The Reid family lived at Smith
Center for a few years in the early nineties while the father was in the bank-
ing business. At that time Albert drew pictures in all his books in his spare

time although the boys called him "sissy" for drawing instead of joining in the sports. His paintings and drawings are principally of early day Kansas frontier scenes and Indian life.[76]

Mrs. Nelson Chubb, formerly Nettie Smith, was born and reared in Center Township. Her parents were Ira and Cora Smith who homesteaded two and a half miles west of Smith Center in 1872. Early in life Nettie developed a talent for drawing and sketching and that has been her main diversion ever since. In 1938 the family moved to Smith Center where the parents lived at their home on West Court Street until their deaths, and where Nettie continued to live. She became an outstanding artist, sketching many scenes in Smith County. She has done all the scenes for the Chamber of Commerce in advertising for Smith Center and the county. She has received numerous prizes at fairs and art displays. She and her husband spend their winters in Arizona, where she loves to sketch and paint.[77]

Bernard (Poco) Frazier was born on a farm near Athol and first made a name for himself at the University of Kansas as a distance runner. He was Big Six Champion two mile runner in 1927, 1928, and 1929. He graduated from the University of Kansas November, 1935. He then went to Chicago to work as an artist in the Midway Studios with Lorado Taft (sculptor). In 1944 he became director of the Philbrook Museum in Tulsa; then he came back to Kansas University to teach and continue his work in sculptoring. He did eight dioramas for the Dyche Museum of prehistoric life in the general area of which Kansas is a part. They were four by six by three feet in size, made to scale and in color. Other works are the Bronze Memorial doors of the Campanile at

76 Mrs. Hattie Baker Collection, op. cit.
77 Compiled from material furnished by Mrs. Hattie Baker at the author's request.

Kansas University, a free standing bear eight feet tall in front of the Missouri State Office Building in Jefferson City, and two large wall sculptures for the Union National Bank in Wichita. In 1941 he won the Western Hemisphere Award for Sculpture on two buffalo called "Prairie Combat." The Joslyn Museum in Omaha has the sculpture of two colts, "The Yearlings," which won the five state purchase prize in Midwest Competition. His latest work in the summer and fall of 1956 was the stone carvings symbolic of the state's history on three faces of the new State Office Building in Topeka. The south face showed a pioneer settler and his family on the trail with a covered wagon and sunflowers. The west face depicted the Spanish thrust into Kansas and featured a captain, priest, and Indians. The east side represents modes of travel by settlers who came to Kansas. His wife, Franczeska Shilling, works with him at Lawrence. She is noted also in the field of art and won the sweepstakes prize for her statue, "Adolescent," at the Kansas Free Fair in 1939.[78]

The Reed Trio, Mildred, Lucille, and Helen, were daughters of Mrs. Nettie Forabaugh Reed and Harry E. Reed. They were born and reared on a farm six miles north of Smith Center. The girls drove to town to attend high school and graduated as follows: Mildred, 1934; Lucille, 1936; and Helen, 1938. After graduation they formed the "Reed Trio" and soon were singing with dance bands in many large cities. They went overseas, entertained at military camps and sang in Paris night clubs. They and their mother now live in California (1960).[79]

---

[78] University of Kansas, Graduate Magazine, Nov. 1935, p. 4; Topeka Capital, July 22, 1956; Topeka Journal, Aug. 6, 1956.

[79] Mrs. Hattie Baker, personal letter to author, April 4, 1960.

Smith County has had an unusual number of residents interested in missionary work, probably a reflection of their early Christian faith and perseverance. One of the very early families in Christian work was the Thompson family at Harlan. The Harlan Sunday School was organized in the Thompson home in 1879 with Mrs. Thompson the first superintendent. Mr. Thompson (given name unknown) had been a Congregational minister in Wisconsin, and preached for the people for awhile, but lived only about a year. His grave and monument are in a little cemetery on the hill north of Harlan. The mother and two boys remained through the pioneer years and the boys attended Gould College. The older son, Frank, went to Africa as a missionary. He went without the backing of a church board, working his way to London, and arriving there without sufficient funds for a night's lodging. A policeman befriended him; his story was presented to the Mission Board of the British Foreign Missionary Society who accepted his application and sent him to Liberia. He returned to Smith County once on a brief furlough, then went back to Liberia to spend his life there. His mother and other brother later joined him.[80]

Melva Z. Livermore of Smith Center did missionary work in India under the Methodist Foreign Missionary Board for more than forty years. Melva was born in Chariton County, Missouri, April 19, 1867, and when a small child came with her parents, Mr. and Mrs. Daniel E. Livermore, to live on a farm four miles north of Smith Center for several years, then moved to Smith Center where she attended school. She taught at Cedar and Lebanon and was county superintendent. She decided to be a missionary and in November 1897 sailed from the east coast for Meeriet, India, where she served through the years

80 Oscar Crouse, op. cit.

until her retirement in 1937. During her forty years of foreign service she was home on furloughs several times and she was always in constant demand for speaking engagements. The Women's Foreign Missionary Society members of Smith County raised the fund of $70.00 to present Melva an honorary anniversary membership in the National Women's Foreign Missionary Society. The citizens of Smith Center had a Ford car sent from the factory to India when it was learned how much Melva needed a conveyance over the territory where she worked. After her retirement, in 1937, she and a missionary friend, Anna Lawson, lived at Pacific Palisades, California, where she died July 1941.[81]

Wilbur Matson, a graduate of Smith Center High School in 1911, taught in the government schools for four years in China, in Singapore and in Ipali. He has been a merchant in Smith Center ever since his return.

Rev. S. H. Patterson, a native of Cedar vicinity, became president of the Radio Prayer League, Inc. and was instrumental in organizing the school lunch program. He went to Denver in 1928 and began radio preaching over KVOD. It was here he organized the Radio Prayer League. When the depression struck in Denver in the 1930's, he sponsored the feeding of 400 school children from five public schools for 4½ years. He applied to President Roosevelt for a WPA program for school lunches. Harry Hopkins was sent to Denver to survey what was being done. His reaction was that it should be all over the United States, and in a short time the project was in operation and still is (1960).[82]

The Faurots, Ruth, Jean, and Albert, moved to Smith Center when their father became pastor of the Presbyterian Church and still consider Smith Center as "home" as they all graduated from school there and the family lived

[81] Mrs. Hattie Baker Collection, op. cit.
[82] Smith County Pioneer, March 29, 1956.

there for about thirty-five years. Jean graduated from Park College and has since received degrees from Westminster Seminary, Philadelphia; McGill University, Montreal, Canada; and a Doctorate from Toronto University. He taught Bible and Philosophy at Missouri Valley College four years and is now Head of the Department of Humanities at Sacramento College, Sacramento, California. Albert graduated from Smith Center High School in 1932, then Park College, and was appointed Missionary of Music at Foochou College in Foochou, China. He served there through the Chinese-Japanese War and also during World War II. When the Communists took over, he was ordered to leave and was transferred to Kobe College, Japan for one year, then to Silliman University at Dumaguette, P. I. He has since studied piano with Mattey in London, and Richard Cantebury at Kansas City, Missouri and received his M.A. from Park College. Ruth Marie, after graduating from Park College, received her M.A. from Kansas University and studied at McGill University, Montreal, Canada. She taught at Smith Center, followed by three years at Scotsbluff Junior College, then received an appointment to the Polytechnical Institute at San German, Puerto Rico. Later she took a leave and received her Ph.D. in English from the University of North Carolina, then returned to Puerto Rico.[83]

James C. Putman, reared on a farm in Smith County and graduated from the Smith Center schools, was one of the founders of the Veterans of Foreign Wars and was the first national commander of that organization. He was the oldest son of Mr. and Mrs. William R. Putman who lived on their homestead two miles west of Smith Center. James Putman's colorful career included participation in three Indian wars, service under Gen. John Pershing in 1890-91 when the latter was an officer in the Sixth Cavalry, service in the Spanish American

---

[83] Letter interview with Dr. Ira N. Faurot, now retired, Nortonville, Kansas.

War, and a worker on the Panama Canal. He also served six years in the
Missouri Legislature. The American Veterans of Foreign Service joined with
several other veterans' groups to form the V.F.W. at Columbus, Ohio, in 1899.
Mr. Putman died at Fayetteville, Arkansas, on October 11, 1956, at the age
of 88 years.[84]

Norman Whiting was a name that not many knew except the residents of
Lebanon, but some historic words that he used became the basis of a hymn that
the famous evangelist, Dwight L. Moody, used in his meetings in the decades
around 1900. Judge C. Myers who recounted the story, was sure that Moody and
Sankey, his song leader, never knew they were talking of a Lebanon man when
they spoke the line and drew a religious truth from the words, "Hold the Fort
for I am Coming." A Mr. Bliss did not know he was writing of a Lebanon man
when he wrote the religious song of this title. Judge Myers quotes the story
of the song from an old volume copyrighted in 1895 that contained a collection
of excerpts from the sermons of Moody thus:

> "Hold the Fort, for I am Coming!" — When General Sherman
> went from Atlanta to the sea through the Southern States — he
> left in the fort in the Kenesaw Mountains a little handful of
> men to guard some rations that he had brought there. And General
> Hood got into the outer rear and attacked the Fort, drove the men
> from the outer works into the inner works, and for a long time the
> battle raged fearfully. Half the men were either killed or wounded;
> the general who was in command was wounded seven different times;
> and when they were about ready to run up the white flag and sur-
> render the Fort, Sherman got within fifteen miles, and through
> signal corps in the mountains he sent the message, "Hold the fort;
> I am coming. W. T. Sherman." That message fired up their hearts
> and they held the fort until reinforcements came. Our friend, Mr.
> Bliss, has written a hymn of this name.... Let us take up the
> chorus.

---

[84] Mrs. Hattie Baker Collection, op. cit.

Ho! My comrades, see the signal
Waving in the sky!
Reinforcements now appearing,
Victory is nigh!
Hold the fort, for I am coming,
Jesus signals still,
Wave the answer back to heaven
By thy grace we will.

Judge Myers says that Norman Whiting was a quiet, dignified "Old Soldier", a slim, kindly person with a white Van Dyke beard who lived with his wife quietly and at peace with the world. Shortly before his death, it was discovered that Whiting, while a signal man with General Sherman, was the young signal corps man who wig-wagged the message to the beleagued fort in the mountains. He spent his remaining years in Lebanon so unobtrusively that it was hard to realize that he could have been the person that sent the message, "Hold the fort; I am coming! W. T. Sherman."[85]

In the field of education the names are legion, from the first pioneer teachers that put up with hardships untold to many who are yet in the work after nearly a lifetime of service. Not being able to give due honor to all of them, this work will compromise by mentioning four who, while they perhaps have not contributed more, have done so in a wider area and are known to more people.

Ida Margaret Ahlborn, Smith Center High School class of 1900, was Professor of Home Economics and Assistant Dean of Women at Kansas State College (University) before her marriage to Dr. Royal J. Montgomery in 1937. She compiled a text book titled Nutrition that is widely used in colleges both in the United States and overseas. A building on the campus at Manhattan, "The Margaret Ahlborn Lodge," was named in her honor. She and her husband both

---

[85] Judge Clyde Myers, op. cit.

came from their home in Grinnell, Iowa, for the Golden Jubilee of Smith Center High School. While there Royal Montgomery, class of 1897, gave the commencement address to the class of 1940. Mrs. Montgomery died October 15, 1957.[86]

Clarence Rarick, who graduated from the Smith Center High School in 1895, was on the faculty of Kansas State College of Hays from 1919-1941. He was born at Glen Elder, Mitchell County, March 1879. The family came to Smith Center while the father, Rev. G. L. Rarick, was minister of the Methodist Church. He was superintendent of schools at Plainville, Rooks County, Stockton, and Osborne from 1904 to 1919. Clarence received his A.B. from Kansas Wesleyan University, 1904, and Ed. D. in 1928. Rarick became Professor of Rural Education and Director of the Extension Service at Fort Hays Kansas State College, Hays, 1919-1934, acting president 1933-1934, and president from 1934 until his death August, 1941.[87]

Frank W. Simmonds was born in a dugout on his father's homestead north of Cedarville, Harvey Township. Here he attended school in a sod schoolhouse with forty or fifty other pupils. During the winter of 1892-93 he worked for his board and attended Smith Center High School where J. N. Mosher, the principal, taught all the high school classes. He secured a county teacher's certificate in the fall of 1893 and taught rural school for three years, then was principal of Cedarville and Gaylord schools for five years. He graduated from the Salina Normal University in 1902 and was superintendent of Mankato schools for eleven years. During this time he served on the Kansas State Board of Education, the county board for teacher's examinations, conducted county teachers' institutes and Summer Chautauquas throughout northwestern

86 Mrs. Hattie Baker Collection, op. cit.
87 Who Was Who in America, Vol. 2, (1945-1950), p. 438; Mrs. Hattie Baker Collection, op. cit.

Kansas, and was president of the Northwest Kansas Teachers' Association. In 1913 he became president of the Lewiston, Idaho, schools where he remained seven years and organized one of the first junior-senior high school systems in the country. During World War I he was a "dollar-a-year" man as U. S. Food Administrator. In 1920 Frank became manager of the New York office of the U. S. Chamber of Commerce. He resigned that position in 1923 to become Deputy Manager of the American Bankers Association in New York and was still in that work in 1932. In 1940 he compiled and published the book, "John and Susan Simmonds and Their Descendants," a story of the geneology of his family and of Smith County.[88]

Basil Cole graduated from the Lebanon High School and taught school for a few years. He then got his college degree at Hays. His wife, Ruth, worked in a beauty shop to assist in the expenses while he studied. He is now Personnel Director of Menninger's Foundation at Topeka and travels for them a great deal.[89]

Carl Cannon, only son of Dr. and Mrs. Willis Cannon, was born in Smith Center and graduated from high school with the class of 1907. His father owned and operated a drug store in the early days and also practiced medicine. Later he purchased an interest in the Smith County State Bank and became vice-president. Carl went East where he was employed in several clerical jobs, first in Pennsylvania and then New York. He became Head Librarian at the City Library of New York City and continued in that position until his health failed about 1955. For his work he received recognition in the Who's Who in America.[90]

---

88 Frank W. Simmonds, op. cit., p. 46-49.
89 Ray Myers, letter to author.
90 Letter interview with Mrs. Hattie Baker.

Another person indirectly in educational work is Dr. Fred H. Hull, a native of Smith County and son of Mr. and Mrs. E. T. Hull of Portis vicinity. He has been on the staff of the Agricultural Experiment Station since 1927 and department head since 1952 at the Florida University. His main work has been in plant breeding. He first succeeded in artificially crossing peanuts and later worked on hybrid corn. The Southern Seedmen's Association named him "man of the year," and he is one of twelve in the United States to be made a fellow of the American Society of Agronomy. He has been a member since 1927, served as secretary, vice-president, and president of the Southern Branch of the Society.[91]

A name familiar to thousands of people who have never heard of Smith County is the Miller Brothers Circus. It is owned and operated by Obert Miller and his sons, Kelly and Dores, all three of whom with their wives are natives of Smith County. Obert started with a small tent show in 1924 and by 1927 was traveling through Kansas and the surrounding states with a "Dog and Pony Show." By 1957 he had organized a regular circus. With him in the business were his two sons, Kelly and Dores, and they continued to expand until in 1957 they had the second largest circus in America and the largest tent show on tour. With the show were 218 animals including a herd of giraffes which otherwise are exhibited in only seven zoological institutions.

Obert Miller was born at Harlan. His father came to the Solomon Valley in 1873 and his mother's family, Buntin, came in 1878. The Millers moved to Smith Center when Obert was four. He grew to manhood there and married Jennie Serena of the Cora vicinity. Kelly's wife was Dale Stevens, a niece of Eva

[91] Smith County Pioneer, February 14, 1957.

Stevens Harlan whose husband was one of the first settlers at Harlan in 1871.
For several years Mr. and Mrs. Walter Stevens traveled with the circus, Walter
as band leader and his wife, Edna, a buyer of supplies. Walter was the son of
Ed Stevens who came to Smith County with his parents in 1872.[92]

Two men by the name of "Wally" made Smith Center known "from Maine to
California" September 22, 1946. One was Wally Boren, the author of the syndicated column, "Wally's Wagon," carried by twenty-five of the largest newspapers in the United States. The other was Waldene (Wally) Ogle, who runs a
popcorn stand called "Wally's Wagon" right out in the paved street on the
busiest corner in Smith Center. Waldene Ogle was born October 3, 1915 in
Smith Center. He weighed but three pounds and contacted spastic paralysis.
He never took a step until six years old; he started to school when eight and
was hauled back and forth in a coaster wagon until in the fifth grade. He
tried a paper route while still in high school (his father died while he was
small; he lived with his mother, Mrs. Lottie Ogle, and sister, Melba) then in
1936 got a popcorn machine. He got a little eight by twelve house on wheels
that could be pulled to the fair grounds or athletic fields for special events;
otherwise it stood on a vacant lot on Main Street between the First National
Bank and Center Cafe. In 1937 Wally graduated from high school; also his lot
was sold. The city mayor, councilmen and townspeople became concerned and decided to locate his wagon on a good foundation right in the street across the
sidewalk from the Pioneer office and across the street from the banks. Homer
Croy, famous author, was in Smith Center checking on "Home on the Range" song
and sent a card to Wally Boren containing the picture, "The Heart of Uncle
Sam", and told him there existed a real "Wally's Wagon." Boren wrote to Ogle,

[92] Mrs. Hattie Baker Collection, op. cit.

and after getting his story, decided to write a column on him and his wagon.
This was published on September 22, 1946. In the meantime his editor suggested that he visit Smith Center for Wally's birthday, October 3, when the
Chamber of Commerce was planning a big party. This he and Mrs. Boren did,
and in later articles he described his visit as "having a funny feeling to
be right in the middle of the country. Whatever way you turn, there is the
same amount of the U. S. in front of you as in the back." He had asked his
readers to send Wally birthday greetings, and over 5,000 arrived. A "thank
you" from Wally Ogle was later published in Boren's column. And so the heart
of the nation has not lost all of its pioneer spirit of friendliness in its
near century of growth.[93]

93 From newspaper clippings of the Smith County Pioneer which contained
reprints of Wally Boren's column from syndicated newspapers and This Week
Magazine, 1946; Mrs. Hattie Baker Collection.

EXPLANATION OF PLATE IV

Fig. 1. Early picture of Smith Center, county seat, Smith County,
         Kansas. (Courtesy of Mrs. Hattie Baker.)

Fig. 2. Main street, Kensington, Kansas, about 1895. (Courtesy
         of Mrs. Lula Crosby.)

Fig. 3. Smith Center's only sod house, 1889. (Courtesy of Mrs.
         Hattie Baker.)

Fig. 4. Building sod post office at Womer, 1892. Men in the
         picture were John Williamson, Ted Williamson, Charles
         Davis, William Sroffer, Mel Womer, Frank Henderson,
         John Williams, Wes Womer, David Watson, Emmet Womer.
         (Courtesy of Emmet Womer.)

Fig. 5. Main street, Lebanon, Kansas, about 1889. (Courtesy of
         L. G. Johnson.)

PLATE IV

Fig. 1

Fig. 2

Fig. 3

Fig. 4

Fig. 5

EXPLANATION OF PLATE V

Fig. 1. Community Hall, Smith Center, built 1922, cost $36,000.
(Courtesy of Mrs. Hattie Baker.)

Fig. 2. Smith Center High School, built 1918. (Courtesy of Mrs.
Hattie Baker.)

Fig. 3. Smith Center Ladies Band, early 1900's.

Fig. 4. Second Smith Center Band, 1880. (Both band pictures
courtesy of Mrs. Hattie Baker.)

Fig. 5. First school building, Smith Center, 1874. (Courtesy
of Mrs. Hattie Baker.)

Fig. 6. G. A. R. Monument at Cedar, Kansas, erected in 1921.
(Courtesy of Mrs. Lula Crosby.)

Fig. 7. Hyde Elevator at Lebanon, Kansas. (Courtesy of W. E.
Lee, Smith County Pioneer.)

PLATE V

Fig. 1

Fig. 2

Fig. 5

Fig. 3

Fig. 6

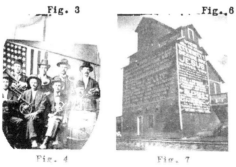

Fig. 4

Fig. 7

EXPLANATION OF PLATE VI

Fig. 1. L. T. Reese, homesteaded near Smith Center, 1872.

Fig. 2. Mrs. L. T. Reese, who came to the county with her parents
in 1877. (Courtesy of Mrs. Hattie Baker.)

Fig. 3. J. R. Durrow, homesteaded adjoining Smith Center, 1873.
Later president of First National Bank of Smith Center
and Central National Bank of Topeka.

Fig. 4. L. C. Uhl, Sr., homesteaded in Center Township, 1872.

Fig. 5. D. H. Crosby, homesteaded adjoining Cedar, 1871. One of
the incorporators of Cedarville.

Fig. 6. Mrs. D. H. Crosby, came to the county with her parents in
1876. (Courtesy of Mrs. Lula Crosby.)

Fig. 7. V. J. Bottomly, homesteaded in Harvey township. One of
incorporators of Cedarville.

Fig. 8. Major J. T. Morrison and wife, pioneers in Cedarville.

Fig. 9. J. H. Johnston, had first store in Cedarville. One of the
incorporators of Cedarville.

Fig.10. George C. McNiece, homesteader in White Rock township and
early newspaper editor.

Fig.11. H. H. Grauerholz and wife, homesteaders in Cedar township
in 1871.

Fig.12. A group of old timers taken in 1903. Identified: E. D. Cooke,
H. R. Stone, D. Weltmer, I. A. Mullen, W. R. Putman, H. H.
Reed, John T. Iden, A. J. Watson, T. C. Wince, W. H.
Thompson, F. M. Carson. (Courtesy of Smith County Pioneer.)

PLATE VI

L. T. Reese
Fig. 1

Mrs. L. T. Reese
Fig. 2

Fig. 3

L. S. LING, Jr.
Fig. 4

Fig. 5

Fig. 6

V. J. BOTTOMLY,
Early settler of Harvey township.
Fig. 7

MAJOR J. T. MORRISON,
deceased, and wife, pioneer of Centerville.
Fig. 8

J. H. JOHNSTON,
Now of Eureka, late of the pioneer
merchants of Centerville.
Fig. 9

GEO. C. MARX,
Pioneer of White Rock township.
Fig. 10

H. H. GRAUBERGER and WIFE,
who landed in Center township in 1871. The wife and mother
of eleven children, passed to her reward, 1908.
Fig. 11

Fig. 12

EXPLANATION OF PLATE VII

Rice Brothers, early Cedar township homesteaders along with their
mother. They arrived in the county in 1873.

Fig. 1.   William Rice.

Fig. 2.   Mad Rice

Fig. 3.   Eliot Rice

Fig. 4.   Harve Rice

Fig. 5.   Scott Rice

Fig. 6,   Mr. and Mrs. Clarence (Cal) Harlan who sang the song,
and 7   "Home on the Range" for the recording used as part proof
         that it was written in Smith County.

Fig. 8.   Mrs. Nettie Smith Chubb, Smith Center artist who has
         illustrated a number of articles and pamphlets on Smith
         County and the song "Home on the Range." (Courtesy of
         Smith County Pioneer.)

Fig. 9.   Bernard Frazier, native of Athol, Smith County, Kansas,
         who made the sculptures of pioneer subjects on the State
         Office Building, Topeka, 1956. (Courtesy of Topeka
         Capital-Journal.)

Fig. 10. Mrs. Hattie Baker, pioneer in the publishing field in
         Smith County.

205

PLATE VII

Fig. 1   Fig. 2   Fig. 3   Fig. 4

Fig. 5   Fig. 6   Fig. 7

Fig. 8

Fig. 9   Fig. 10

CHAPTER VII

HISTORICAL HIGHLIGHTS

In each town, city, or state there are objects or incidents that make such deep impressions in the culture of the people that a knowledge of them is extensively found many decades or even centuries later. Thus the Liberty Bell and the Declaration of Independence have become symbols of freedom, the covered wagon and log cabin have become symbols of the pioneer on the frontier. Six developments of the past have become symbols of pride in Smith County and have welded a people of different social backgrounds into one. Although each individual or his family may not have had personal contact with these "Historical Highlights," they are a part of the history of the county and are a part of each individual's heritage.

It is particularly appropriate that each of these six "Highlights" belonged to different areas in the county: the Geographic Center of the United States located in the east area near Lebanon, the Dutch Mill built in the northern part at Reamsville, the place of the origin of the song "Home on the Range" in the northwest corner, the Naval Band from the extreme western area at Kensington, the Memorial Hospital, while a county project, located in the exact center at Smith Center, and the Smith County Historical Society coordinating the whole with a representative in each township. It is also fitting that the time span should extend from the beginning of the county with the first settlement — through the years of development — to the period nine decades later when the present generation began the attempt to record the history of the past. Ninety years is not a long time in the centuries of civilization, but miraculous changes have been wrought in this thirty mile square labeled "Smith County." A trackless prairie country crossed with some lazily meandering streams and used by the Indians for a hunting ground has been transformed into a rich farming area with comfortable homes, excellent schools and churches, and progressive, industrious people. Ruts of winding trails can occasionally be seen near the oiled highways, but no traces remain of the sod schoolhouses and sod homes that have been replaced by modern buildings. Memories seldom are called to mind of the oxteams and wagons that once traversed these prairies. Electric lights gleam brightly on the most isolated farms; tractors with many horse power skim over the ground where the oxen with the breaking plow once plodded. These and a thousand other marks of progress have spelled the advance of civilization, and Smith County has kept pace with that progress!

Smith County Memorial Hospital

The Smith County Memorial Hospital, located on South Main Street in Smith Center is the proud possession of everyone in the county. The hospital was built mainly by tax funds voted by the people of Smith County in a bond election held April 16, 1946. The contract for the new building was signed February 15, 1950 and it was finished at a total cost of $351,328.53 with $200,000 from tax levy, $140,000 from federal aid, and $11,328 from gifts of individuals and organizations. The building is 228 feet long and an 84 foot east wing. It is a twenty-six bed hospital, completely modern with radiant heating, air conditioning, oxygen piped to each room, and all other conveniences for patients, nurses, and doctors. A county Hospital Association was organized and the men appointed to serve as members of the first hospital board were: Glenn M. Stoops, Smith Center, chairman; Rev. A. Eggerling, Kensington, pastor of St. John's Lutheran Church, secretary; James Roush, Lebanon, treasurer; Harry Lloyd, Gaylord, and Fred Simmons, Smith Center.

The Memorial Hospital was dedicated on Sunday afternoon, June 3, 1951. It was named as a memorial to the Smith County Veterans of World War II who made the supreme sacrifice and their names (see Appendix) were inscribed on a plaque at the north end of the building. Hundreds of people from this and surrounding counties stood in respectful silence while members of the American Legion Posts and Veterans of Foreign Wars in the county dedicated the plaque. The high school band provided music, and Dr. J. L. Lattimore, Topeka, President of the Kansas Blue Cross, gave the address. Dr. B. Hardman, President of the Smith County Medical Association, John Shaver, architect, and others also spoke. The hospital contract for operation was given to the Great Plains Lutheran Hospital Association. Medical doctors at the time of dedication were Hector Morrison, F. H. Relihan, Victor Watts, Lafe Bauer, Robert Sheppard, D. A. Hardman, I. E. Nickell, and R. C. Windscheffel, dentist, and J. J. Patzel, optometrist. The death of Dr. Morrison June 6, three days after he had attended the dedication ceremonies, brought sadness to the county. He had been a physician in the county for fifty years, first practicing at Womer.[1]

Geographical Center of the United States

Smith County had a unique claim to fame as the official geographical center of the United States -- the real "Heart of the U.S.A." Soon after the site was developed with a motel, park, monument and oiled road, two new states, Hawaii and Alaska were added to the Union. However, it is still the geographical

---

[1] Mrs. Hattie Baker Collection; Kansas City *Times*, June 4, 1951.

center of the forty-eight states, or of the contiguous states. Many people
apparently wanted the thrill of being able to stand and look in any direction
and know there was just as much of the United States "in front of you as in
back," as Wally Boren, eastern columnist, once wrote. In 1959, 29,000 visitors
came to the "center", including visitors from 24 foreign countries.[2] The news
that it was the geographical center was first announced under a 1913 dateline
from Washington, D. C.: "A point ten miles north of Smith Center, Kansas is
the geographical center of the United States. This fact has been established
by experts of the geological survey."[3] The official location was given as
latitude 39 degrees, longitude 98 degrees, 35 minutes west. A number of other
spots had vigorously claimed the honor through the years, including Ft. Riley.
The geographical center in 1922 belonged to A. C. Roberts who had farmed the
site for a generation and his father before him had also farmed it. The exact
site was about eighty rods north of the Rock Island Railroad tracks.[4] People
often confuse it with the geodetic center of North America, located on Meade's
ranch eighteen miles southeast of Osborne or about sixty miles south of the
geographical center. It was located in 1901 by the U. S. Coast and Geodetic
Survey and is important to map makers and surveyors for surveys of one sixth
of the world's surface. One of the shortest highways in Kansas, one mile long,
runs from US 281 west to the monument, located one mile north and one mile west
of Lebanon.[5] Most of the development as a tourist attraction has been as the

[2] Smith County Pioneer, December 24, 1959.
[3] Kansas City Star, May 11, 1913.
[4] Council Grove Guard, September 22, 1922.
[5] Topeka Daily Capital, April 21, 1955; J. Nelson Chandler wrote a story
called "Three 'Strikes' in Kansas" in which he featured the Dutch Mill,
Higley's Cabin, and the Geographic Center at Lebanon. It was illustrated
with sketches by Nettie Smith Chubb, Smith County artist, and published in
the May 1955 issue of Ford Times.

result of the Hub Club of Lebanon.

Smith County Historical Society

Smith County citizens organized their Historical Society November 22, 1958, and the membership grew to more than 400. The first officers were Emmet Womer, president; W. E. Lee, vice-president; Mrs. Margaret Nelson, secretary; Mrs. Claude Diehl, treasurer; and directors Ray Myers and Lou Felton, Lebanon; I. A. Nichols, Harlan; Walter Hofer, Cedar; and Oscar Rice, Kensington. Annual memberships were set at one dollar with anyone 79 years or older given an honorary life membership. The main purpose of the organization was to write the history of Smith County, and at the first annual meeting, January 23, 1960, a report was given that the project was well under way with over 600 pages written. Lincoln Township was the banner township with ninety-nine per cent membership. All of the officers were re-elected for another year and it was voted to have the meetings near to Memorial Day so many from a distance would be in the county and could attend. Talks on aspects of the history of Smith County and the value of the historical society were given by Ray Myers, veteran reporter and writer from Lebanon; Mrs. Vera (Crosby) Fletcher, Kansas State University, Department of History; and A. L. (Bert) Headley, retired newspaper editor on the Smith County Pioneer for over forty years. It was reported in March, 1960, that twenty per cent of the honorary members of the Historical Society had died during 1959.[6] This means there are one-fifth loss of the older people available to pass on the history directly because an honorary member in 1959 had to be at least seven years old

_____

[6] Topeka Daily Capital, March 27, 1960.

at the time Smith County was organized. This fact well illustrates the most often expressed thought about the organization of the Historical Society. Elmer Stump, member from Lebanon, wrote in his manuscript for the Society, "The only objectionable feature is — if only it would have been started thirty or more years ago." A letter to the Pioneer from George Morgan, a seventy-five year old resident, now of Manhattan, expressed the same thought.

> It is of no little interest that I read in last week's issue of your old home paper of the plans of some of our civic minded people to write up some Smith County history. If I were asked, I would very promptly answer that this little matter is away past due and that there are many items of real interest to practically everyone of us that have already escaped and will escape forever our records, and consequently most of us will never know about them.[7]

The Kensington Band

The Kensington Band was "headline news" in 1918-1919, both in Kansas and in Smith County. This once famous band should not become a forgotten fact in the realms of time, and a written record of its accomplishments is of utmost importance to the historical record of Smith County.

Official interest in the organization of military bands originated in an order by General John Pershing in May 1918, to Walter Damrosch to organize and train bands "as a part of military efficiency." General Pershing said, "I would like our army band to play so well that people will say when we march up Fifth Avenue after peace has come, 'Here is another proof of the justice of military

[7] George (Brad) Morgan, Personal letter to Smith County Pioneer and sent to the author by Emmet Womer, President of the Historical Society. George Morgan also stated his father, Frank L. Morgan, was among the early settlers of Smith County and hauled lumber from Hastings, Nebraska to Smith Center. After the railroad went through the south side of the county, he hauled from Gaylord. He homesteaded on the half section of land about two miles southwest of Smith Center and it was there George was born. Other information, Smith County Pioneer, February 4, 1960, January 21, 1960.

training.'" This led to the withdrawal of bandsmen from the ranks of stretcher
bearers where they had been serving, a decided campaign for the enlistment of
bandsmen and to a definite training program being organized in each branch of
the service for military bands.[8]

Clarence W. Osborn came to Kensington from Pennsylvania about 1915 to
be musical instructor in the Kensington High School. It soon became apparent
that he was an outstanding musician. He began to take an active part in local
activities outside of the school, becoming band leader for the local Commercial
Club. Perhaps part of this interest was due to the fact that he had met and
married a local girl, Miss Goldie Martin.[9] The Commercial Band showed such
exceptional results that Osborn was appointed director of the Twelfth Bat-
talion State Guards Band made up of musicians from Kensington, Gaylord, Athol,
and Cedar.

In June 1918, several members of the Kensington Band along with other
musicians from Smith Center and Lebanon decided to go to Kansas City and
enlist as a unit.[10] Ordinarily this would not have been news except for
notices of enlistments in the local paper, but an enlistment mistake put
them on the front pages of the Kansas City papers. They enlisted in both
the navy and marines!

> The 35 piece Kensington, Kansas band lost after application
> at the navy station in Kansas City and frantically searched for
> all Saturday afternoon turned up yesterday at the office of the
> marine corps and enlisted as a unit. A mistake on the part of
> the band leader in confusing the marines with the navy led to
> the applications being made at the wrong station. On discovering

8 "New Status of Military Bands," Literary Digest, Sept. 28, 1918,
p. 30-31.

9 H. V. Dilsaver, Kensington, Kansas, in letter to author.

10 C. W. Osborn, Band Director, Kensington, Kansas, in a letter to the
author, April, 1960.

the mistake the leader applied to Lieut. H. G. Hornsbostel of the marine corps. Lieut. Hornsbostel wired to Washington for permission to enlist the band. As the application was granted, the men will become the official band of the Fourteenth Regiment and will receive their training at Paris Island Marine Camp. In accordance with word from Washington, Dr. Harry Prentiss, examining officer for the marines, will go to Kensington to examine the men in the band.[11]

But the band was not in the marine service to stay. Four days later the Kansas City papers' patrons were again trying to find Kensington on the maps. "Who's Band Is This Now?" was the headline on July 13.

To be marines or not to be. The navy recruiting station says not, in speaking yesterday afternoon of the Kensington, Kansas band which has been the cause of much local notice because of its inability, up to date, to decide whether to join the navy or the marines. First the band voted in favor of the navy, but last Saturday when an inspector came to look the band boys over, the unit had temporarily disappeared. On Monday they were identified at the marine recruiting station, where they had just received permission from Washington to join the marine corps as a unit. Then the band went home.

The marine corps sent two doctors out to Kensington to inspect the members of the band and immediately began to round up some thirty more musicians to send along with the Kensington unit to make a full regimental band of fifty pieces. Meanwhile two navy inspectors tried a little follow-up game, supposedly to get the facts in the mix-up straightened out. Yesterday the following telegram came to the Navy recruiting office in Kansas City: "Prospects look bright for navy getting the band."

The navy has a hunch it will sign the boys up before tonight as prospective members of the 1,700 man band at the Great Lakes training station, particularly since the band's strong point, so far discovered, is an ability to change its mind quickly.[12]

Apparently the men sent out by the navy intended to do more than a mere "follow-up" as the Kansas City paper intimated. The local papers reported that "a musician representing the John Philip Sousa band of the Great Lakes Naval Training Station," a physician, and Prof. C. W. Osborn were in the various towns on July 11 checking on band members.[13] It would seem that in 1918 the

---

11 Kansas City Journal, July 9, 1918.
12 Ibid.
13 Kensington Mirror, July 11, 1918; Smith County Pioneer, July 11, 1918.

navy "landed" before the marines in this instance. The Kansas City Star had

the headline on July 13 that the "Navy gets the 'Lost Band'."

> The Kensington, Kansas band — the "lost band" which has
> been the subject of attack and counter-attack between the navy
> and marine corps recruiting stations in their efforts to obtain
> the band — has landed finally in the navy. Thirty members,
> the entire strength, were enlisted today and granted two-weeks
> furlough after which they will go to the Great Lakes Naval
> Training Station. In celebration of the enlistment the band
> paraded the downtown streets /of Kansas City/ today with a large
> banner inscribed, "Kensington Band, on the Way to the Navy." The
> band serenaded the Star.[14]

The Navy also sent a Navy bandsman, a Mr. Brown, to Kensington for ten

days and he and Osborn spent that time enlisting fifty more men from Kansas and

Missouri. "On July 2, 1918, these musicians assembled in Kansas City, and

were sent to the Great Lakes Naval Training Center, Illinois.[15] The band's

arrival was noted at Great Lakes. "A complete band of sixty-one pieces all

organized under Drill Master Osborn arrived at Great Lakes Tuesday from Kansas

and paraded the main drill field.... The aggregation which is called the

Kensington Band has been organized for some time and decided to join the navy

in a body.[16] Nothing much was written concerning the band for the next five

months. Some of the men came home on leave occasionally, including Clarence

Osborn, which was noted in the county papers. It was probable the thirty mem-

bers of the band from Smith County were "lost" again among the 1,700 bandsmen

at the Naval Training Station but such was not the case. Clarence Osborn men-

tions that the band was kept together as a unit and was known as the Kensing-

ton Band. He was also kept in the position of leader. Mr. Osborn modestly de-

scribed the honor paid to the band when he said, "We were at Great Lakes five

14 Kansas City Star, July 13, 1918.
15 C. W. Osborn, op. cit.
16 Great Lakes Bulletin, July 31, 1918.

months when the Band was chosen as the Band to go on the U.S.S. George Washington with President Wilson to France. He made both trips with President Wilson. I was the director of this band."[17] The Kansas City and Topeka papers greeted the announcement with headlines. The Kansas City Times reported:

> A Kansas Band for Wilson. The Kensington Musicians Selected to Make the Trip Overseas. The Kensington, Kansas Band of twenty-two pieces which was lost by the marines and found by the navy in a heated recruiting duel last July in Kansas City, was today paid the first compliment yet bestowed upon a navy band from the Great Lakes Naval Training Station.

> Headed by Bandmaster C. W. Osborn of Kensington, the band "shoved off" this morning for New York to board the U. S. S. George Washington. It will be the honor band which will accompany President Wilson to Europe next week. The Band came to Great Lakes composed of "rookie musicians." Today they were chosen from among twenty-three other bands as the best product of finished musicians ever introduced at the station by Captain William A. Moffett, commandant. Before departing, Capt. Moffett told the musicians from Kensington that he expected them to "live up to the excellent reputation they had made while in training," and that each man was individually responsible for the great honor that had been bestowed upon them.[18]

Nowhere was there a complete list of the names of the personnel of the band. However, it has been possible to trace some of them. Russell Frazier of Athol was a member of the original band. Mr. Osborn mentions there were five members from Kensington, including Ed Rutter, Ernst Wilson, Raymond Hayes, Edwin Hilbrink and himself. From Smith Center were Alvin Luse, Jerry (Dooley) Underwood, Russell Clark, and Jack Werts. There were two members from Lebanon — John Amos and Larry Cherry. Cherry, a barber and member of the local band, died of Spanish influenza in the service and may not have made the trip. George C. Houdek of Cuba was another member. The bass horn player at Kensington, Ed Rutter, a son of a Civil War Veteran, was over age for

[17] C. W. Osborn, op. cit.
[18] Kansas City Times, Nov. 30, 1918.

enlistment but Osborn took him along anyway and he was accepted.

The U. S. S. George Washington was the second largest ship afloat at the time it was used for President Wilson's trip to France. It was a former German liner and had been taken over by the United States as a troop carrier. It could carry 7,000 troops a trip, was 722 feet long, weighed 37,000 tons, was ten decks high, and carried a crew of 1,300 men. A picture of the band of twenty-one pieces taken on board ship had names and instruments played.[19] Clarinets were Kendig, Solo; Whitecamp, first; Hunter, director; Aurdder, third; Theis, third; Foster, picolo. Cornets were St. Peter, Solo; Underwood, first; Anderson, third; Hobbs, Houdek, and Anderson, alto. Trombone was played by Buzzard and Clark, tuba by Walker and Rutter, drums by Wilson and Hilbrink.

After the war, Clarence Osborn re-assembled the members of the band and toured the country playing concerts and State Fairs. They were known as "President Wilson's Official Peace Band from Kensington, Kansas." The Osborns went to Pennsylvania to live, but returned to Kensington in the nineteen fifties to make their home. There are only two other living members of the eleven bandsmen that Mr. Osborn could trace, Russell Clark and Jack Werts.

The Old Dutch Mill

In the spring of 1873 a young man named Charles G. Schwarz from Grauenhagen, Michelenburg, Germany came to the United States, then in 1876 had enough money to return for his family, Mrs. Schwarz and their son, Conrad. Charles was trained as a flour miller, and expected to have a job waiting in Ashland, Nebraska, but the mill was closed down. The family decided they wanted a homestead

---

[19] Mrs. Edwin Hilbrink now lives at Phillipsburg, Kansas. She furnished the pictures of the band (see pictures, page 234) taken on board the ship.

and came to the Reamsville vicinity in Smith County in 1877 and built a sod house twelve by sixteen feet. He began planning the mill about 1878 and began cutting a pair of burrs out of native stone from across the line in Franklin County, Nebraska. Most of the timber was cut during the winter of 1881-1882 by Charles and his brother and hewn by hand for the upright posts. The timbers were hauled to a location about a mile north of the present site of Reamsville. "Sod Town", as it was then called, consisted of a frame store, and three residences, a blacksmith shop, and schoolhouse, all of sod. A scarcity of water in Sod Town led to the decision to move to the present site of Reamsville and farmers for miles around donated their help in hauling the timbers to the site. The town soon followed and the name changed in 1882 to Reamsville.

Charles and his brother Alfred made spikes $3\frac{1}{2}$ inches to 8 inches long and bolts up to 24 inches long in Alfred's blacksmith shop, mostly from worn out wagon wheel tires, to fasten the mill together. In 1881, Mrs. Schwarz's brother and family, William Markman, came from Germany. He was a miller and millwright and his aid was valuable in helping finish the mill. On May 1, 1882, Schwarz got his final citizenship papers, made final proof on his homestead, and immediately put a loan on it to build the mill. Alfred did the same.

The raising of the mill frame was a major undertaking. The eight posts were 12 inches by 12 inches and about forty feet long. The mill was octagon in shape, forty feet in diameter at the bottom, tapering to eighteen feet at the top. The height to the turntable was forty-two feet and to the top of the roof was fifty-four feet from the foundation stone. For harnessing the wind a huge fan was built with a spread of sixty feet. A sail cloth could be spread or taken up as the wind velocity got higher or lower. The tailwheel was ten feet in diameter. The building was five stories high and shingled from top to bottom. Mrs. Alda Bennett, a daughter of Charles Schwarz, describes the interior thus:

> On the first floor was father's office and work room and some of the machinery used in operating the burrs; on the second floor were the burrs and other machinery; third and fourth floors were mostly grain bins and the top or fifth floor was more machinery. This is where was found the large wheel with wooden cogs, all made by my father. When the mill was first built, grain was elevated from the first floor by hand.
>
> In the spring of '83 the mill was started. It had been predicted that the project would be a failure, that sufficient power and speed could not be secured to pull those burrs and grind corn meal but when the mill was finally ready and did start to grind meal and feed successfully, it was the wonder of the country and grain came from considerable distances. Corn meal and graham flour was ground on shares, and the corn meal was said to be of such excellent quality that it was sold in all adjoining towns in Kansas, also in Riverton and Franklin, Nebraska, and was shipped to other states.[20]

A July 26, 1885 item in the Reamsville Dispatch stated that Alfred traded his interest in the Star Mill to Jack Thornton for 200 acres of land in Illinois. A later item says the grist mill, Holland type, has just been finished at the cost of $3,500. Then in the fall of 1885 Thornton sold out to Charles. The sail cloth had not been taken in, January 12, 1887 when a blizzard and wind struck suddenly. The main shaft, a white elm log squared to twenty-four inches, broke where it was rounded for the bearing and all four fans came down. During the summer of 1887 Schwartz rebuilt this from pine timber ordered special and hauled from the railroad at Gaylord, twenty-five miles away. Conrad Schwarz, son of Charles, reported that the homestead and mill were then traded to a man named Josiah Platt in 1888 for the Eagle Mill near Riverton, Nebraska, and the family moved there.[21] It took about a year

---

20 Mrs. Alda Bennett, Franklin, Nebr. Sentinel, September 1, 1932.

21 Interviewed by author in Topeka, Kansas, February, 1960.

to build a dam and rebuild the mill at Riverton. Then December, 1890, the
Riverton mill was burned, apparently to cover a theft of flour. The insurance
was contested in court for three years. This left the family practically des-
titute and Charles and Conrad cut and sold firewood that winter to pay for
groceries and flour. Schwarz made a trip back to Reamsville and was so dis-
gusted with the way Platt had let the old mill deteriorate that he went back
and traded a team of horses and something else (Conrad could not remember
what) for the old mill, repaired it and ran it again. In 1913 he quit running
the mill by wind and installed a kerosene engine. It was closed in 1920 because of Mr. Schwarz's failing health. Mr. and Mrs. Schwarz moved to Topeka
to live with their son, Conrad.[22] Mr. Schwarz, who was born December 1840,
died November 1929, at the age of almost 89 years. Mrs. Schwarz lived until
March 1936, age 89. They had five children, Henry, Conrad, and Herman,
Matilda (Tillie), Mrs. Alda Bennett, and Emma, Mrs. H. C. Hohner.

In 1937 the surviving relatives of the Schwarz family offered the mill
to anyone who would restore and preserve it as there were only five such mills
ever built on the Kansas plains. The city of Smith Center took the offer and
in January, 1938, it was moved to a small park in Smith Center by Les Neal
and Bernard Glenn, then repaired, refinished and the fans rebuilt. All the
expenses of lumber, and material were paid for by the city and much of the
labor was done by the NYA boys under the supervision of Logan Leonard. Then
March 16, 1955 the old mill caught fire in some way and the "smoke rising
high brought consternation to everyone." The siding was destroyed and the upright timbers badly charred. The Topeka Capital reported that "only a

---

22 Conrad Schwarz had started working out after the fire, then attended
Topeka Business College after a summer in the harvest fields. He became
founder and president of the Schwarz Basket and Box Company in Topeka.

skeleton remains and it is beyond repair. The only similar one left now
is at Wamego." But they did not know the determination of Smith County residents. It was estimated that restoration would cost between two and three
thousand dollars, depending on volunteer labor. Donations were soon coming
in. Two of the grandchildren of Charles Schwarz, Arnold Hohner and Elmo
Bennett, electricians by trade, donated the wiring and labor as part of the
repair. By June 1, 1955, the Old Dutch Mill had been restored and was open
to the public again.[23]

"Home on the Range"

In 1872 on the bank of Beaver Creek in Smith County a crude one-roomed
cabin of logs and limestone was erected by Dr. Brewster Higley. It must have
been built better than average because it stood the test of time. It was not
until 1941 that anyone took any note of the cabin used by the tenants on the
farm for a chicken house, but twenty years later, it is not unusual to pick
up a magazine or paper and find a picture of it on the cover, and it is
recognized without a caption all over the United States. The story of this
cabin and its inhabitants reads like a work of fiction but the best part was
that some of the participants were still living when the concluding chapter
was written.

---

23 J. Nelson Chandler's story, "Three 'Strikes' in Kansas", featured
the Mill along with the geographic center and Higley's cabin in the May 1955
issue of Ford Times. Other sources were Mrs. Alda J. Bennett, "Wind Driven
Grist Mill Built a Half Century Ago Still Stands," which is an article written
by the daughter of the builder for the Sentinel, Franklin, Nebraska, Sept. 1,
1932; seven-page manuscript in the Mrs. Hattie Baker Collection; Topeka Daily
Capital, March 28, 1955, April 21, 1955, March 20, 1955; Smith County Pioneer,
September 23, 1954; interview by the author with C. H. A. Schwarz, a son, now
86 years old and living at 719 Taylor Street, Topeka, February 18, 1960.

Brewster Higley was born in Meigs County, Ohio in November, 1823. While
staying with an old doctor and attending Rutland, he developed an interest in
medicine. He attended the University of Columbus and State Medical College
of Indiana, graduating in 1848. He was Demonstrator of Anatomy in the State
Medical School for two terms, and one year at Ann Arbor, Michigan. He then
moved his family to La Porte, Indiana and began private practice in that area
in partnership with his uncle, a Dr. Everts. He practiced there for about
twenty-six years. October 1849, he married Maria Winchell, who bore one son,
September 1851. He died within a few days. Mrs. Higley died in 1852. In
August 1853, Higley married Eleanor Page. They were parents of one son,
Brewster Higley VII.[24] His second wife died in late 1854 or early 1855, and
in 1858 he married Catherine Livingston, and to this marriage was born Estelle
"Stella" in 1859 and Arthur Herman in 1861, the two children he sent for when
in Smith County. His wife was injured and died June 3, 1864. In February
1866, Dr. Higley married Mercy Ann McPherson, a widow. The family lived at
Union Mills and Indian Point, both small towns near La Porte. When the doctor acquired the addiction to drink that is thought to have been a contrib-
uting factor to his coming to Kansas is not known. That the losses of his
wives and the problem of small motherless children could have been some in-
stigation is realized. Witnesses also have stated that he and his fourth
wife were very incompatible, and at Indian Point he pawned even his medical
instruments to buy drink. He finally sent his children to relatives in
Illinois and left for an unannounced destination, apparently Kansas. Nine
years after their marriage, Mrs. Mercy Higley got a divorce by default, effective February 1875. That he drank to excess at times, becoming moody and

24 Brewster Higley VII was living at Shawnee, Oklahoma, at the age of
93 years, in 1947.

melancholy, when he first came to Kansas is a matter of record. Otherwise, he was "quiet and retiring." It is thought he came to the frontier and a solitary life to fight this habit and apparently succeeded because he afterwards married for the fifth time and lived normally with a family. In Smith County he soon became known for his fine medical ability and he rode far and wide over the prairies practicing his profession. Several of his patients were alive to attest to his ability when his name was saved from oblivion. He was the doctor present when Mrs. Margaret Nelson, who wrote the book, Home on the Range, was born.[25]

Higley was also known for his musical ability and among Reamsville items is one telling that "Brewster Higley and Daniels furnished the music for a dance at the home of Mr. Whittier."[26] He had also written other poetry before the composition that eventually made him famous. For example, "A poem still exists in manuscript, inscribed to 'Dryden, Eng. Poet,' nine pages long and penned in old-fashioned heavily-shaded script. He wrote at least three other songs, one of which became popular at the close of the Civil War."[27] An old scrapbook now in possession of Harry Higley has "mostly in his [Dr. Higley's] methodical hand, twenty-five excellent poems which he wrote at various times," some penned on foolscap like the doctor used for his famous poem and perhaps written about the same time. There are several published poems

---

[25] Several others whose doctor at birth was Dr. Higley were at the dedication of the cabin in 1954; namely, Mrs. Joe Schenk, Franklin, Nebr.; J. C. Walter, Mrs. Bert Junzi, and O. E. Rice, Kensington; Mrs. Roy Wolfe and Mrs. Amos Ormsbee, Smith Center; M. U. John, Athol; Mrs. Arthur Cowan, Topeka; Elsa Walker, Trenton, Missouri; and Harvey Brewster Stoner, Kirwin. (Smith County Pioneer, July 9, 1954.)

[26] Reamsville Dispatch, November 7, 1889.

[27] Kirke Mechem, "Home on the Range," Kansas Historical Quarterly, Vol. 17, 1949, p. 20.

clipped to the pages, and several more marked "published" in the margin.
Missing are "The Katydid's Secret" and "Army Blue," which was made into a
popular song just after the Civil War.[28]

He married Sarah Clemens at Smith Center, March 8, 1875. To this marriage was born four children, Sanford who died in 1878; Achsah, born 1877;
Everett, born 1880; and Theo, born 1882. He also sent for his two children
by his third wife, Stella and Arthur Herman, who were fourteen and sixteen
at the time. His daughter, Estelle or "Stella" as Higley called her, taught
school in a sod schoolhouse on the John Dyer homestead on West Beaver for two
winters. Higley was elected the first register of deeds in Smith County, and
later served one term as clerk of court. It was apparently at this time that
he moved to a house just north of Smith Center.

Before this last marriage and while he lived alone on the Beaver in a
log cabin,[29] Trube Reese took a man with a gunshot wound to the Higley residence for treatment. After a dinner prepared by Higley, Reese pulled one of
his books off the shelf and the foolscap papers with the words to "My Western
Home" fell out. Reese, upon reading them, suggested getting Dan Kelley to set
them to music. The next time Dr. Higley went to Gaylord, he took them along
and showed them to Kelley, and the tune was composed for "Oh, Give Me a Home
Where the Buffalo Roam."[30] It was first played by the Harlan orchestra, which

28 J. W. Williams, op. cit., p. 48.
29 It is believed in Smith County that Higley lived in the log cabin,
which was built with a log-raising and celebration, July 4, 1872, when he
wrote "Home on the Range" but which Kirke Mechem, Kansas State Historical
Society, maintains was written in a dugout.

30 The song was first published in the Smith County Pioneer in 1873,
under the title "Western Home" which is no longer extant. The Kirwin Chief
publication of February 26, 1876, was a reprint from their issue of March 21,
1874, a copy of which is also missing from the files, so the 1876 version is
the earliest one in print.

consisted of Gene Harlan and Dan Kelley playing violins and Cal Harlan a guitar, at a party and dance at the residence of Judge John Harlan. It met instant acclaim and became one of their most popular numbers. This orchestra played in several counties and as far away as Hays City, one hundred miles southwest.

Daniel Kelley was born February 6, 1843, at North Kingston, R. I. He was a bugler in the army and was mustered out as a sergeant major. He came to Gaylord, Kansas in 1872, and two years later married Lulu Harlan, by whom he had four children, all boys. He gave his occupation as carpenter, but seemed more in demand as a musician. However, items in local papers record that he received contracts for building a hotel and another time for four buildings. Mention was made of his fine Solomon Valley farm, and livery stable in Gaylord. He moved to Waterloo, Iowa in 1889, and died there October 23, 1905, at the age of 62.[31]

Although a favorite ballad locally and sung at schools and programs, "Home on the Range" was not officially noticed in Smith County until forty-one years later a reprint was made in the Smith County Pioneer. One writer records that nothing in the history of the song is so remarkable as the way it spread over the entire frontier.[32] An article in the Cattleman, suggests this was because the Kansas buffalo range was becoming seriously depleted and the big hunt moved down into Texas. As "both buffalo and hunters migrated with the changing seasons, the new melody covered some 50,000,000 acres of the un-tamed West and...became a song hit 1,500 miles west of Broadway!"[33] The song

---

[31] Kirke Mechem, op. cit., pp. 23-24. Dan Kelley was an uncle by marriage of Mrs. Lottie Harlan Wagner and Mrs. Grace Harlan Homer of Smith Center, both daughters of Cal Harlan, member of the Harlan orchestra that first played the song.

[32] Ibid., p. 20.

[33] J. W. Williams, "Home on the Range," The Cattleman, Aug. 1947, p. 21.

continued spreading over the cattle trails from 1877 to 1890. Finally John Lomax, who was collecting western ballads for his book Songs of the Cattle Trail and Cow Camp, published in 1910, interviewed in 1908 an old Negro cook at San Antonio who had gone on the trail drives to Kansas and recorded his version of "Home on the Range." Strange to report, the words, outside of a few geographical terms common to Smith County, were remarkably similar to the Higley original of thirty-five years previous. No particular attention was given to Lomax's publication, especially in Smith County. Then in 1932 reporters sang the song while waiting to see President-elect Franklin D. Roosevelt and he remarked that it was his favorite. It became a hit, it was rated as tops on the radio for six months, it was recorded, it was used in motion pictures — all without royalties because there was no copyright and the author was unknown. Admiral Byrd reported that he sang it at the South Pole after his phonograph froze up so he could not play it.[34]

Then came front page news! William and Mary Goodwin filed suit in the courts of New York for one-half million dollars damages against thirty-five individuals and corporations, including the National Broadcasting Company, for infringement of copyright. Their home was Tempe, Arizona, and they claimed they had written the song as "My Arizona Home" and copyrighted it February 27, 1905. Music Publishers Protective Association hired Samuel Moanfeldt, a New York lawyer, to discover if possible the origin of the song. His search took him all over the western states, and convinced him the song had originated in the cow country long before the Goodwins claimed to have written it, but he needed evidence he could take into court. He finally came to Dodge City, where he got affidavits from Putt Hill and Heinie Schmidt,

---

34 Kirke Mechem, op. cit., pp. 11-12.

oldtime stage drivers, that they had heard the song before 1880. Newspapers
carried stories of Moanfeldt's search, and one was read by Miss Florence
Pulver, Osborne, Kansas, who wrote a letter asking that proper credit be given
Dr. Higley as author. Mr. Moanfeldt came to Osborne where he also met Mrs.
George Parke, wife of a pioneer storekeeper and banker of Gaylord, who had
known Dr. Higley well as he attended her when her daughter was born. Moanfeldt
also had obtained an article which appeared in the Kansas City Star, March 25,
1935, written by Mrs. Myrtle Hose of Osborne, that she had an article from the
Pioneer in a scrapbook with a reprint of the words as first printed in 1873.
His search in this area led him to Trube Reese who had first read the poem,
and to the Cal Harlans who had first sung the words to the tune written by
their brother-in-law. Mr. Harlan, then 87 years old, and Mrs. Harlan made a
wax recording for Moanfeldt, singing the words in the old Smith County version.
Mrs. W. H. Nelson, whose husband was editor of the Pioneer for many years, told
of coming to the county as a bride in 1875, of knowing Higley well, and that
her husband sang the song in Pennsylvania in 1875 when he came there to marry
her, telling that it had been written by a friend of his by the name of Higley.
With affidavits and photostats obtained in Smith County Moanfeldt easily won
his case. To further substantiate the case, ten years later a copy of the
Kirwin Chief, February 26, 1876, that had a reprint of the poem under the
title, "Western Home," was found in the archives of the State Historical Society, Topeka. More important for Smith County, though, Higley and a homestead
in Section 17, Pleasant Township, fourteen miles northwest of Smith Center,
suddenly became historically important twenty-five years after the author's
death.

Dr. Higley had moved his family to Van Buren, Arkansas in 1886 where he could hunt and fish. In 1891, the Oklahoma Strip was opened and the next year the Higleys moved twenty-five miles southeast of Oklahoma City and then moved for the last time in 1893 to the new town of Shawnee. During the last "eighteen years of his life, he saw the town grow up around him large enough to bid against Oklahoma City as a possible capital when Oklahoma became a state."[35] He died May 10, 1911 and was buried at Shawnee, Oklahoma, a year after his song was published by Lomax but as far as is known he never saw a copy.

In 1940 Mrs. Cora Skinner Ream, former Gaylord pioneer, wrote a featured article for the Kansas City *Star* about the Estey organ with which her father had surprised his family in 1876. He had hunted buffalo, taken the skins to Waterville, Kansas by wagon and sold them to pay for the organ which he had ordered from Brattleboro, Vermont. It was the first instrument of its kind in the county, and, as it was only about four feet long, it was often loaded into the wagon and taken to parties or the schoolhouse for social gatherings. One of the favorite songs was "Home on the Range," since the Dan Kelley family was a neighbor of the Skinners.[36]

Smith County celebrated "Homecoming on the Range" in connection with their Old Settlers Meeting, September 18, 1941. They held a historical pageant commemorating the writing of "Home on the Range" under the direction of Mrs. Renna Hunter, member of the staff of the Kansas Industrial Development Commission. They also gave prizes for the best rendition of the song. It was

[35] J. W. Williams, op. cit., p. 46.

[36] Mrs. Cora Skinner Ream, Kansas City *Star*, July 14, 1940. The Estey organ has since been donated to the Kansas Historical Society.

considered an outstanding success.[37]

Following the establishment of the fact that "Home on the Range" was written in Smith County, Dr. I. E. Hickell, State Representative from Smith Center, introduced a bill into the House of Representatives to make it the official state song. The bill was introduced in the State Senate by Hal Harlan, Manhattan, son of Gene Harlan who was a member of the Harlan Orchestra. It was officially adopted June 30, 1947 as the state song of Kansas, using the original Higley words.

The Smith Center Rotary Club, on the recommendation of Melvin Collier, decided to restore the old cabin on its original site. The owners, Mr. and Mrs. Pete Rust, who had lived on the place since 1935, agreed. Emmet Homer offered to furnish the logs from an old building erected by his father in the 70's. Floyd Gray, Lebanon, assisted in laying them. The State Highway Commission helped with road signs and the county highway department worked on the road, so it really turned into a county project. The renovation was completed in 1954 and a marble plaque was put on the east end of the cabin. A dedication program was held Sunday, July 25, 1954, with approximately 1,500 people in attendance. The principal address was given by Governor Edward Arn. Among guests in attendance were two grandsons of Dr. Higley; several of the people termed "his babies"; Mrs. Cordilla Bates, 101 year old lady from Franklin, Nebraska who was attended at the birth of her daughter by Dr. Higley; Don Richards, Kansas Industrial Development Commission, who was to write a story for the forthcoming issue of To the Stars, (Sept.-Oct. 1954); and Kirke Mechem, Lindsborg, former secretary of the Kansas State Historical Society who

[37] Smith County Review, September 11, 1941; September 18, 1941.

did considerable research on the origin of the song.[38]

Thus, as the history of the county developed from broad prairies unknown except to the Indians, in a similar manner the Kansas state song came
from the banks of a little creek that wended its way across these same prairies.
As the county came out of obscurity to take its place in a prosperous state,
so the cabin and the author was saved from oblivion in the realm of time.
Thus it seems fitting to end this ninety year history with an original word-
ing of the song that Mechem describes as "a perfect blending of man's nos-
talgia for home with his dreams of some far-away and fairer land. This
ambivalent masterpiece has turned out to be the ideal expression of the
love which Kansans feel for their unpredictable state."[39]

---

[38] A number of relatives of Dr. Higley have visited Smith Center or
made themselves known there since the authorship of the song has been established. His youngest daughter Theo, Mrs. Ed Brumley, now lives in
Shawnee, Oklahoma. Her husband is a retired farmer and they recently celebrated their sixtieth wedding anniversary (Smith County Pioneer, August,
1959). She said her mother died first and her father four months later. He
said the "house was like a tomb." (The death certificate lists Higley's
cause of death as grief.) There are five grandsons living, namely: D. M.
Higley, Tampa, Florida; Arthur Higley, Tulsa, Oklahoma; and Warren Higley,
Tampa, Florida, sons of Arthur Higley, one of the children who came to Smith
County; and Harry and Floyd Higley of Shawnee, Oklahoma, sons of Brewster
Higley VII. He was still alive in 1947 at the age of 93 and had a great-
grandson, Brewster Higley IX. D. M. Higley also has a son, Melvin. Another
visitor in Smith Center was Bernard Higley, Columbus, Ohio, a cousin. James
E. Sanderson, Union Mills, Indiana, came to Smith Center to get data. His
grandmother, Zeruah Higley Sanderson, was a sister of Dr. Higley. Another
Rotary Club is also taking note of Dr. Higley. The Oklahoma Orbit, Shawnee
Oklahoma, reported that a roadside marker was being erected near Shawnee,
Oklahoma, Dr. Higley's burial place, by the Oklahoma Historical Society. It
was the result of a contribution by the Shawnee Rotarians of $100 for this
purpose. Harry A. Smith, member of the Pottawatomie Historical Society, led
the move (Smith County Pioneer, August 6, 1959). It was reported at the first
Smith County Historical Meeting that approximately 2,600 people visited the
Higley cabin in 1959.

[39] Kirke Mechem, op. cit., p. 34.

HOME ON THE RANGE
as printed in the Smith County Pioneer
by Editor Levi Morris in 1873

Oh, give me a home where the buffalo roam,
Where the deer and the antelope play
Where never is heard a discouraging word,
And the sky is not clouded all day.

Oh, give me the gale of the Solomon vale,
Where life streams with buoyancy flow.
On the banks of the Beaver, where seldom if ever
Any poisonous herbage doth grow.

Oh, give me the land where the bright diamond sand,
Throws light from its glittering stream,
Where glideth along the graceful white swan
Like a maid in her heavenly dream.

I love the wild flowers in this bright land of ours,
I love, too, the curlew's wild scream.
The bluffs of white rocks and antelope flocks
That graze on our hillsides so green.

How often at night, when the heavens are bright,
By the light of the glittering stars,
Have I stood there amazed and asked as I gazed,
If their beauty exceeds this of ours.

The air is so pure, the breezes so light,
The zephyrs so balmy at night,
I would not exchange my home here to range
Forever in azure so bright.

The chorus added by the Harlan orchestra:

A home, a home where the buffalo roam,
Where the deer and the antelope play;
Where never is heard a discouraging word,
And the sky is not clouded all day.

EXPLANATION OF PLATE VIII

Fig. 1. The Old Dutch Mill built by Charles Schwarz in 1882 with
         the help of his brother. The two-room sod house was
         built in 1881. (Courtesy of Conrad Schwarz.)

Fig. 2. The Dutch Mill in the park in Smith Center, April 1960.

Fig. 3. The Charles Schwarz family, Golden Wedding, June 1921.
         Mr. and Mrs. Schwarz, Tillie, Emma, Henry, Conrad, and
         Herman. (Courtesy of Conrad Schwarz.)

Fig. 4. Officers of the Smith County Historical Society, 1959.
         Mrs. Margaret Nelson, secretary and author of the book,
         "Home on the Range," Emmet Womer, president, Ray Myers,
         Lou Felton, I. A. Nichols, and Walter Hofer.

Fig. 5. Geographic center of the forty-eight states near Lebanon,
         Kansas. (Courtesy of the Smith County Pioneer.)

Fig. 6. Smith County Memorial Hospital, Smith Center, Kansas,
         built 1951. (Courtesy of Mrs. Hattie Baker.)

PLATE VIII

Fig. 2

Fig. 1

Fig. 3

Fig. 4

Fig. 5

Fig. 6

EXPLANATION OF PLATE IX

Fig. 1. Kensington Band on board the U.S.S. George Washington, December, 1918. Personnel listed in text. (Courtesy of Mrs. Edwin Hilbrink, Phillipsburg, Kansas.)

Fig. 2. President Woodrow Wilson and Mrs. Wilson on board the U.S.S. George Washington. (Courtesy of Mrs. Hilbrink.)

Fig. 3. Daniel E. Kelley, pioneer of Smith County who wrote the music for "Home on the Range."

Fig. 4. The Higley cabin on Beaver Creek, Smith County, Kansas. Taken April, 1960.

Fig. 5. Dr. Brewster Higley, pioneer Smith County doctor who wrote the words of "Home on the Range."

Fig. 6. Relatives of Dr. Higley — his son, Brewster Higley VII, grandson, Harry Higley, and great-grandson, Brewster Higley, of Shawnee, Oklahoma. (Courtesy of The Cattleman, Ft. Worth, Texas.)

PLATE IX

Fig. 1

Fig. 2

Fig. 3

Fig. 4

Fig. 5

Fig. 6

EXPLANATION OF PLATE X

Story map of the song, "Home on the Range," locating the high
points of the history of the song. (Courtesy of The Cattleman.)

PLATE X

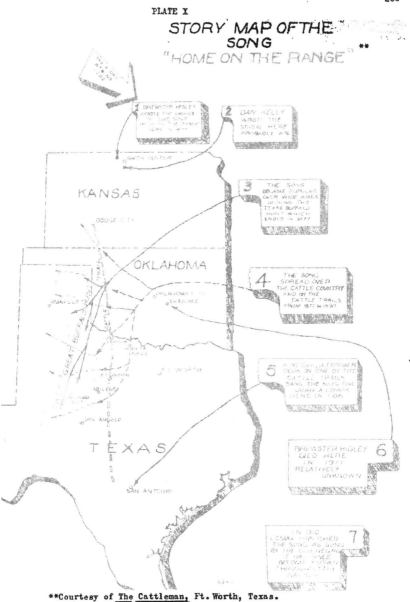

**Courtesy of The Cattleman, Ft. Worth, Texas.

EXPLANATION OF PLATE XI

Sketches drawn by Mrs. Nettie Smith Chubb based on the song,
"Home on the Range." Mrs. Chubb is a native of Smith Center.

PLATE XI

238

Smith County's Own Song

Written by Dr. Brewster Higley, pioneer physician,
in his little homestead cabin near Smith Center in 1873.

O, give me a home,

, give me a home where the buffalo roam,
Where the deer and antelope play,
)ere seldom is heard a discouraging word
And the sky is not clouded all day.

CHORUS

A home, a home where the deer and antelope play,
Where seldom is heard a discouraging word
And the sky is not clouded all day.

And the skies are not cloudy all day.

CONCLUSION

The history of Smith County is typical of most of the agricultural counties in the north central part of Kansas. The wave of industrialism that swept over the United States passed by this county and left it an agricultural section inhabited by the white race, as there never has been a record of more than fifteen Negroes in the county and in 1959 there were none. No Mexicans became permanent residents. The foreign population has always been a small percentage and in 1950 it was less than two per cent. The greatest gain in population was in 1875, three years after the organization of the county in 1872, with an increase of 4,500 people for a single year. The peak of the population was in 1900 with 16,384 reported. From that date the population has steadily decreased with the greatest emigration from the county in the "dust storm years" of the 1930's. This is in direct contrast to the state population records which have shown a steady increase in population. Smith County had more residents than the average Kansas county in 1900 but 6,570 fewer than average in 1940. The total population has leveled off the last ten years at about 8,000 people with 8,016 in 1959.

The basic source of economic wealth is from agricultural production with corn the main crop until 1938. In 1938 the greater acreage harvested became wheat and it has remained so since. A chief concern of the farmers is the weather. The key climatic factor is the amount and variability of precipitation as Smith County receives an average rainfall of twenty-two inches which is barely sufficient for crops if it comes at the right season of the year to be most useful. There have been many periods in the past when moisture was insufficient or came at the wrong time of year and drouths resulted. The Kirwin Dam Irrigation Project along the Solomon Valley may bring new wealth and security for a limited number of farmers in the county. There is little opportunity for such development elsewhere in the county because there are no other major waterways. Climatic hazards directly affected the entire economic structure of the county. This was seen in the exodus of settlers following the "Easter Blizzard" of 1873 and the "Great Blizzard of 1886." The roads were crowded with settlers returning East after the grasshopper invasion of 1874; however, many returned to their homesteads the following spring. The greatest number of people left, however, when the dust storms hit in the 1930's. Farm sales were held so frequently during 1937, 1938, and 1939 that two or three were scheduled daily. In 1930-1940 there were five times as many deeds issued to life insurance companies, the Federal Land Bank, Federal Farm Mortgage Company, and other companies as had been recorded to that time. In 1940 the Federal Land Bank and Federal Farm Mortgage Corporation secured deeds to 10,177 acres. If this trend had continued in the same proportion, Smith County would have belonged to companies in less than forty years, but it was reversed with the return of more prosperous conditions in the 1940's and farmers began re-purchasing farms.

Today Smith County is a local unit of prosperous, industrious people in 900 square miles of farmland. It is crisscrossed with a good system of transportation, two minor hard surfaced highways, one major highway, and two railroads. The county has three weekly newspapers, thirty-two operating school districts, four high schools, many rural and town churches, and nine towns ranging in population from 77 to 2,410. There are two tourist attractions, the Higley cabin built by the author of "Home on the Range," the Kansas state song; and the "Hub" or geographic center of the contiguous forty-eight states. Many natives of Smith County have won recognition for outstanding accomplishments in art, literature, politics, education, and other fields.

Certain conclusions have been reached from this study.

1. Smith County settlers were motivated by a desire for homes and farm land. There is little record of cattle ranchers and none of range wars such as are found in many other counties.

2. Settlers came to Smith County as a result of advertising literature and due to the fact that many settlers came to the end of the railroad, then spread out over the frontier, the region of which Smith County was a part in the 1870's.

3. The pattern of life was similar to other regions of the frontier. The same type of loneliness, lack of neighbors, crudities of living and homes, lack of doctors, and few comforts of civilization as well as the lack of water and timber and the difficulty of farming sod ground were found in all the counties in the Great Plains area. The settlers made good use of available materials in constructing homes and buildings. They had the advantage of settling after the Homestead Law was well established and received the benefit of the amendments added to the original law.

4. The first settlements remained, perhaps because there were fewer cases of Indian atrocities than found in many other areas; because these people were very poor in many instances and had come here to establish homes, and as such they "stuck" it out.

5. The tendency has been from farm ownership to tenant farming since 1880 with the low point of ownership reached in 1940. Since then ownership has increased with a tendency to larger farms and fewer owners.

6. General farming has been and still is the dominating industry in the county.

Most people who have lived in Smith County have a strong feeling of loyalty toward the area. Many of the residents in 1960 can think of no place they would rather live. To them — and to many who have moved away — Smith County always will be "home".

BIBLIOGRAPHY

Books and Pamphlets**

Adams, F. G. The Homestead Guide. Waterville, Kansas: F. G. Adams, Publisher, 1873.

Andreas, A. T. (ed.), History of the State of Kansas. Chicago: A. T. Andreas, 1883.

Beardslee, Etta. Lebanon's Golden Jubilee, 1887-1937. Lebanon: Lebanon Times, 1937.

Billington, Ray Allen, Westward Expansion. New York: Macmillan Co., 1960.

Beebe, Charles (publisher), Kansas Facts. 2 vols. Topeka: Charles Beebe, 1929.

Blackmar, Frank (ed.), Kansas: A Cyclopedia of State History. 2 vols. Chicago: Standard Pub. Co., 1912.

Bright, John D., Kansas, the First Century. 4 vols. New York: Lewis Historical Pub. Co., 1956.

Burch, L. D., Kansas As It Is. Chicago: C. S. Burch & Co., 1878.

City of Gaylord, 1886-1936. Pamphlet, K.S.H.L.

Clark, Thomas D., Frontier America. New York: Chas. Scribner Co., 1959.

Connelley, William, A Standard History of Kansas and Kansans. 5 vols. Chicago: Lewis Publishing Co., 1918.

Crawford, Samuel J., Kansas in the Sixties. Chicago: McClurg & Co., 1911.

Fremont, Brevet Capt. J. C., Report of the Exploring Expedition to the Rocky Mountains and to Oregon and North California in 1843-1844. Washington: Blair and Rives, 1845.

Gledhill, A. E., Among He Sens. Lamar, Colo.: Lamar Register Press, 1939.

Greeley, Horace, An Overland Journey. San Francisco: H. H. Bancroft & Co. 1860.

Hodge, Frederick, Handbook of the American Indians, V. 2. New York: Pageant Books, Inc., 1959.

** K.S.H.L. is Kansas State Historical Library.

Howes, Charles, This Place Called Kansas. Norman, Okla.: Univ. of Oklahoma, 1952.

Hutchinson, C. E., Resources of Kansas. Topeka: C. E. Hutchinson, 1871.

Kansas Industrial Development Commission, To the Stars, Vol. 10, No. 4. Topeka: July-August, 1955.

Martin, John A., The Development of Kansas, Topeka: Topeka Pub. House, 1886.

Millbrook, Minnie D., Ness, Western County, Kansas. Detroit: Millbrook Pub. Co., 1955.

Nelson, Margaret, Home on the Range. Boston: Chapman and Grimes, Inc., 1948.

Paxson, F. L., History of the American Frontier. New York: Houghton, Mifflin & Co., 1924.

Prowant, L. A., Stanzas for Kansas. Wichita: Privately printed, 1937.

Rand, McNally, Pioneer Atlas of the American West. Chicago: Rand, McNally & Co., 1956.

Richardson, Albert, Beyond the Mississippi. Hartford: American Pub. Co., 1867.

Ross, Harry, What Price White Rock. Burr Oak (Kansas): Burr Oak Herald, 1937.

Shannon, Fred A., The Farmer's Last Frontier. New York: Rinehart & Co., 1959.

Simmonds, Frank W. John and Susan Simmonds. Rutland, Vt.: Tuttle Pub. Co., 1940.

Tuttle, Charles, New Centennial History of the State of Kansas. Madison: Interstate Press, 1876.

Whittemore, Margaret, Historic Kansas. Lawrence: Univ. of Kansas Press, 1954.

Who Was Who in America, Vol. 2 (1945-1952). Chicago: A. N. Marquis Co., 1950.

Wilder, D. W., The Annals of Kansas, 1541-1885. Topeka: F. D. Thacher, 1886.

Willard, James and Goodykoontz, C. B., The Trans-Mississippi West. Boulder: Univ. of Colorado, 1930.

Womer, Margaret Mitchell, That You May Know. Smith Center: Smith County Pioneer, 1935.

Works Projects Administration, Kansas, A Guide to the Sunflower State. New York: Viking Press, 1939.

Theses

Abel, Annie, "Indian Reservations in Kansas and the Extinguishment of Their Titles," M. A. thesis, Kansas University, 1900.

Blake, L. E., "The Great Exodus of 1879-1880 to Kansas," M. S. thesis, Kansas State University, 1942.

Esterley, Charles, "The Trend of Farm Population and Land Ownership in Smith County, Kansas, 1900-1940," M. S. thesis, Ft. Hays State College, 1941.

Gill, Helen, "The Establishment of Counties in Kansas," M. A. thesis, Kansas University, 1903.

King, Rebecca, "Identification of Foreign Immigrant Groups in Kansas," M. S. thesis, Kansas State University, 1946.

Newell, Fred, "Survey of the Administration of Secondary Schools in Smith County, Kansas," M. S. thesis, University of Southern Calif., 1946.

Sauer, Howard, "The Frontier of Settlement for 1860," M. A. thesis, State University of Iowa, 1931.

Staack, Henry, "The Frontier of Settlement in Kansas, 1860-1870," M. S. thesis, State University of Iowa, 1925.

Venable, Robert, "The Kansas Frontier, 1861-1875," M. S. thesis, University of Oklahoma, 1936.

Wade, Joseph, "History of Kansas Trails and Roads," M. S. thesis, Kansas State College of Pittsburg, 1947.

Waldron, N. B., "Colonization in Kansas from 1861-1890," Ph.D. thesis, Northwestern University, 1932.

Manuscripts and Other Collected Material

Allen, Erroll, "Incidents of Homestead Days," Mns., K.S.H.L.

Annual Catalog of Gould College, Osborne, Kansas, 1887.

Baker, Mrs. Hattie, "Historical Sketches of Smith Center and Smith County," in author's possession.

Barnes, A. R., "Early Days on Beaver Creek," Mns., K.S.H.L.

Barr, Virginia Harlan, "Reminiscences of Early Days in Kansas," Mns., K.S.H.L.

Cowan, Bess, "Reminiscences of Edna Chase Cowan," Mms., K.S.H.L.

Headley, A. L., "History of Smith County," Mms., K.S.H.L.

"History of the Mahin Family," Mms., K.S.H.L.

Kansas State Census Records for Smith County, 1870, 1875, 1878, 1959.

Kirkendall, Hattie and Lutz, Isabell Reed, "History of Methodist Church, 1877-1927," Mms., K.S.H.L.

Phillips County Review, Kirwin Dam Dedication, June 10, 1955.

Myers, C. Clyde, "Biographical Sketch of Myers Family," Mms., K.S.H.L.

Myers, C. Clyde, "Historical Sketches of Lebanon and Salem," Mms., K.S.H.L.

Myers, Ray, "Historical Sketches of Lebanon and Oak Township," Mms., K.S.H.L.

Original Smith County Charter, in Smith County Clerk's office, Smith Center, Kansas.

Ream, Mrs. Cora, "Frontier Memories," Mms., K.S.H.L.

Records of County Clerk, Smith County, Smith Center, Kansas.

Records of Register of Deeds, Smith County, Smith Center, Kansas.

Records of Superintendent of Schools, Smith County, Smith Center, Kansas.

Schwarz, Conrad, "Charles Schwarz and the Dutch Mill, Reamsville, Kansas," Mms., K.S.H.L.

Slagle, Mrs. Minnie, "Organizing a Library," Biographical Scrapbook, Vol. 9, K.S.H.L.

Smith County Clippings, 2 vols., K.S.H.L.

Smith County Old Settlers Homecoming Assoc. Souvenir, 1912, K.S.H.L.

Spurrier, Elmer, "Historical Sketches of Logan Township," K.S.H.L.

Stump, Elmer, "Historical Sketches of White Rock Township," K.S.H.L.

Newspapers

Council Grove Guard, 1922.

Downs News, 1939, 1960.

Franklin (Nebraska) Sentinel, 1932.

High Plains Journal, Dodge City, Kansas, Jan. 21, and Jan. 28, 1960.

Kansas City Journal, 1918.

Kansas City Star, 1913, 1940.

Kansas City Times, 1950-1951.

Kensington Mirror, 1918.

Lebanon Times, 1960.

Osborne County Farmer, (Osborne, Kansas) 1880.

Phillips County Review, June 9, 1955.

Reamsville Dispatch, 1884-1885.

Red Cloud (Nebraska) Chief, 1903.

Smith County Journal (Smith Center, Kansas), 1914.

Smith County Pioneer (Smith Center, Kansas), 1876-1960.

Smith County Review (Smith Center, Kansas), 1941.

Topeka Daily Capital, 1905-1960.

Topeka State Journal, 1917, 1960.

Periodicals

Heritage of Kansas, Vol. 2, No. 2. Kansas State Teachers College, Emporia, 1958.

Kansas State Historical Society, Collections, 17 vols. Topeka, 1881-1928.

Kansas State Historical Quarterly, 7 vols. Topeka, 1902-1949.

Musician, "American Army Bands in Europe," May, 1918, p. 317.

The Cattlemen, Texas and Southwestern Cattle Growers Assoc., Fort Worth, 1947.

Who's Who in the Kansas Legislature, Topeka, 1929, 1932, 1937.

Government Publications

Flora, S. D., Climate of Kansas, Weather Bureau Report, Kansas State Board of Agriculture, Topeka, 1948.

Kansas State Board of Agriculture Reports, Vol. 4-44, Topeka, 1874-1956.

Seventh Session of Legislature, Laws of Kansas. Leavenworth, 1867.

Twelfth Biennial Report of the Adjutant General of the State of Kansas, Kansas Troops in the U. S. Volunteer Service in the Spanish and Philippine Wars, 1898-1899. Topeka, 1900.

United States Census Reports, Washington, D. C., 1880-1950.

Wedel, Waldo, An Introduction to Kansas Archaeology, Washington, D. C., 1959.

State and National Statutes

General Statutes of Kansas, 1867, Ch. 40, Art. 4, Sec. 2-3; Ch. 112, Sec. 1-4, Lawrence, 1868.

39th Congress, 2nd Sess., 1866-1867, Report of Secy. of Interior, Exec. Doc. No. 1, Vol. 2. (Library reference no. Serial Doc. 1284.)

42nd Congress, Sess. 2, Statutes at Large, Vol. 17, Ch. 85.

42nd Congress, 3rd Sess., U. S. Statutes, 1872-1873, Vol. 17, Ch. 277.

Statutes at Large, Vol. 5, Ch. 16.

Statutes at Large, 1862-1863, Vol. 12.

Letters and Interviews

Morgan, George B. Manhattan, Kansas, to A. L. Headley, Smith Center, Kansas, Jan. 20, 1959.

Smith, Jane F. Archivist, Natural Resources Records Division, Washington, D. C., to author, March 18, 1960.

Register of Deeds, Smith County, Smith Center, Kansas, to the author, March 28, 1960.

Letters to author with information used:

Baker, Mrs. Hattie, Smith Center, Kansas, who had a collection of historical notes on Smith County and Smith Center and access to files of the Smith County Pioneer; Dec. 30, 1959, January 7, 1960, March 28, 1960, March 30, 1960, April 2, 1960, April 3, 1960.

Boyd, Walter, Kensington, Kansas, March 28, 1960.

Burns, Gene, Portis, Kansas, March 6, 1960.

Cowan, Bess, Topeka, Kansas, March 23, 1960.

Crouse, Oscar, Harlan, Kansas, March 4, 1960.

Dilsaver, H. V., Kensington, Kansas, March 11, March 17, March 31, 1960.

Faurot, Ira, Nortonville, Kansas, April 1, 1960.

Gledhill, F. H., Portis, Kansas, March 2, 1960.

Hainke, Robert, Kensington, Kansas, March 17, 1960.

Headley, A. L., Smith Center, Kansas, April 7, 1960.

Hilbrink, Mrs. Edwin, Phillipsburg, Kansas, April 7, 1960.

Hinshaw, Mrs. Mabel, Smith Center, Kansas, February 8, 1960.

McIlvain, Arthur, County Clerk, Smith Center, Kansas, April 28, 1960.

Myers, Ray, Lebanon, Kansas, February 26, 1960, March 8, 1960.

Osborn, C. W., Kensington, Kansas, April 9, 1960.

Overmiller, Willis, Smith Center, Kansas, March 2, 1960.

Rice, Mrs. Theo, Athol, Kansas, March 7, March 30, April 10, 1960.

Strong, J. Lincoln, Smith Center, Kansas, March 3, 1960.

Watts, Dr. Victor, Smith Center, Kansas, April 6, 1960.

Womer, Emmet, Smith Center, Kansas, president of the Smith County Historical Society, Jan. 2, 1960; Jan. 18, 1960; Jan. 27, 1960; Feb. 19, 1960; March 4, 1960.

Interviews

Mrs. Hattie Baker, Smith Center, Kansas, Jan. 9, 1960; Jan. 23, 1960;
    April 6, 1960.

Mrs. Margaret Nelson, Smith Center, Kansas, Jan. 9, 1960; Jan. 23, 1960;
    April 6, 1960.

Mr. Conrad Schwarz, Topeka, Kansas, April 11, 1960, February 2, 1960.

Mr. and Mrs. Emmet Komer, Smith Center, Kansas, Jan. 9, 1960; Jan. 23, 1960;
    April 6, 1960.

APPENDIX

Smith Center, Kansas
March 28, 1960

Mrs. Vera E. Pletcher
History Dept.
Kansas State University
Manhattan, Kansas.

Dear Madam:

Below is the answer to your first question:

1. The NW$\frac{1}{4}$ 18-4-11
The Patent was issued to A.P.Hester from the U.S. recorded
Dec. 1, 1887, after his Receiving Receipt was recorded May 8
1885.

2. Receiving Receipt to Nancy A. Custer on E$\frac{1}{2}$SE$\frac{1}{4}$ was recorded
Jan. 14, 1884, Patent recorded Dec. 3, 1887.
On W$\frac{1}{2}$SW$\frac{1}{4}$ 20-4-11 the Rec. Rec. recorded same as above, Patent
recorded Dec. 13, 1887.

3. Rec.Rec. to John H. Watson recorded Jan. 2, 1886.

4. None of our entires are divided as you have them (and so
many of the names are not the same either).
SW$\frac{1}{4}$ 18-4-11 Rec. Rec. recorded to Johan A. McCullough, Patent
recorded Sept. 8, 1892.
SE$\frac{1}{4}$ Patent to Hans P. Clemann recorded Nov. 17, 1910.

5.SW$\frac{1}{4}$SW$\frac{1}{4}$ 7-4-11, Rec. Rec. recorded Dec. 10, 1880, to
Wm. P. Shepperd, Patent recorded June 10, 1892.

NE$\frac{1}{4}$SW$\frac{1}{4}$ 7-4-11, Patent to Alvin C. Culley recorded Feb. ', 1884.

SE$\frac{1}{4}$SW$\frac{1}{4}$ Patent to Charles W. McCullough recorded July 7, 1892.

NW$\frac{1}{4}$SW$\frac{1}{4}$ 7-4-11, Rec. Rec. to Geo. W. Kyger recorded Nov. 16, 1883,
Patent recorded April 27, 1920.

6. S$\frac{1}{2}$NW$\frac{1}{4}$ - N$\frac{1}{2}$SW$\frac{1}{4}$ Patent to Chrales W. Jeffrey recorded Mar. 1, 1875.

7. Patent to Clarence Blinn recorded Aug. 24, 1882.

8. Patent ·. Victor Blinn recorded Aug. 5, 1881.

9. Patent Patent to Rufus M. Brown recorded Sept. 1, 1874.

10. Rec. Rec. to James R. Clark recorded Feb. 10, 1879, Patent
recorded Nov. 28, 1893.

11. Rec. Rec. to Julius C. Harris recorded April 2, 1880,
Patent recorded Nov. 8, 1881.

12. Rec. Rec. to Wm. W. Coop on E$\frac{1}{2}$ & NW$\frac{1}{4}$SW$\frac{1}{4}$ recorded Jxxxix
April 18, 1882, Patent recorded Jan. 10, 1910.

SW$\frac{1}{4}$SW$\frac{1}{4}$ to James L. McColm Rec. Red. recorded Mar. 22, 1888,
Patent recorded Dec. 21, 1909

GENERAL SERVICES ADMINISTRATION

National Archives and Records Service
Washington 25, D. C.

March 18, 1960

VIA AIR MAIL

Mrs. Vera E. Pletcher
Department of History
Kansas State College
Manhattan, Kansas

Dear Mrs. Pletcher:

In your letter of March 9, 1960, you requested information concerning homestead entries in Smith County, Kansas.

An examination of the records of the former General Land Office, now in the National Archives, shows that the United States Land Office at Junction City, Kansas, administered land transactions in the area of Smith County, Kansas, until January 16, 1871. An examination of the monthly abstracts of homestead entries made at the land office at Junction City, Kansas, shows the following homestead entries in the fall of 1870 for land located in Smith County:

1. Homestead entry number 9234, October 29, 1870, Josiah Crick, the NW¼ of Section 18, Township 4 South, Range 11 West.

2. Homestead entry number 9235, October 29, 1870, Henry M. Blue, the E½ SE¼ Section 19, and W½ SW¼ Section 20, Township 4 South, Range 11 West.

3. Homestead entry number 9236, October 29, 1870, Daniel B. Hopkins, the NE¼ of Section 19, Township 4 South, Range 11 West.

4. Homestead entry number 9237, October 29, 1870, Chancy Williams, the E½ SW¼ and W½ SE¼, Section 18, Township 4 South, Range 11 West.

5. Homestead entry number 9238, October 29, 1870, James M. Thompson, the SW¼ of Section 7, Township 4 South, Range 11 West.

6. Homestead entry number 9375, November 9, 1870, G.W. Jeffrey, the S½ NW¼ and N½ SW¼ of Section 2, Township 5 South, Range 14 West.

Mrs. Vera E. Pletcher

7.   Homestead entry number 9394, November 10, 1870, Clarence Blinn, the NW$\frac{1}{4}$ of Section 25, Township 4 South, Range 14 West.

8.   Homestead entry number 9395, November 10, 1870, Victor Blinn, the W$\frac{1}{2}$ SW$\frac{1}{4}$ Section 25, and E$\frac{1}{2}$ SE$\frac{1}{4}$ Section 26, Township 4 South, Range 14 West.

9.   Homestead entry number 9396, November 10, 1870, Rufus N. Brown, the SW$\frac{1}{4}$ of Section 24, Township 4 South, Range 14 West.

10. Homestead entry number 9416, November 11, 1870, Herman Potter, the SE$\frac{1}{4}$ of Section 35, Township 4 South, Range 15 West.

11. Homestead entry number 9417, November 11, 1870, Bella G. Merrill, the W$\frac{1}{2}$ NW$\frac{1}{4}$ and W$\frac{1}{2}$ SW$\frac{1}{4}$, Section 32, Township 4 South, Range 14 West.

12. Homestead entry number 9544, November 18, 1870, James R. Richard, the SW$\frac{1}{4}$ of Section 25, Township 5 South, Range 12 West.

The abstract of homestead applications shows only that entries were made by the persons named. To determine if they completed their homestead requirements and received patents to the land it will be necessary to have Final Certificate numbers. It may be possible to secure these numbers from the Bureau of Land Management, Department of the Interior, Washington 25, D.C. If you write to that Bureau, please include all of the information furnished in this letter. With the numbers of the final certificates we will be glad to make a further examination of the records and provide an estimate of the cost of reproductions.

Sincerely yours

Jane F. Smith
Archivist in Charge, Interior Branch
Natural Resources Records Division
The National Archives

State of Kansas, Smith County, ss.

Office of Probate Judge of Said County.

BE IT REMEMBERED, That on the 16th day of September A.D. 1878 there was issued from the office of said Probate Judge, a Marriage License, of which the following is a true copy:

MARRIAGE LICENSE.

STATE OF KANSAS, SMITH COUNTY, September A.D. 1878

To Any Person Authorized by Law to Perform the Marriage Ceremony, Greeting.

You are hereby authorized to join in marriage Daniel H Crosby of Cedarville aged 31 years, and Sarah V Young of " aged 17 years, and of this License you will make due return to my office within thirty days.

SEAL. John C. Harlin Probate Judge

And which said marriage License was afterwards, to wit on the day of A.D. , returned to said Probate Judge, with the following certificate endorsed thereon, to-wit.

STATE OF KANSAS, Smith COUNTY, SS.

I, E W King do hereby certify that in accordance with the authorization of the within License, I did on the 19 day of September A.D. 1878 at my Office in said County, join and unite in Marriage the above named Daniel H Crosby and Sarah V Young Witness my hand at my office the day and year above written.

Attest: E W King Justice of the Peace of Harvey Town

State of Kansas, Smith County, ss.

I, Probate Judge in and for said County do hereby certify that the foregoing is a full and correct copy of the Complete Record

in the matter of

APPENDIX A

Roster of the Kansas Posts of the G.A.R., 1894**

Kensington Post No. 381, Kensington, Kansas

    Baire, J., U. S. Inf. pri.
    Bunnell, George, Ind. Inf. pri.
    Boggs, William, Pa. Inf. pri.
    Brown, Joseph, Kans. Inf. Corp.
    Burtch, John, Ia. Inf. sgt.
    Diggins, Fred, Ill. Inf. pri.
    Dyer, John, ———
    Eberhm, Pri, O. Inf. corp.
    Gates, W. B., Ia. Inf. pri.
    Langston, A., Ind. Inf. pri.
    Moore, H. Ind. Inf. pri.
    May, A. P., Ia. Inf. pri.
    May, S. S., Ia. Inf. pri.
    Martin, Charles, Ia. Inf. bugler
    Peters, Lewis, Ill. Inf. pri.
    Watts, Fred, Wis. Inf. pri.

Gaylord Post No. 355, Gaylord, Kansas

    Armitstead, J. G., Ia. Inf. pri.
    Brake, William, Tenn. Inf. pri.
    Curtis, B. M., Mo. Inf. pri.
    McEllfresh, J., Mo. Cav. pri.
    Foote, J. H., Ill. Inf. pri.
    Hervey, J. R., Ia. Inf. pri.
    Harding, J. N., Wisc. Cav. pri.
    Keys, William, Ill. Inf. ———
    Lenall, J. J., Ind. Inf. sgt.
    Lambert, Elisha, Ind. Inf. corp.
    Longcor, William, Ia. Inf. pri.
    Newell, Perrcy, Ia. Inf. corp.
    Redinger, F. D., Ill. Inf. pri.
    Ratcliffe, J. G., ——— Inf. pri.
    Stranathan, W. B., Ia. Inf. sgt.
    Stanley, J. H., Ill. Inf., Wisc. Inf. pri.
    Wright, William, Ia. Inf. pri.
    Young, Allen, Ind. Inf. pri.

    ** Roster of the Kansas Posts of the G.A.R., 1894, Kansas
State Historical Library, no publisher.

APPENDIX A (cont'd.)

Lebanon Post No. 240, Lebanon, Kansas

Bonecutter, David, Ill. Inf. pri.
Bruker, J. C., Ia. Inf. pri.
Buchanan, W. Ia. Inf. pri.
Coaly, John, Ill. Inf. Sgt.
Chery, John, Ky. Cav. pri.
French, J. F., Vt. Inf. pri.
Foszey, A. J. Ind. Inf. pri.
Gates, A. H. Ia. Inf. sgt.
Gibones, James, Ind. Inf. corp.
Heister, E. S., O. Inf. pri.
Jones, Ched, Mo. Inf. pri.
Mason, A. L., Ill. Inf. corp.
McNall, C. E., Ia. Inf. pri.
North, J., Ia. Inf. pri.
Rowles, Caleb, Mo. Inf. sgt.
Rogers, W. N., Ia. Inf. pri.
Smith, Nathan, Ia. Inf. pri.
Srader, Joseph, Mo. Inf. pri.
Strickland, William, Ind. Inf. pri.
Smith, E. W., O. Inf. sgt.
Thompson, Mathew, Misc. Inf. pri.
Trueblood, Francis, —— Inf. pri.
Vanocker, George, Mich. Inf. corp.
Walker, William, Ind. Inf. corp.
Warner, M. V., Ia. Inf. pri.
Welden, Clark, Ill. Inf. corp.

Charley Aldrich Post No. 184, Cedarville, Kansas

Crosby, D. H., Wisc. Inf. pri.
Chapman, Jasper, O. Cav. pri.
Campbell, J. A., Ill. Inf. pri.
Clandell, J. T., Ind. Inf. pri.
Draper, N. B., Wisc. Inf. pri.
Engstrom, A. Ill. Inf. pri.
Gibson, Garrett, Ill. Inf. Pri.
Howe, C. J., Ia. Inf. corp.
Haynes, F. V., Ind. Inf. pri.
Johnstone, J. H., O. Inf. sgt.
Lowry, J. C., Ill. Inf. pri.
Likens, Samuel, Ind. and Ill. Inf. pri.
Morrison, J. T., O. Inf. capt.
Noncmaker, S., Pa. Inf. pri. and Pa. H. art. pri.
Pegg, S., O. Inf. pri.
Quick, S. W., Ill. Inf. pri.
Robertson, J. W., Ill. Inf. pri.

APPENDIX A (concl.)

Rankart, M., N. Y. Inf. pri.
Rea, T. M., Pa. v.r.c. sgt.
Simmonds, W. H., O. Inf. pri.
Simmonds, C. D., O. Inf. pri.
Sweat, S. L., Ind. Inf. pri.
Stranathan, Samuel, Ia. Inf. pri.
Swing, John, alias PerotRa, John, Mo. Cav. pri.

Robert Anderson Post No. 45, Smith Center, Kansas

Beacom, J. W., Ia. Cav. pri.
Barrett, B. B., ———
Byram, J. N., ———
Burgess, A., Ia. Inf. pri.
Clemens, J. D., Ind. Inf. pri.
Dierdorf, Joseph, ———
Ferris, J. H., ———
Goodale, J. C., Ill. Inf. pri.
Guthrie, A. A., Ia. Cav. pri.
Gilson, L., ———
Hawkins, O. S., Wisc. Inf. pri.
Henderson, James, Ia. Inf. pri.
McDowell, J. S., Pa. Inf. capt.
May, F. M., Mo. Inf. pri.
Mollison, John, Ill. Inf. pri.
Merriman, A., Ia. Inf. pri.
Olds, E. L., Mich. Cav. corp.
Putman, W. R., Ill. Inf. pri.
Reed, H. H., Ill. Inf. lt.
Smith, Ira B., O. Inf. pri.
Shockly, John, Ill. Inf. pri.
Welch, E. S., N. Y. Inf. pri.

APPENDIX B

Roster of the United States Volunteer Men from Smith

County in the Spanish and Philippine Wars**

1898-1899

Aims, Eli
Boner, Albert
Bosworth, Elmer
Bozarth, Franklin
Brady, Charles
Brooks, Levi
Burgess, Otis
Byers, Thomas
Calkin, Charles
Chandler, Walter
Culley, James
Eustace, James
Galloway, Americus
Gasho, Charles
Galusha, George
Galusha, John
Heald, Joseph
Henderson, John
***Hollingworth, Lennie
Howig, Charles
Joy, Alfred
Kimball, Orville
McLean, Renel
Merriam, John
Miller, George
Pickering, Arthur
Putman, William
Renfro, Frank
Rhodes, Daniel
Smith, Frank
Thackrey, Harry
Thackrey, Samuel
Whiteley, William
Williamson, William

_____

** Twelfth Biennial Report of the Adjutant General of the
State of Kansas. Topeka: State Printing Office, 1900.
*** Died in service, Camp Hamilton, Kentucky.

APPENDIX C

Memorial List for the European War, 1917-1918,
Smith County, Kansas.***

Baker, Charles   Kingsbury, LaRue
Baker, Ed   Moler, Ray
Beldon, Ralph   Lanney, Frank
Brown, Gordon   Lewellen, Willard
Carson, Albert   Marran, Frod
Chase, Walter   Marshall, Frederick
Cherry, Henry   May, Frank
Cole, Harold   Nevill, Clarence
Cole, Joseph   Persell, Asa
Chase, Russell   Petty, Charles
Curtis, Allie   Riley, Joe
Farley, Elmer   Rice, Ronald
Hall, Vernon   Robertson, Archie
Hooper, Wilbert   Scott, Archie
Hopkins, Willie   Slaby, John
Hornkohl, Joseph   Shook, Freddie
Ifland, Conrad   St. Claire, John
Jennings, Lewis   Wiggins, Charles
Jensen, Marious   Yoder, William
Barnes, Lloyd   Tracy, Robert
                      Troyer, Robert

APPENDIX D

Memorial list for World War II, Smith County,
Kansas.***

Benge, Edgar	Mathes, Robert
Bohlen, Henry	Monroe, Robert
Campbell, Ivan	Mugridge, Carl
Campbell, John	Mugridge, Duane
Casteel, Marvin	McElderry, Duane
Cleminson, William Jr.	McLeod, Stanley
Clingman, Paul	Nonamaker, Harold
Colburn, Max	Olson, Everell
Creamer, Clifton	Pfander, Stanley
Curry, Leroy	Pitzer, Dwight
Dean, Donald	Rice, Dean
Detwiler, John	Rice, Waverly
Doyle, Bernard	Rupp, Bernard
Duston, Roger	Schoen, Leonard
Griffith, Francis	Schlatter, Walter
Grauerholz, Merton	Seabright, Robert
Gaddis, Walter	Strickland, Charles
Hartsook, Carl	Swift, Thaine
Herndon, Duane	Van Staalduine, Donald
Hubbard, Darrell	Waddle, Ernest
Jones, Delmar	Werts, William
Jones, George	Withington, Racey
Jones, Paul	Wolf, Alvin
Lyon, Russell	Yocum, Merton
Luther, Hubert	

*** From the Memorial Tablet on the plaque of the
Smith County Memorial Hospital.

APPENDIX E

Corporators of town of Cedarville, May 1, 1874.***

O. A. Harvey	T. M. Helm
V. J. Bottonly	Stephen King
James Fordice	F. D. Morse
J. L. Masterson	E. P. Hobbs
James Johnston	Lewis Plummer
D. H. Crosby	C. J. Hohner
B. J. Bottonly	

*** Secretary of State Corporation Charter Book, Vol. 6, Archives Division of the Kansas State Historical Society, Topeka, Kansas.

APPENDIX F

Census of 1870, Smith County, Kansas.###

Name	Age	Place of birth
King, Daniel	51	N. Y.
King, George	30	N. Y.
Glait, Jessee	42	N. Y.
Woods, Lewis	22	Ky.
Graham, John	39	N. Y.
Salter, John	39	Ind.
Porter, Isaac	37	Ky.
" Sarah	38	Ky.
" Isaac	12	Mo.
" John	9	Mo.
" Alexander	2	Mo.
Matteson, James	29	Ireland
" Margaret	60	Ireland
" William	33	Ireland
Ford, William	26	Ill.
McDaniel, John	25	Ky.
Kindy, Joseph	25	Penn.
" Alice	22	Penn.
" John	1 mo.	Mo.
Calvert, Hiram	26	Ill.
Davis, Willard	26	Ill.
" Martha	23	Ill.
Edington, Joshua	27	Ky.
Babbitt, Charles	27	Ill.
Humphrey, James	30	Eng.
Bradley, Barnett	21	Ky.
McAllister, John	27	Ohio
" Jane	24	Ohio
" George	5	Ill.
" John	2	Ill.
Heath, William	31	N. Y.
" Mantra	24	Ill.
" Thorman	3	Ill.
" George	35	N. Y.
Lessier, Napoleon	30	H. Y.
Haight, Simon	26	Ind.
Riley, William	22	Ind.
Spencer, John	27	Ind.
Gove (or Gore), James	23	Penn.
" Mary J.	22	Penn.
" Mary A.	2	Penn.
Murphy, William	25	Ill.
Van Schok, John	33	N. Y. Physician
Rodgers, George	30	N. Y.

APPENDIX F (concl.)

Name	Age	Place of birth
Allen, Willis	30	Ind.
" Reuben	25	Ind.
Holland, Brice	26	Penn.
Pickett, Oliver	27	Penn.
Jones, Adolphus	21	Penn.
Broad, William	32	England
" Maria	30	England
" William	7	Ill.
" John	3	Ill.
Avery, George	22	England
Earp, Samuel	31	England
" Margaret	22	England
" John	2	Ill.
Goddard, James	21	Ky.
" Scott	27	Ky.
Somers, Napoleon	21	Ohio
" James	23	Ohio
Griffith, George	29	Ohio
Huntley, William	27	Ohio
" Pelina	25	Ohio
" George	4	Ohio
" John	1	Ohio

Persons who died during the year ending June 1, 1870:

| Matteson, William | 62 | Ireland | Pneumonia |
| Goddard, Josephine | 23 | Ind. | Accidental drowning |

Also tabulated were 17 dwellings, 17 families, 22 white males, 4 white females. /Apparently children were not counted in this tally./

Signed by A. B. Lutton, Asst. Marshal, Belleville, Kansas, August 2, 1870.

*** Census of 1870, County of Smith, Archives Division of the Kansas State Historical Society, Topeka, Kansas.

A HISTORY OF SMITH COUNTY, KANSAS TO 1960

by

VERA EDITH CROSBY PLETCHER

B. S., Kansas State University, 1956

AN ABSTRACT OF A THESIS

submitted in partial fulfillment of the

requirements for the degree of

MASTER OF ARTS

Department of History, Political Science, and Philosophy

KANSAS STATE UNIVERSITY
OF AGRICULTURE AND APPLIED SCIENCE

1960

Smith County is in the north central part of Kansas, bordered on the north by Nebraska, and on the other three sides by counties quite similar in physical features, and economic and industrial development. The economy, except for a few minor industries, is based wholly on agriculture. The towns, none large enough to be classed other than rural, range from hamlets to a population of approximately 2,400 at Smith Center, the county seat. Since there have been no industries to bring in "outsiders," the majority of the people are descendants or related in some way to the early settlers of the area and are intensely proud of their county. The purpose of this thesis has been to give a brief survey of the history of Smith County from the pre-settlement days to recent times, including the history of the settlement of the various towns, and some representative families and people who have contributed to its development. As no extensive reports of historical nature have ever been written for Smith County, this work is in the nature of a pioneer effort in the field, and it has been the writer's intention to use as many primary sources as possible, and to preserve material that in a few years will no longer be available from any of the generation that were among the families of the first settlers in the county. This has been possible due to the personal contacts the writer has with the county through her grandparents, her parents, her husband's family, and her girlhood in the county.

The material has been handled topically. The seven main topics have been (1) the physical and biological features and the natural resources of the county; (2) the Indians, their contact with the whites and early land claims; (3) organization and first settlements; (4) origin of first settlers, incentives for their migration and population trends; (5) a survey of economic, political, educational, social conditions, and climatic hazards found in the

county; (6) the development of schools and transportation, with consideration to "ghost" towns and representative Smith Countians; and (7) a consideration of six outstanding or unique features in the county. The written
material is amplified with fourteen maps, nine tables, numerous explanatory
footnotes and pictures. No effort has been made to consider extensively
outside activities that vastly influenced developments within Smith County.
Realizing that history in an area does not develop in a vacuum, the author
has indicated the outside influence where they directly affected activities
within the county, but the major concern has been Smith County itself.

Research for this thesis required many trips to Topeka where much
material was found in the library of the State Historical Society in the
Newspaper and Archives Division and the Kansas collections. Four trips
were made to Smith County to interview people, to check records at the
courthouse, and to attend the annual Smith County Historical Meeting for
1959. Correspondence with dozens of individuals in the county and others
from the county but living in various places added much valuable information.
The inter-library loan service of Farrell Library gave access to theses that
had background material for the area. Scarcity of material was not the problem. From the numerous sources and vast amount of material, choice of the
most pertinent to the purpose of the thesis became a major concern, and at
the same time preserve readability and continuity. Another serious obstacle
was the problem of verification of material due to discrepancy in reports.

Certain conclusions were reached from this study. Smith County was settled by settlers desiring homes and farms. Settlers came as a part of the
influx of immigrants from the eastern and north central states following the
Civil War to areas just beyond the limits of the railroad terminals. The

pattern of life was similar to other regions of the Great Plains frontier. The first settlements remained established despite the hardships and hazards of the times. General farming has been and still is the dominating industry in the county.